T0284989

daughter,

mother,

grandmother,

and whore

A book in the series
LATIN AMERICA IN TRANSLATION /
EN TRADUCCIÓN / EM TRADUÇÃO
Sponsored by the Duke–University of North
Carolina Program in Latin American Studies

DUKE UNIVERSITY PRESS
Durham and London   2024

The Story
of a Woman
Who Decided
to be a *Puta*

daughter,

mother,

grandmother,

and whore

Gabriela Leite   *Translated by Meg Weeks*

FOREWORD BY CAROL LEIGH

INTRODUCTION BY LAURA REBECCA MURRAY,
ESTHER TEIXEIRA, AND MEG WEEKS

© 2024 DUKE UNIVERSITY PRESS

All rights reserved. Printed in the United States of America on
acid-free paper ∞
Project Editor: Lisa Lawley
Cover design by Aimee Harrison
Text design by Courtney Leigh Richardson
Typeset in Untitled Serif and Fira Sans by Copperline Book Services

Library of Congress Cataloging-in-Publication Data
Names: Leite, Gabriela Silva, author. | Weeks, Meg, [date] translator,
writer of introduction. | Leigh, Carol (Sex worker), writer of foreword. |
Murray, Laura (Laura Rebecca), writer of introduction. | Teixera, Esther,
writer of introduction.
Title: Daughter, mother, grandmother, and whore : the story of a woman
who decided to be a puta / by Gabriela Leite ; translated by Meg Weeks ;
foreword by Carol Leigh ; introduction by Laura Murray, Esther Teixera,
and Meg Weeks.
Other titles: Filha, mãe, avó e puta. English | Latin America in
translation/en traducción/em tradução.
Description: Durham : Duke University Press, 2024. | Series: Latin
America in translation | Includes bibliographical references and index.
Identifiers: LCCN 2023048053 (print)
LCCN 2023048054 (ebook)
ISBN 9781478030508 (paperback)
ISBN 9781478026273 (hardcover)
ISBN 9781478059516 (ebook)
Subjects: LCSH: Leite, Gabriela Silva. | Prostitutes—Brazil—Biography. |
Sex workers—Brazil—Biography. | Sex workers—Civil rights—Brazil. |
Sex workers—Political activity—Brazil. | BISAC: SOCIAL SCIENCE /
Ethnic Studies / Caribbean & Latin American Studies | SOCIAL SCIENCE /
Human Sexuality (see also PSYCHOLOGY / Human Sexuality)
Classification: LCC HQ126.2.L45 A3 2024 (print) |
LCC HQ126.2.L45 (ebook) | DDC 306.74092 a B—dc23/eng/20240402
LC record available at https://lccn.loc.gov/2023048053
LC ebook record available at https://lccn.loc.gov/2023048054

Cover art: Photograph of Gabriela Leite by Paulo Santos. Courtesy
of the Arquivo Público do Estado do Rio de Janeiro.

Contents

daughter, mother, grandmother, and whore
The Story of a Woman Who Decided to be a *Puta*

Foreword

CAROL LEIGH

I was always a great admirer of Gabriela Leite. When I was first invited to write a foreword to the English translation of her memoir, I wanted to make sure I could comment in a way that would speak both to all those who knew and loved her and those who never had the opportunity to meet her.

The timing of the invitation was also significant, as my own end-of-life-cancer journey brings me to this reunification with Gabriela, nearly ten years after her death in 2013. I was diagnosed with cancer in 2015, and Gabriela's journey was always part of my own relationship with the disease. As an older sex worker, the kind of ideas she had at the end of her life meant a lot to me. In fact, my prostitution philosophy was the natural outgrowth of being raised in community with women like Gabriela and being informed by their philosophies. I am mostly known for coining the term *sex work* in the late 1970s, but I consider myself a younger sister of that first generation of whore leaders, of which Gabriela was a part.

What a great fortune for a political activist to find oneself on the precipice of a new movement. When I think of my own work, I feel lucky to have been in the right place at the right time. In writing this foreword, I looked back to decipher the inception and trajectory of our movement and the contributions of our early leaders. I often make myself dizzy trying to answer questions such as "How did this movement emerge?" and "Who are we as a movement?" I recall the lengthy philosophical discussions from the early days of sex-worker activism, which always seemed to ping-pong between two questions in particular: "Why do they hate and criminalize us?" and "What makes us so important to them that we 'deserve' the honor of being the primary target of their hatred?"

These questions permeated the 1989 World Whores' Summit in San Francisco, where I first met Gabriela. It was a time when formal international organizing of sex workers was relatively new. Margo St. James and Gail Pheterson were based in San Francisco, which has a hearty history of activist prostitutes.

Margo was the first public political whore to come forth in the United States in 1973, forming COYOTE (Call Off Your Old Tired Ethics), and Gail was an activist, a psychologist, and a researcher. Together, in the early 1980s, they began organizing the World Whores' Congresses, which took place in Amsterdam in 1985 and Brussels in 1986. At this time global communication among prostitutes' rights activists was expanding greatly, evolving along with international communication methods. Sex work always has had a particular relationship to migration and international networking, as stigmatized prostitutes were forced to leave home to escape recognition. So, we were indeed World Whores.

After the Amsterdam and Brussels conferences, Margo, Gail, and fellow COYOTE leader Priscilla Alexander organized the 1989 San Francisco conference based on the work established in Europe. They invited sex-worker leaders and allies from around the world, including Gabriela.

When I first saw Gabriela, she almost seemed like a sister; her demeanor reminded me of my mother and aunts, and I thought we even looked alike. She was very friendly and had a beautiful smile. In my eyes, she shone; I was immediately struck by the character of her beauty, her warmth, clarity, and humble intelligence.

Gabriela had come to the summit after a huge success in Brazil. As the first public political prostitute in her country, Gabriela and her colleagues had just established the Brazilian Network of Prostitutes in 1987. In the late 1980s, she was also at the beginning of her career working for NGOs, and she would go on to found the prostitutes' advocacy organization Davida in 1992. The AIDS crisis had emerged in the 1980s and there was international support and funding for sex workers as health educators. Like a number of other sex-worker activists at the time, however, Gabriela's emphasis went beyond the mechanics of AIDS education, addressing a wide range of issues and insisting that health should not be separated from political empowerment.

At the time of the summit, I had become an avid videographer, recording conferences, interviews, and demonstrations. In that role, I was fortunate to spend some time getting to know Gabriela and documenting her political passions. I was particularly concerned with abolitionist attacks on our work and related debates among feminists, and I was struck that our rhetoric in the United States had a lot in common with her concerns about police violence, the media's role in the AIDS crisis, and stigma. She answered my questions exactly how I would have.

In one interview, I asked her about the red-herring accusation that prostitution could never be a choice—an assertion as reductive and classist then as it is today. Does one choose to work at McDonald's? This line of thinking drove me crazy. Gabriela explained to me that there is *some* choice, even when choices are limited. "It's dangerous to start from a position that people have no choices in life," she explained. "Because, if we do that, we only look at them as victims and victims have no choice *and no voice*."[1]

Prostitutes' rights were a revelation for so many of us. Like other pioneering global whore leaders, Gabriela developed her occupation, role, and philosophies in an environment of increasing sexual freedom and expression. In the 1960s and 1970s, women's roles were shifting, and the earliest inkling of a prostitutes' rights movement was beginning to emerge, even against the backdrop of a repressive military dictatorship in Brazil. That handful of first-wave whore leaders such as Gabriela was just beginning to work as prostitutes. As we see in this memoir, Gabriela proudly embraced her sexuality, leaving behind the shame that imprisons most of us and stepping forth courageously to speak out as a prostitute.

I often think about what made Gabriela so valuable in the prostitutes' rights movement, and I always come back to the fact that she was largely a strategist. Then again, as I reflect, so many of the early leaders of our movement were primarily strategists. It was so much the norm that I joke that the sex-worker-as-general should be another sex-worker archetype. But the thing that was different about Gabriela, what inspires us so deeply, was that she was so effective. Ultimately, I think this effectiveness stems from the combination of her brilliant, strategic mind with her fierce emotional strength, courage, and unwavering commitment to the movement. In a sense, I think her memoir provides us with a road map to this effectiveness, showing us how she developed these skills in the context of her household politics. Gabriela had suffered from the power struggles within her family, and she became a tough, rebellious child who strove to create a life for herself beyond the limitations of her family.

The Whore's-Eye View
In her role as a strategist, Gabriela understood that the prostitution stigma is central to our oppression. This is another intersection at which I felt my sisterhood with Gabriela, as the whore's-eye view offers front-row seats in the theater of society's hypocrisies.

---

1 Carol Leigh, dir., *Outlaw Poverty, Not Prostitutes*, 1990.

Like Gabriela, I was concerned with the power of language, both as a poet and as a feminist. In my play *Scarlot Harlot*, first performed in the early 1980s, the main character struggles to find the courage to come out as a prostitute. "Sex workers unite! We won't remain anonymous!" she exclaims as she finally tears the paper bag from her head. I had heard that there was tension in the naming of the Brazilian Prostitutes' Network, as Gabriela had embraced the words *prostituta* and *puta* as her identity rather than *sex worker*, which had become the prescribed term in NGO contexts. She believed that *puta* was a rich, evocative word with a history and culture, and that *sex worker* was thrust upon her in NGO circles to sanitize prostitution. I know what she meant. Many of us feel that prostitution, sex work, whoring, and so on is larger than labor, and that it can be reductive to only use that term to describe not only our work but also our roles, our activities, and our identities. Like Gabriela, I also feel strongly about the word *whore*, and I embrace it. The word itself is transgressive, providing the jolt needed to provoke people into listening to us.

Scarlot Harlot, in which I launched the term *sex worker*, was an embrace of the rights of prostitutes/sex workers *as well as* a satire on political correctness. The term *sex work* can be comedic. For example, when Scarlot Harlot tells her mother she is a sex worker, Mom replies, "What?!? You're working in a dildo factory?"

The Whore is an archetype, or many archetypes rolled into one. The Whore of Babylon, the Whore Goddess(es), the Sacred Whore—*whore* contains within it archetypes of victimization, disrespect, abuse, and deceit. But it can also bring to mind the power that comes from being different. Because of this, my peers and I embrace it. It is the word I use most casually, as a term of endearment. Margo St. James once told me that *whore* also means "beloved."

Then there is *puta*, a word embraced by prostitutes across the Americas. In the United States, trans Latina sex workers have reclaimed the term and formed a new movement of *putas*. I suggest *puta* has an English meaning, too: it means "whore," but a little nicer. Perhaps to us it seems more romantic because it's in another language.

The term *sex work*, however, has been politically advantageous for us. I coined it at a more serious juncture, in the 1970s, as a response to a workshop titled "The Sex Use Industry." That phrase was obviously stigmatizing! Plus, as a feminist, I thought we should be referring to *what women do* from our own perspective, not men's. Men use the services and women do the work, so it should be called sex *work*! It was obvious to us.

So, for us, *sex worker* ended up being a more useful term than *prostitute*. While we used *prostitute* in formal interviews and in the media until the 1990s, we didn't particularly like it, preferring euphemisms like *working girls* and others. When *sex worker* was added to the lexicon, it unlocked a certain political potential for us, and with it blossomed a huge international movement.

While I understand what possibilities this term opened up, I agree with Gabriela that we cannot forget the provocative spirit of the whore and the power that comes from embracing the terms that have been used to stigmatize us. *Puta* owns the stigma and metamorphosizes it. Gabriela was among those who would not be limited by convention and expectation. Like many, she reminds us that we should not be hemmed in by terms of reference. The *puta* is more than a worker; she is a powerful part of culture and our collective psyche. Throughout her career, Gabriela constantly sought to reclaim the terms *puta* and *prostitute* as part of a political strategy to fight the stigma surrounding prostitution and develop and implement strategies inspired in the red-light districts of Brazil.

Whore Leadership and Looking Ahead

Gabriela's history has spread through much of the field of sex work studies in volumes of research, but this is the first time an English readership is able to read her in her own words. Her memoir communicates to sex workers and students of sex work understandings that are sorely missing from the short history of our politics. What does Gabriela represent at this time in terms of whore leadership? I would say that it is the strength and wisdom acquired in adversity, a deep love and respect for humanity and culture, a pride that allowed her to follow her instincts, and a deep commitment to freedom.

The stark honesty of Gabriela's memoir reaches beyond stereotypes and allows us to witness the factors that shaped her. It is also a warning about the limitations of advocating solely around an idea of prostitutes as workers. Gabriela warns us from inside the NGO, existing on the border between prostitutes' communities and the government, that the risk of sanitization accompanies the incorporation of sex workers into mainstream categories. She saw the results of the problematic co-optation of the prostitute movement, and, in doing so, she opened the doors even wider for a fuller expression of provocative and transgressive activism outside the confines of government-funded prevention projects, such as the clothing line Daspu.

As I write this in 2022, we are on the one hand alarmed by the current political climate in both the United States and Brazil, in particular the rise of fascism and violent right-wing extremism. At the same time, while formal politics are falling apart, the policies for sex workers are becoming more just. We have recently had some victories for decriminalization, such as the introduction of a bill in the New York state legislature to decriminalize sex work and the endorsement, finally, of decriminalization by many major human rights and research groups. And at the start of the COVID-19 pandemic, I was also inspired by the community-building and community-care efforts I witnessed in sex-worker communities around the world. In times of distress, people pull together.

To conclude my foreword and introduce the pages that follow, I would say that this compelling memoir is deeply rooted in the physical details of Gabriela's existence, offering an almost painterly grasp of the scenery of everyday life, from family relationships to brothel etiquette to the bohemian world of urban Brazil. We particularly need stories like Gabriela's to offer us guidance as we confront ongoing taboos and change laws and practices in our communities and countries. Gabriela possessed the attributes we need to recognize as we fortify our future. What courage these pioneers mustered, to overcome the profound social stigma, to step forth and speak out as prostitutes!

Translator's Note

MEG WEEKS

When I first decided to translate Gabriela Leite's memoir, originally published in 2008 in Portuguese, I was well aware of the gravity of the project. Through my doctoral research on the history of the sex workers' movement in Brazil, I fully grasped Gabriela's importance for both Brazilian prostitutes and other sexual minorities, as well as for international mobilizations of sex workers beginning in the 1970s. Although I never knew her personally, I felt as though I did, as I was intimately familiar with the audiovisual and material traces of her that I had discovered in the archives. Yet, despite the proximity I had established through my research, bringing her words into English was an exhilarating, novel experience, one that in turn unlocked new understandings and insights for my scholarship. The two projects—this translation and my scholarly monograph—have advanced hand in hand, borrowing literary and intellectual depth from one another and shepherding one another into existence.

A particular challenge I encountered in translating Gabriela's writing stemmed precisely from my own knowledge as a researcher, which at times conflicted with her recollections as recorded in this memoir. In addition to confronting various linguistic puzzles, I grappled with the inconsistencies and unreliability of the genre of memoir; how should I approach the episodes that I suspected Gabriela misremembered, embellished, or exaggerated? Ultimately, I decided that "correcting" the text did not fall within my purview as a translator, although the experience did provoke interesting reflections on the nature of memory and the stubbornly idiosyncratic quality of oral history. In any case, it is worth keeping in mind the permeability of testimonial literature as one reads Gabriela's life story.

Another challenge that I confronted was choosing how best to render in English Gabriela's frank treatment of race and gender, which often employs language that does not neatly conform to that of contemporary racial justice and feminist movements. To one equipped with US sensibilities, Gabriela's tendency to identify a person's race only when they are a person of color may come across as distasteful. Moreover, she subscribed to what at times seemed like an essentialist view of gender at odds with many second- and third-wave feminist understandings of the often oppressive nature of gender as a social construction. While race and feminism in the Brazilian context will be discussed in the book's introduction, I want to touch upon this issue briefly. While she was undoubtedly an advocate of gender and racial justice—an insurgent feminist in my view, though she did not consistently identify with the term—one of Gabriela's most steadfast commitments throughout her life was to speak plainly and candidly. In fact, she frequently professed an aversion to "political correctness," especially as the international prostitutes' movement came to favor the term *sex work* and foreground a more technocratic, pro-work orientation that she felt sanitized the transgressive ethos of a political formation on the margins of society. This penchant for unbridled speech and provocation was aimed not just at her peers, however; it sought to expose hypocrisies and fragilities across the political spectrum, from conservative moralists and Catholic ideologues to dogmatic second-wave feminists and orthodox leftists.

In addition to annotating the memoir itself to identify historical and cultural phenomena, I also make ample use of footnotes to define Brazilian terms that I chose to leave in the original Portuguese due to their fundamental untranslatability. Because I am not only a translator but also a scholar of Brazilian history and of the Brazilian sex workers' movement in particular, I believe that the following introduction, coauthored with my collaborators Laura Murray and Esther Teixeira, will serve as a means of contextualizing Gabriela's life and work without speaking for her—a crucial distinction considering that self-representation was one of the first and most vociferous demands of the movement she helped found. And, as you will observe in her memoir, she was more than capable of speaking for herself.

Acknowledgments

LAURA REBECCA MURRAY,
ESTHER TEIXEIRA, AND MEG WEEKS

We would like to thank Evelin Almeida, Alessandra Leite, Tatiany Leite, Flavio Lenz Cesar, Carol Leigh, Coletivo Puta Davida, Lourdes Barreto, Leila Barreto, Friederike Strack, Angela Donini, Amanda Calabria, Lourinelson Vladmir, Anderson Sampaio, Sara Freeman, Elisa Wouk Almino, Abraham Adams, the Harvard University Department of History, the Memória da Vida: Organization and Dissemination of the Archive of the Brazilian Prostitutes' Movement project at the Federal University of Rio de Janeiro, Sheila Silva, Gabriel Alencar, and the rest of the staff at the Arquivo Público do Estado do Rio de Janeiro.

Introduction

LAURA REBECCA MURRAY,
ESTHER TEIXEIRA, AND MEG WEEKS

From Otília Silva Leite to Gabriela

Introducing Gabriela Leite's memoir to the English-speaking world is a task we undertook with great care and joy. In the pages that follow, we offer the broader context in which she lived and worked for readers less familiar with Brazil, its attendant cultural references, and the broader sex-worker movement. That said, while our goal is to elucidate her social and political milieu, we also wish for the text to stand on its own as the unvarnished life story of an iconoclast, a pioneer, and a provocateur.

Born Otília Silva Leite in São Paulo in 1951 to an indigenous farmworker mother and a casino-worker father, Gabriela experienced a sheltered middle-class childhood. While her early years were steeped in conservative Catholicism and parental discipline, she nursed from a young age a voracious intellectual appetite and a rebellious spirit. After being exposed as a teenager to great masters of history and literature such as Sérgio Buarque de Holanda and Machado de Assis, she sought broader horizons as a philosophy student at the University of São Paulo, Brazil's most prestigious university, eventually opting for a sociology degree after her first year.

Gabriela began her university studies at the height of Brazil's military dictatorship, which, after coming to power in a coup in 1964, had entered its most repressive phase by 1968. She balanced her coursework with a part-time job as a secretary at a large company, but was increasingly drawn to more visceral, authentic experiences, as she had grown tired of the pretensions and hypocrisies of her peers and the traditional Left. Fueling Gabriela's decision to embrace a new identity as a prostitute were her frustrations at what she perceived to be the false moralism of middle-class society and her own desire to live differently. In the early 1970s, she began her career in prostitution, first in an upscale nightclub and later in a working-class brothel in São Paulo's bohemian Boca do Lixo neighborhood. She even took on a new name, "Gabriela," inspired by the seductive and free-spirited protagonist of Jorge Amado's 1958 novel *Gabriela, cravo e canela* (*Gabriela, Clove and Cinnamon*).

At the time, São Paulo was home to a counterculture that was striving to preserve itself in the nation's tense political climate, yet artists and intellectuals continued to flock to Boca do Lixo's storied bars, clubs, and cinemas. While at first Gabriela struggled to adapt, she eventually embraced the work of prostitution and soon found herself reveling in the human richness and raw social energy of her newfound environment. Throughout her career, Gabriela took pride in providing companionship, advice, comfort, and friendship to her clients, often likening the prostitute to the psychoanalyst and confidante. Observing and participating in a diverse range of sexual practices satisfied the profound curiosity toward sex and the human condition she had nurtured since her adolescence. Over the next two decades, Gabriela would also become a community organizer, health-policy adviser to the federal government, and nonprofit director, all the while ardently defending her community, one of the most stigmatized and neglected groups in Brazilian society.

Gabriela consistently asserted that she enjoyed working as a prostitute, while noting that her life was not free from violence and exploitation. Much of this abuse, according to her and many other sex-worker activists, stems from the precarious legal standing of the profession. In Brazil, neither selling nor buying sex is a crime, as long as both the sex worker and client are over eighteen. However, as Gabriela explains in her memoir, Brazil's 1940 Penal Code (which is still in effect today) criminalizes third parties who profit from prostitution, either through the running of a brothel or "living off the earnings" of prostitution, rendering commercial sex establishments ripe for exploitation, corruption, and violence, inflicted by the police in particular.[1] The complete decriminalization of adult prostitution would be a primary demand of the Brazilian sex workers' movement during Gabriela's lifetime, although, as of the publication of this book, it has yet to come to fruition.

Always quick to recognize the structural roots of violence, Gabriela was one of the leaders of the first cohort of grassroots activists to protest police brutality targeting sex workers and homosexuals in São Paulo in 1979 and 1980. At first energized by these initial shows of collective action, she was dismayed when her colleagues seemed uninterested in organizing a more enduring movement to protest the injustices they suffered. Their reluctance, however, was justified. Since 1964, Brazilians had lived under the iron fist of a socially conservative military regime, which had seized power from a

---

1 Blanchette, Mitchell, and Murray, "Discretionary Policing."

democratically elected, left-leaning government to forestall what the political establishment feared was the country's descent into Cuban-style socialism. Supported by the US government in its global campaign to thwart the spread of communism, the Brazilian military dictatorship proceeded to suspend elections; arrest, imprison, and torture political dissidents; and censor the press. This repression manifested itself in law enforcement as well, with local police employing harsh measures to purge city streets of what it perceived as unsightly and morally offensive activities, specifically persecuting gay men, *travestis*, and sex workers.[2] An uptick in police brutality in the late 1970s catalyzed the first organized actions of Brazilian prostitutes, introducing them to gay activists, Afro-Brazilian groups, and feminists, all of whom were clamoring for regime change and an overhaul of their country's calcified social order. This moment coincided with the acceleration of what historians call Brazil's "political opening," which, marked by the passage of the Amnesty Law in 1979 that allowed political dissidents to return from exile, inaugurated a period of great social and political effervescence.[3]

In the early 1980s, Gabriela left São Paulo and spent several years living and working in the Zona Boêmia of Belo Horizonte, Brazil's sixth-largest city and the capital of the state of Minas Gerais. While the city was smaller and more provincial than her hometown of São Paulo, Gabriela recalls how she enjoyed the traditional glamour of its prostitution trade, reputed to be one of the most lucrative in the country. Originally planned as a brief vacation from the brisk pace in Belo Horizonte, a trip to Rio de Janeiro in 1983 turned into a permanent relocation. Immediately upon arrival in Rio, Gabriela became enamored with the city's colorful charm, breathtaking scenery, and spirit of *malandragem*, the playful trickery historically attributed to the city's samba musicians and petty criminals. In no time, she established herself in Vila Mimosa, Rio's working-class red-light district and the successor to Mangue, a storied region of brothels frequented by some of Brazil's most illustrious artists and intellectuals since the nineteenth century. The defiant and irreverent spirit of Mangue, which had, after many attempts to resist displacement, been razed by the city government in the late 1970s to make way for the con-

---

2 *Travesti* is a Brazilian Portuguese word that refers to someone who identifies with the female gender but does not necessarily identify as a woman or seek to change their anatomy. The term, previously highly stigmatized and frequently associated with prostitution, has been appropriated and resignified by the trans movement and has a strongly political connotation.

3 Fausto, *Concise History of Brazil*, 306.

struction of a new City Hall complex and subway system, was kept alive in Vila Mimosa, where the city's prostitution establishments remained until the mid-1990s. While Vila Mimosa bore little of the charm and renown of the districts in São Paulo and Belo Horizonte, the space maintained what Gabriela reverently called the "two great mysteries inscribed on the profession over time: seduction and the mysterious climate of the red lights."[4] It was only once she was ensconced in Vila Mimosa that she was finally able to organize a local and later national movement of prostitutes demanding decriminalization, an end to the stigma that had long marked their community, and comprehensive human rights.

On the national stage, Gabriela's early years in Rio were a time of great political mobilization. By the early 1980s, the military generals who presided over the federal government in Brasília had indicated that they were amenable to a return to civilian rule and, in 1982, had allowed for the resumption of multiparty direct elections for all offices except the presidency. The following year, Gabriela received an invitation from the country's first Black city councilwoman, Benedita da Silva, to participate in the first Meeting of Women from the Favelas and Urban Periphery. The meeting, which brought together domestic workers with community leaders and other grassroots activists, would forever change the course of Gabriela's life. It was there that she first publicly identified herself as a prostitute, a move that both shocked and enchanted the crowd and led to a groundswell of media attention.

Concurrently, Brazil's feminist movement was gaining momentum and would later achieve important milestones in the Constitution of 1988, the crowning achievement of the transition to democracy that was ratified three years after Brazil formally restored civilian governance. And while Black feminists have criticized the mainstream feminist movement for its middle-class sensibilities and Eurocentric tendencies, Gabriela was quick to associate her political demands as a sex worker seeking civil rights with the demands of poor women with little schooling.[5] It was within this renewal of grassroots politics and civil society that Brazil's sex-worker movement began to take shape alongside other sectors mobilizing on the Left.

In 1984, one year after Benedita da Silva's invitation, a second gathering, this time organized by the Catholic Church, would prove to be another important catalyst for Brazil's national sex-worker movement, particularly through the lifelong partnership that would develop between Gabriela and fellow ac-

4 Gabriela Leite, Coluna da Gabi, *Beijo da rua*, May 1994.
5 Carneiro, "Mulheres em movimento," 117–33.

Figure I.1. Archival photograph of Gabriela Leite. Source: Davida—Prostitution, Civil Rights and Health Archive at the Public Archive of the State of Rio de Janeiro (APERJ).

tivist Lourdes Barreto. The previous decade, progressive clergy from the Conferência Nacional dos Bispos do Brasil had founded the Pastoral da Mulher Marginalizada (Ministry for Marginalized Women, or PMM), a program to develop the self-esteem of prostitutes deeply informed by a Latin American tradition of liberation theology. Despite the crucial platform that the ministry provided, the relationship between the PMM and the Brazilian prostitutes' movement to which it would give rise became conflictual once Gabriela began attending meetings in the mid-1980s. The crux of their disagreement lay in the fact that the Catholic Church and its radical feminist allies espoused a neo-abolitionist view of prostitution, contending that commercial sex represented the apogee of patriarchal exploitation and advocating for its eventual abolition. Lourdes and Gabriela quickly recognized in each other a shared rejection of the notion that prostitutes were necessarily victims of said exploitation, a realization that led them to break away from the PMM and form an autonomous movement of sex workers in 1987.

Brazil's Sex Workers' Movement Grows and Gains International Traction
The previous decade, when the prospect of an independent movement of sex workers in Brazil was still merely a dream of Gabriela's, an international

Figure I.2. Photograph of Gabriela Leite with Lourdes Barreto. Rio de Janeiro, 1995. Photograph by Flavio Lenz. Source: Lourdes Barreto's personal archive.

movement of sex workers was quickly gaining ground. In 1975, a group of French prostitutes had gone on strike and occupied several churches across France, catalyzing a broader European struggle for the decriminalization of prostitution and sex workers' rights. Two years prior, in the United States, Margo St. James, a charismatic and media-savvy sex worker from California, had founded COYOTE (Call Off Your Old Tired Ethics), a group that staged playful and flamboyant social events as well as advocated for decriminalization and the notion of prostitution as legitimate work. By the late 1970s, San Francisco had become a hub for sex-worker organizing, with St. James working closely with activists such as Annie Sprinkle, Priscilla Alexander, and Carol Leigh. Leigh, who coined the term *sex work* during that period, authored a beautiful foreword to this book shortly before she passed away in 2022.

In 1985, St. James, feminist academic and activist Gail Pheterson, and representatives of the Dutch prostitutes' organization the Red Thread collaborated to plan and host the First World Whores' Congress, held in Amsterdam. At the Congress, sex-worker participants formed the International Committee for Prostitutes' Rights (ICPR) and released a charter outlining their demands for comprehensive labor rights, health care, and education for sex workers. The ICPR convened a second international meeting the following year in Brussels, and another in 1989 in San Francisco, which Gabriela attended as a representative of Brazil's burgeoning sex-worker movement. At the 1989 meeting, which Carol Leigh remembers in her foreword, women from the Global South such as Gabriela shared visions of political and economic emancipation informed by their nations' legacies of militarism, colonial and neocolonial extraction, and global geopolitical stratification. In doing so, they pushed the ICPR to articulate a more nuanced view of labor and sex under late capitalism, yet, as Gabriela insisted, one that left room for discussions of pleasure, joy, and agency.

Two years earlier, in 1987, Gabriela and Lourdes had organized a national meeting of Brazilian sex workers in Rio de Janeiro, an event that marked the founding of the Brazilian Network of Prostitutes, or RBP. At that time, the fast-spreading HIV epidemic was starting to provoke fear and panic in the country, and the Ministry of Health quickly categorized sex workers as a "risk group." The advent of AIDS greatly colored the event's proceedings, and activists expanded their initial focus on fighting police violence and defending their right to work to include a discussion of the rampant stigma by which prostitutes were held to be vectors of disease.

The following years brought many changes for Gabriela. She increasingly dedicated herself to activism and her work at the Institute for Religious Studies (ISER), a nongovernmental ecumenical organization that, like the PMM, was influenced by leftist ideals of liberation theology. In 1989, the recently established National AIDS Program invited Gabriela and Lourdes to participate in the development of the first HIV prevention program for sex workers in Brazil. It was the beginning of a long relationship between the Ministry of Health and the sex-worker movement that would be both fruitful and fraught with conflict. Gabriela and Lourdes's insistence on associating pleasure with prevention, in addition to drawing attention to the central role of stigma in increasing sex workers' vulnerability to HIV, provided a platform for the development of some of the world's most progressive and provocative approaches to HIV prevention.

Figure I.3. Sex-worker leaders at the First National Meeting of Prostitutes, Fala, mulher da vida (Speak, woman of the life), held in Rio de Janeiro in 1987. Source: Davida—Prostitution, Civil Rights and Health Archive at the Public Archive of the State of Rio de Janeiro (APERJ).

Figure I.4. Still of Gabriela Leite from the film *Amores da rua* (Street love), directed by Eunice Gutman, with photography by Inês Magalhães. Source: Davida—Prostitution, Civil Rights and Health Archive at the Public Archive of the State of Rio de Janeiro (APERJ).

"Cada um tem seu jeito, sexualmente. O problema é que o cara pode ter seus grilos. Aí acho que a mulher tem que ajudar: conversar, fazer carinho, pegar..."

"A gente fala que só transa por dinheiro. Mas às vezes acontece um acidente de trabalho, que é quando a gente goza." (Depoimentos de prostitutas)

Figure I.5. The first HIV-prevention brochure produced for sex workers in Brazil in 1989, titled *Fala, mulher da vida* (Speak, woman of the life), written by Flavio Lenz and produced by ISER in a project coordinated by Gabriela Leite. This material, which was drawn from interviews with prostitutes, reads (*left column, top to bottom*): "Everyone has their own tastes, sexually. The problem is that some guys have hang-ups. So that's when a woman needs to help them: talk to them, caress them, and touch.... We say that we just have sex for money, but sometimes a workplace accident happens, which is when we orgasm." Source: Davida—Prostitution, Civil Rights and Health Archive at the Public Archive of the State Rio de Janeiro (APERJ).

In 1988, the movement launched *Beijo da rua*, a newspaper edited by Flavio Lenz, a journalist and ISER employee who would go on to be Gabriela's partner until her death in 2013.[6] *Beijo da rua* was the first print journal in Brazil created by and for sex workers, founded in order to express a collective "political voice" for the community, which saw itself portrayed in traditional media "either as victims . . . degenerates and sluts, or as vectors of disease."[7] The first edition, which affirmed that "prostitution isn't a police matter," contained poetry, interviews, and news from the *zonas*, or red-light districts, of Brazil. For twenty-five years, Gabriela published her Coluna da Gabi (Gabi's column), in which she reflected on various topics including prostitution, sexuality, health, philosophy, and politics in Brazil. In her inaugural column, Gabriela makes clear that her goal in launching the paper was to demonstrate that prostitution was an integral part of her country's social fabric and, as such, should not be treated as a problem to be solved: "The prostitute is not a slut or the result of savage capitalism, but rather an expression of a society that is scared to death of facing its sexuality and consequently feels deeply threatened when the prostitute shows her face."[8]

Over the next decade, the Brazilian sex-worker movement expanded, with activists founding dozens of organizations across the country, many with funding from the Ministry of Health and the direct involvement and support of Gabriela and Lourdes. In Vila Mimosa, Eurídice Coelho founded the first sex-worker organization in Rio de Janeiro, the Association of Prostitutes of the State of Rio de Janeiro. Gabriela participated in the founding of that organization and, several years later, in 1992, would publish her first autobiography, *Eu, mulher da vida* (I, woman of the life); become a grandmother; and launch Davida—Prostitution, Civil Rights and Health, the organization she led until her death. Davida would soon grow into one of the most important prostitutes' rights organizations in Brazil, widely recognized as a vanguard for its unequivocal rejection of the discourse of victimhood, its use of cultural idioms such as theater and music in HIV-prevention projects, and its strong defense of prostitution not only as work but also as a platform for advancing broader sexual and human rights in partnership with other social movements, artists, and academics.

6 A full run of *Beijo da rua* is available for consultation at Rio's Biblioteca Nacional.
7 Lenz Cesar, Pereira de Andrade, and Aquino, "*Beijo da rua*, um jornal com a voz das prostitutas," 2015.
8 Gabriela Leite, Coluna da Gabi, *Beijo da rua*, December 1988.

Figure I.6. Gabriela and Flavio at the Club Gloria in São Paulo before a Daspu fashion show, July 16, 2006. Photo by Roberta Valerio.

Figure I.7. The first cover of the newspaper *Beijo da rua*, 1988. *Translation of right column:* "Prostitution isn't a matter for the police • The girls' sex • New life in Recife • God and the devil in the Zona do Mangue • Poetry • Prostitutes don't go in crowds to the polls." Source: Public Archive of the State of Rio de Janeiro (APERJ).

Figure I.8. Eurídice Coelho in the entryway of Vila Mimosa before it relocated in the mid-1990s. Source: Rio de Janeiro Association of Prostitutes Archive at the Public Archive of the State of Rio de Janeiro (APERJ).

Figure I.9. Launch of Gabriela's first book, *Eu, mulher da vida* (I, woman of the life). Davida founding member and sex-worker activist Doroth de Castro is next to Gabriela, and Flavio Lenz is kneeling on the floor. Source: Davida—Prostitution, Civil Rights and Health Archive at the Public Archive of the State Rio de Janeiro (APERJ).

Figure I.10. Gabriela autographing her first book with Rafael Cesar, Flavio Lenz's son—her "almost-son," as she affectionately called him. Photograph by Flavio Lenz.

Figure I.11. Gabriela with her granddaughter, Tatiany, and her daughter Alessandra, Rio de Janeiro, 1992. Photograph by Flavio Lenz.

Figure I.12. Davida members at the organization's founding meeting in July 1992 at the Mirim Samba School in the Estácio neighborhood of Rio de Janeiro. *Pictured, from left to right*: Gabriela Leite, Waldo Cesar (president of Davida from its founding until his death in 2007), Felipe Cesar (Flavio Lenz's brother), Maria Luiza Cesar (Flavio's mother), Doroth de Castro, and Regina Leite (Gabriela's sister). Photo by Flavio Lenz. Source: Davida—Prostitution, Civil Rights and Health Archive at the Public Archive of the State of Rio de Janeiro (APERJ).

By the early 2000s, officials at the Ministry of Labor and Employment were well aware of the Ministry of Health's successful HIV campaigns in partnership with sex-worker organizations. Thus, in 2002, the former invited Gabriela, along with other representatives of the Brazilian Network of Prostitutes, to participate in a workshop to formalize *profissionais do sexo* (literally, sex professionals) as an official profession within the Brazilian Classification of Occupations (CBO). The CBO designates which professions qualify for federal government benefits such as pensions and financial assistance in case of illness, and, as such, the inclusion of sex workers in the database was considered a tremendous achievement for the movement. Another watershed event in 2002 on the national stage was the election of Luiz Inácio Lula da Silva as Brazil's president. A charismatic former labor union organizer and cofounder of the left-wing Workers' Party with an unmatched talent for political strategy, Lula grew up in Brazil's impoverished Northeast and never finished secondary school. The Workers' Party candidate was a symbol of resistance for Brazil's

Figure I.13. Gabriela Leite with sex-worker leaders at the 1994 National Meeting of Sex Workers, organized by Davida and held in Rio de Janeiro. Davida leader Doroth de Castro is at Gabriela's *right*, and Lourdes Barreto is at the *far right*. Source: Davida—Prostitution, Civil Rights and Health Archive at the Public Archive of the State of Rio de Janeiro (APERJ).

popular classes, and his election ushered in an era of hope among those who had supported him since his early days organizing against the dictatorship.

Lula's first term coincided with an event that had a profound symbolic effect on sex-worker activism and HIV prevention around the world. In 2003, as part of President George W. Bush's Emergency Plan for AIDS Relief (PEP-FAR), the US government introduced a contractual clause stipulating that all entities receiving US government funds adopt a statute explicitly opposing prostitution. At the time, the Brazilian Ministry of Health was negotiating the terms of a large grant that would benefit local NGOs, eventually including Davida. As the very legality of the clause was being challenged, and US organizations were not obligated, at the time, to sign what would come to be known as the "anti-prostitution pledge," the Ministry of Health arranged for the first installment of funding to be paid through an international organization.[9]

9 In 2005, the Alliance for Open Society International questioned the constitutionality of the USAID (United States Agency for International Develoment) policy, claiming it was a violation of First Amendment rights (*Agency for Int'l Development v. Alliance for Open Society Int'l, Inc.*). Other international NGOs mobilized around the case, and in 2013, the US Supreme Court ruled the policy was an unconstitutional restriction of the rights of US-based organizations.

Intense negotiations between the Ministry of Health, USAID, international NGOs, and Brazil's well-established HIV/AIDS and sex-worker movements ensued in a variety of settings, including national-level meetings over the next few years. As is characteristic of high-profile negotiations involving myriad interests, unequal power dynamics, and large amounts of money, the precise details of these negotiations are remembered differently by different actors. Ultimately, they culminated in Brazil's HIV/AIDS program taking a strong stance and refusing to implement the mandate, eventually rejecting nearly forty million dollars in HIV-prevention funds that had been allocated to the country. The final decision, made in partnership with Davida, the Brazilian Network of Prostitutes, and the broader HIV/AIDS movement, was heralded by the international community and applauded by sex-worker activists globally as an act of defiance vis-à-vis neoimperial foreign policy.

That same year, the creation of Daspu, a clothing line for sex workers, would also contribute to both Gabriela and Davida's national and international fame. Much of the media attention the line received stemmed from a lawsuit brought by the luxury São Paulo clothing store Daslu for copyright infringement and defamation. Many actors and media personalities came out in favor of Daspu, publicly positioning themselves against the high-end retailer, which came to symbolize conspicuous consumption and Brazil's extreme inequality. By featuring both sex-worker and non-sex-worker models on its catwalks, Daspu created a space of safety, ambiguity, and obfuscation that led many sex workers who might not otherwise have been willing to come forward, walk the runway, and confront the prejudices that surround prostitution. Daspu collections designed in partnership with professional designers played on the cultural symbols of sex and prostitution, always featuring cheeky and provocative T-shirts with phrases like "We're Bad But We Could Be Worse." With Daspu, as Gabriela states in her memoir, "Beauty triumphs over hypocrisy."

While Daspu brought an injection of energy and funding to Davida, Brazil's broader political context would become increasingly hostile and repressive toward issues at the core of the prostitutes' movement. Gabriela, always a prescient observer of national politics, noted as she was penning this memoir in the late 2000s that she felt that things were "moving backward" with regard

Non-US organizations, however, still had to sign the "anti-prostitution pledge." The constitutionality of applying the policy to foreign organizations was subsequently challenged, yet in 2020 the Supreme Court ruled, in a majority decision written by Justice Brett Kavanaugh, that foreign organizations operating abroad "possess no rights under the US Constitution" (see https://www.supremecourt.gov/opinions/19pdf/19-177_b97c.pdf).

Figure I.14. Gabriela celebrating Davida's birthday and the founding of Daspu at Davida's headquarters in Rio de Janeiro, July 15, 2005. Behind Gabriela is a reprint of the cover of the *Fala, mulher da vida* (Speak, woman of the life) educational material. Photograph by Flavio Lenz.

to prostitution. In 2010, disheartened and disappointed with the movement's dynamics with the government, Gabriela decided to run for the lower house of Congress representing the Green Party. True to her rebellious spirit, Gabriela's campaign centered on issues many politicians avoided, such as HIV/ AIDS, abortion, and prostitution. While her bid was not successful, she made history as the first public sex worker to run for federal office in Brazil.

In the years before her death, Gabriela increasingly focused on sexual rights and the need to treat the issue of prostitution beyond the limited and often stigmatizing scope of public health. In 2011, at the Brazilian Network of Prostitutes' regional conference in Belém, activists made a decision to no longer apply for federal funding for AIDS projects. In their statement, leaders expressed their sense that the "risk group" framework they had fought so vehemently against in the late 1980s had returned. In 2013, the extent to which the Ministry of Health's approach to HIV prevention had changed became even clearer when the government censored a public information campaign developed for International Sex Workers' Rights Day (June 2).

Figure I.15. Jane Eloy models the Daspu wedding dress at the 27th São Paulo Biennial in 2006. Characteristic of Daspu's humorous and playful approach to its designs, the wedding dress, a collaboration between Davida and artist Tadej Pogačar, is made of sheets and pillowcases from Rio de Janeiro sex motels and accessorized with a necklace and veil made from condoms.

Figure I.16. Gabriela Leite at her 2010 campaign launch. Still from the documentary *A Kiss for Gabriela*, directed by Laura Rebecca Murray.

Sex-worker organizations responded with public protests and strong statements of condemnation, and Gabriela coauthored an article with Flavio Lenz and Laura Murray expressing her sharp critique of the Ministry of Health.[10]

Throughout her life, Gabriela strove to identify and uncover hypocrisies and veiled prejudices surrounding prostitution, gender, and sexuality. Gabriela's indignation at the injustices she witnessed fostered many of her life's most consequential decisions, and this attitude is evidenced in many of the experiences she shares in this memoir. In particular, Gabriela's ardent defense of the word *puta* and her preference for the unvarnished *prostitute* over the more politically palatable and de rigueur *sex worker* are exemplary of her personal philosophy. For her, the word *puta* represented an attitude toward life and a way of doing politics, unapologetically and irreverently so. Her penchant for the term, which is traditionally used as a slur in Portuguese, was rooted in her disdain for attempts to sanitize and make more respectable the profession of the whore. Moreover, she bristled at its use in the common derogatory expression *filho da puta* (literally, "son of a whore," though roughly equivalent to the English expression "son of a bitch"). Gabriela believed it unfair that the children of her colleagues—whom she considered to be devoted mothers, differently from how she saw herself—represented one of the worst epithets in the Portuguese language.[11] She believed that reclaiming and resignifying the word *puta* disrupted the effects of stigma by forcing people to see whores as mothers, protectors, feminists, and workers while defending prostitution within a framework of sexual rights, specifically the right to deviate from normative expressions of gender and sexuality.

The movement's insistence on foregrounding sexuality, pleasure, and combating stigma in all spheres of its activism has been its greatest strength in weathering political upheaval and economic crises over the past four decades. This animating ethos, however, has also been one of its greatest challenges in sustaining funding, particularly as the political climate in Brazil became increasingly conservative and real estate prices in Rio de Janeiro soared as the city prepared for the 2014 World Cup and 2016 Summer Olympic Games. In 2010, Davida decided to move its offices to the Hotel Paris, a building used for prostitution in downtown Rio. Gabriela had always dreamed of Davida having offices in the *zona*, yet the relocation was short lived, as the hotel was sold

10 Leite, Murray, and Lenz. "Peer and Non-peer," 7–25.
11 Um Beijo para Gabriela, "Why Gabriela Likes the Word *Puta*," YouTube video, June 12, 2013, 3:52, https://www.youtube.com/watch?v=CvKkGPiXv0o.

Figure I.17. Gabriela at the theatrical presentation of *Daughter, Mother, Grandmother, and Whore* at the Brazilian AIDS Conference in São Paulo, 2012. Still from video shot by Angela Donini.

to a French company, which promptly evicted its occupants. As a result, Davida transitioned to operating online and from activists' homes. Facilitating the organization's ongoing activities were institutional partnerships such as those with the Observatório da Prostituição / Prostitution Policy Watch (an initiative bringing together Davida activists and researchers from the Federal University of Rio de Janeiro), the Brazilian Interdisciplinary AIDS Association (ABIA), the Brazilian Network of Prostitutes, and the Public Archive of the State of Rio de Janeiro (APERJ), to which Gabriela donated Davida's extensive textual and audiovisual archive in 2013.

Gabriela passed away from lung cancer in October of 2013, approximately a year following her diagnosis. Over the following years, Davida underwent a series of organizational restructurings, continuing to operate online and through its institutional partnerships, even without a physical headquarters in Rio de Janeiro. The group started collaborating more directly with CasaNem, an LGBTQIA+ shelter and radical sociocultural education project founded by Indianarae Siqueira, a self-described "travestigênere puta" activist who has also run for public office. As Gabriela notes in her first memoir, *Eu, mulher da vida*, published in 1992, Brazil's sex-worker movement was largely focused on cisgender women, an orientation that continued throughout her

Figure I.18. The cover of the June 2014 *Beijo da rua* issue produced in honor of Gabriela. The artwork, by Davida member Sylvio Oliveira (who designed many of Daspu's T-shirts), states, "I'm not here to fool around."

lifetime, making this more recent collaboration especially significant.[12] In the 2010s, Daspu also continued its activities, putting on fashion shows throughout Brazil. Davida was particularly active and vocal around the 2014 World Cup and 2016 Olympic Games, publishing editions of *Beijo da rua*, still edited by Flavio Lenz, about both "megaevents" that denounced both police violence and displacements and produced counternarratives to the moral panic surrounding prostitution at the time. Shortly before the COVID-19 pandemic arrived in Brazil, Davida activists held a meeting at the CasaNem and decided to restructure the organization as a collective, changing its name to Coletivo Puta Davida.

In 2022, the Brazilian Network of Prostitutes celebrated thirty-five years of activism. Lourdes Barreto continues to be a leader and an international

12 Leite, *Eu, mulher da vida*, 151.

Figure I.19. Sex workers and allies after a Daspu fashion show at the 2018 Women of the World (WOW) conference in Rio de Janeiro, 2018. Indianarae Siqueira, wearing a white dress, sits in the first row, and Lourdes Barreto is seated in a wheelchair, also in the first row. Photograph by Gabi Carrera.

icon of sex-worker activism, publishing a memoir herself in 2023.[13] In the years following Gabriela's death, sex-worker activists in Brazil also formed two additional national networks, the Unified Sex Workers' Central (CUTS) and the National Association of Sex Professionals (ANPROSEX). During the COVID-19 pandemic, all three networks provided essential supplies, information, and support to their communities across Brazil. These activities drew on long-standing practices of mutual aid; in fact, activists and allies who lived through both the HIV/AIDS epidemic and COVID-19 in Brazil frequently compared the central role sex workers played in both health crises. In contrast to its actions during the HIV epidemic, however, the federal government did not pursue partnerships with social movements during the COVID-19 pandemic. In response, sex workers and their allies widely denounced the egregious negligence of far-right president Jair Bolsonaro, elected in 2018 amid a groundswell of social conservatism in the country.[14]

13 Barreto, *Lourdes Barreto*.
14 Santos et al., *Sex Work*.

The Ten Commandments: How to Be a Professional Puta

Drawn from a series of interviews that were conducted and edited by the Brazilian journalist Marcia Zanelatto, Gabriela's memoir tells the story of her deeply unorthodox life, from the middle-class neighborhoods and Catholic schools of São Paulo to the brothels and samba schools of Rio and later to major international stages. Interspersed throughout the book's two hundred pages is a subversive parody of the Ten Commandments, which Gabriela appropriates to provide advice to prostitutes drawn from her arsenal of professional wisdom. Rather than focus on divulging intimate details about her relationships with clients, Gabriela chooses instead to situate herself and her fellow prostitutes within the complex fabric of Brazilian politics, culture, and society.

In straightforward prose, Gabriela's memoir identifies sex workers as active participants in their country's political and cultural opening of the 1970s, 1980s, and 1990s, a process that resulted in an overhaul of Brazil's fundamental legal order and a reconfiguration of civil society. For Gabriela and her colleagues, this struggle continued into the 2000s and 2010s, as there was still much work to do to ensure that Brazil became meaningfully—not just nominally—democratic. In addition to narrating her life trajectory, Gabriela paints a rich portrait of marginal spaces and people in São Paulo, Belo Horizonte, and Rio de Janeiro, a bohemian underworld shunned by middle-class society but cherished and lovingly portrayed in the pages that follow. This bohemia became crucial to Gabriela's philosophy of sex and politics, a physical as well as metaphorical space on the margins of society from which she and her colleagues could critique the falsities and moralism of the bourgeois mainstream.

Throughout her career, Gabriela spoke with frankness and pride about her profession in an attempt to confront and dispel age-old prejudices surrounding sex work, female sexuality, and sexual practices that were not monogamous, procreative, or strictly heterosexual. And while other grassroots mobilizations in Brazil sought proximity to the federal government via labor organizing and unionization, the sex-worker movement, led by Gabriela and her colleague Lourdes, would always remain somewhat wary of the state as a vehicle for social, economic, and political mobility. To this day, Brazilian prostitutes continue to question the meaning of democracy in a nation in which many racist, classist, and patriarchal power structures from the colonial period have remained intact, even after the end of the dictatorship nearly forty years ago. With her characteristic irreverent humor and sharp political critique, Gabriela, a true organic intellectual, recounts a lifetime of political

Figure I.20. Gabriela speaking at an event at Praça Tiradentes, one of Rio de Janeiro's red-light districts, December 4, 2008. Photograph by Flavio Lenz.

militancy against a backdrop of massive social upheaval as Brazil grappled with the legacies not only of authoritarianism and state violence, but also of slavery, patriarchy, and Catholic social conservatism.

Looking Back while Looking Ahead: Activist Scholarship

As scholars from three different disciplines—anthropology, history, and literature—we wanted this introduction to highlight the memoir's importance to diverse bodies of knowledge. We believe that Gabriela's memoir has unique merit as a historical account of a rapidly shifting period in Brazilian politics and society, a beautifully rendered example of testimonial literature, and a portrait of complex cultural and sociological dynamics against the backdrop of the international AIDS epidemic and the burgeoning sex-workers' rights movement. While Laura knew Gabriela personally and worked with her closely for nearly a decade, Esther and Meg came to know her through their own scholarly research and the conversations with her daughters, Alessandra and Evelin, and her partner, Flavio, that were critical to bringing the publication of this translation to fruition. We hope that our different relationships to the protagonist of this story provide a variety of epistemic and personal points of entry through which readers can approach the text. More-over, we chose to join forces on this project due to a shared commitment to bring together scholarship and political activism, a marriage that has a long and fruitful history in Gabriela's life and work, albeit not always a frictionless one. In fact, partnering with allies from a variety of fields and backgrounds was always a priority for Gabriela. The social movement she helped build ad-vocated not only for human rights but also for valuing sex workers as writers, artists, cultural critics, and researchers, as producers of knowledge who also deserve a place in the canon of feminist thought.

Furthermore, we hope that her work, together with this introduction, may help shed light on Brazil's long-standing patterns of social conservatism and far-right extremism that gained new life with Bolsonaro's election in 2018. Never defeatist, Gabriela would surely want her memoir to be seen, as Carol Leigh suggests in her foreword, as an elucidation of the strategies that may be most effective in resisting closed-mindedness, bigotry, and oppression. On a more uplifting and final note, one of the most moving experiences of the process of bringing Gabriela's work to an English readership was work-ing with Carol Leigh on her poignant foreword, which was the last piece of writing Carol authored before her death in November 2022. As Carol wrote so eloquently, this book offers a "whore's-eye view" of the absurdities of com-monly held attitudes toward sex, gender, and work—a unique perspective that may just unlock the type of radical critique we need most at this critical juncture.

BIBLIOGRAPHY

Barreto, Lourdes. *Lourdes Barreto: Puta Biografia*. Edited by Leila Barreto and Elaine Bortolanza. São Paulo: Editora Paka-Tatu, 2023.

Blanchette, Thaddeus, Gregory Mitchell, and Laura Murray. "Discretionary Policing, or the Lesser Part of Valor: Prostitution, Law Enforcement, and Unregulated Regulation in Rio de Janeiro's Sexual Economy." *Criminal Justice and Law Enforcement: Global Per-spectives* 7, no. 2 (2017): 31–74.

Carneiro, Sueli. "Mulheres em Movimento." *Estudos Avançados* 17, no. 49 (2003): 117–33.

Fausto, Boris. *A Concise History of Brazil*. Cambridge: Cambridge University Press, 1999.

Leite, Gabriela Silva. *Eu, mulher da vida*. Rio de Janeiro: Editora Rosa dos Tempos, 1992.

Leite, Gabriela Silva, Laura Murray, and Flavio Lenz. "The Peer and Non-Peer: The Poten-tial of Risk Management for HIV Prevention in Contexts of Prostitution." *Revista bra-sileira de epidemiologia* 18 (2015): 7–25.

Lenz Cesar, Flavio, Ana Beatriz Pereira de Andrade, and Henrique Perazzi de Aquino. "Beijo da rua, um jornal com a voz das prostitutas." In *Anais do 7º Congresso Interna-cional de Design da Informação / Proceedings of the 7th Information Design Interna-*

tional Conference / CIDI 2015 (Blucher Design Proceedings, no. 2, vol. 2), edited by C. G. Spinillo, L. M. Fadel, V. T. Souto, T. B. P. Silva, and R. J. Camara, 460–67. São Paulo: Blucher, 2015.

Santos, Betania, Indianarae Siqueira, Cristiane Oliveira, Laura Murray, Thaddeus Blanchette, Carolina Bonomi, Ana Paula da Silva, and Soraya Simões. "Sex Work, Essential Work: A Historical and (Necro)Political Analysis of Sex Work in Times of COVID-19 in Brazil." *Social Sciences* 10, no. 1 (2020): 2.

Souza Nucci, Guilherme de. *Prostituição, lenocínio e tráfico de pessoas: aspectos constitucionais e penais*. São Paulo: Thomson Reuters Revista Dos Tribunais, 2014.

The Story
of a Woman
Who Decided
to be a *Puta*

daughter,

mother,

grandmother,

and whore

The Greatest Lesson

I love men. I love being around them, and I have never met an ugly one. They are all handsome, each one with his own characteristic smell, his walk, his gaze. They harbor an immense love for their mothers and for their own bodies. Fat or thin, they all have beautiful bodies, even when they have little potbellies. Sometimes I ask myself how they manage to walk: Does the dick in between their legs get in the way? I haven't worked up the courage to ask this question, at least not yet.

Another thing I love is saying what I think, with no filter. Those who read this book will immediately notice this about me. I have learned a thing or two in my time on earth. One of them is the importance of having an opinion, of speaking up when you don't like something. It took me a while to acquire this right, and, for that reason, I will never give it up. I spent a good part of my life fighting for it, and now I am spending another part trying to convince my prostitute colleagues that it belongs to them as well.

There is a third thing that I cherish. In fact, perhaps it is the thing I value most highly: freedom. Freedom to think differently, to dress differently, to behave differently. I don't know where my passion for freedom came from exactly—my life is full of many certainties, as well as infinite doubts and contradictions—but it is here to stay.

My destiny up until this point was guided by these three loves. And, as we all know, love doesn't only bring happiness. It causes a great deal of pain as well, in ourselves and in those who are close to us. I know that, because of my obsession with breaking chains—be they political, cultural, moral, or psychological—I have hurt some people who are dear to me.

But I believe that I have also helped countless prostitutes to lead more dignified lives. I was, am, and will continue to be responsible for my actions. What one thinks of them depends on one's outlook on life. As long as I can still exercise my freedom, I have nothing to worry about.

This is the greatest lesson I have learned. I, daughter, mother, grand-mother, and whore.

The Whore's First Commandment: You shall be discreet. You shall never point to a man in the street and say that he is your client.

Coca-Cola and Pills

"Get out! Get out!" the prostitute screamed at the guy. "Get out!" The scene was tense. Visibly out of her mind, the woman had the man by the arm, try-ing to pull him out of the packed elevator. The guy was a client in a building dedicated entirely to prostitution, in São Paulo in the 1970s. The prostitute was me.

Drugs always circulated in the world of the whores, in one form or another, but they had never really been my thing. In that time, however, I don't really know why, I ended up addicted to pills. Maybe it was my lack of knowledge, or just my willingness to try anything. The girls in that building, number 134 of Rua Barão da Limeira, were in the habit of taking Pervitin or other uppers.[1] One day, I was tired and a colleague asked me if I wanted to try half of a pill. I took it and I loved it. I liked the electricity, the activated feeling it gave me. After that day I started taking more and more. When I finally stopped, I was taking an average of five pills per day.

Every morning when I arrived at the building, I ate a fresh roll with butter and drank a black coffee that Cecília, our madam, prepared in the apartment where we received our clients. There was a kid who would do our shopping so that we wouldn't have to change clothes constantly just to go to the bakery. I used to ask him to bring me a large Coca-Cola. We weren't allowed to have drugs or alcohol in the apartment, but there was a guy who walked the hall-ways selling pills. I would crush the pill with the bottom of a cup, mix it into the Coke, and gulp it down.

1 Pervitin was the brand name of licit methamphetamine produced by the German pharma-ceutical company Temmler in the twentieth century.

I worked hyperalert. Often my clients would say to me: "Your eyes are crazy, girl! What are you on?" After work, I would go to a nearby restaurant to eat, usually just a watercress salad. And then I would get high again at night.

One Sunday, business was slow and I ended up taking a couple of pills at once. All of a sudden, I saw the elevator stop on my floor, packed with men. I grabbed one of them and yelled at him to get out. He said that he didn't want to, so I started pulling the guy by the arm. "Get out!" I screamed. The man tried to shake me off, and everyone started yelling at me to let go of him. And I, having taken uppers to be able to see more and more clients, had it in my head that I was going to get that man out of the elevator no matter what. The man in question was a regular guy, nothing special. I was compelled simply by my own compulsion to work. The elevator operator started yelling at me, saying that he was going to close the door, and I responded: "Close it and I will break this bastard's arm!" Poor guy!

After this scandal, I realized that I had gotten myself into a predicament. Many girls have gone through similar things, hitting their clients, sometimes even having psychotic breaks. I decided to stop taking pills. My habit hadn't even been going on that long and I already didn't recognize myself. What would be in store for me if I continued like that? I didn't know, no one knew. But it most likely was nothing good. With great effort, I stopped taking pills.

At first my productivity fell a bit. But it was worth it. Without the pills, I was able to chat with my clients. And being able to chat is one of the secrets of being a good prostitute. At first, it is difficult to understand how our world works. As the years passed, however, I was able to make sense of it. Or part of it, at least.

You can't treat a client like a boyfriend, I learned. But it was by lending them an ear, letting them tell you what they like and what they want, that I started to learn the secrets of the profession. Men are extremely fragile; that whole story about how they are great connoisseurs of female sexuality is a big lie. They know only about their own urgent desires and fantasies. And these, most of the time, are treated like things to be hidden, weaknesses that shouldn't be shared with anyone. Including—and, in fact, especially—with the women they love.

I learned from my clients that we should always fake orgasms, because that's what they want. They like to believe that the women they fuck come, even prostitutes. Even if it's just a little quickie lasting five minutes. There are those who like to think that by paying a bit extra, the prostitute will come. As if orgasms depended on money.

The elevator episode was one of the most impactful moments in the story of my life. But this story started many years before, all the way back when my parents, Oswaldo and Mathilde, met.

A Short-Lived Fairytale

Women and children are the first to stop sinking ships.
—ANA CRISTINA CÉSAR

My parents met on the coffee and cattle farm belonging to my paternal grandparents in Araras, in the state of São Paulo. My mother's father, Seu Chico, was the foreman of the farm and lived there with my grandmother, Dona Benedita, and their six children. They all worked on the farm from the time they were little. My father, on the other hand, grew up infatuated with casinos and lived with his parents in a mansion in the Vila Mariana neighborhood of São Paulo.

One fine day, having grown tired of his bohemian lifestyle, my father decided to spend a season on the family farm, where he had spent little time in the past. When he arrived there, he met Mathilde, a girl of seventeen, black-haired, slim, with tawny skin and downcast eyes. My father, who was twice her age, fell completely in love.

My mother's family was enthusiastic about the possibility of a marriage to the boss's son, and the young Mathilde, despite not feeling anything for Oswaldo, was obligated to go forward with the union. Even though she was forced to marry, to this day Dona Mathilde's eyes shine when she remembers her wedding party. She keeps the photos with the care and affection of a woman in love. These are the mysteries of a shared life.

It appears that in the beginning they lived well together. They moved into the house in Vila Mariana and my mother got pregnant, but the baby, very weak because of the anemia my mother had lived with for a long time unawares, only lived for a few days. He was her only boy. A few months later, my father began traveling around to casinos across Brazil and my mother was left alone in the mansion in Vila Mariana, cohabitating with her in-laws. "I am sure that even on the trip here men flirted with you, because you are beautiful although you insist on saying that you're ugly." My father said this to me the last time we were together and, in one way or another, many times over the course of our lives together. My friends have told me that I idolize my father. Perhaps this is true.

Oswaldo Leite was born in São Paulo into an elite family descended from the state's earliest settlers. He was the eldest son of the famous captain Juquita, or José Leite Filho, coffee baron and combatant in the Constitutionalist Revolution of 1932.[2] According to family legend, my father never had a job in his youth. When he finally realized that he had gotten to know all the tricks of the casinos from having gambled so much, he discovered his profession: croupier.

This is how I remember my father. Bohemian, crazy about his job, elegant, and sweet-smelling. He loved a lavender scent called Atkinsons that I would recognize immediately if someone were wearing it today, though I think they've stopped making it. How I miss that polite and affectionate man who gazed at me from behind his thick glasses. He was an inspiration and a protector.

I grew up when girls didn't have the freedom to do much of anything, yet he always understood the problems this caused for me. He understood my urge to spread my wings, my future plans, and my secret desire to be tall and beautiful. Once I was a grown woman, every so often I would vent to him about my insecurity about my height and he would joke, "Relax, there's no rush, you'll grow a bit more." He added: "And if you don't grow, there is always the illusion of high heels. You're already there—look at the size of your heels!"

My father worked in clandestine casinos and would stay away from home for a month or two at a time. When he came back, I would invariably be on a hunger strike. Since I was a child, I have had a strong personality, and when my mother prohibited me from doing something, I would rebel by refusing to eat.

In truth, I was really lucky. My hunger strikes never lasted more than one or two days. All it seemed to take for him to show up was for me to make the decision to fast.

My mother would complain to him about my behavior and I, locked in my room, would hear my father say, "Be patient, she is a girl. She is discovering life and you don't give her a break." My mother would get furious, saying that

2 The Constitutionalist Revolution of 1932 was an uprising of the people of the state of São Paulo against the government of Getúlio Vargas, which had seized power in a coup in 1930. The conflict, which resulted in several thousand deaths, was an expression of discontent at the eroding power of São Paulo elites in the national political arena. While the rebels ultimately lost the military offensive, they were able to broker the drafting of a new federal constitution in 1934.

he was too lenient with me: "Then why doesn't Gina, who is almost the same age as her and is also discovering life, act the same way?" My father would get quiet, climb the stairs, enter our room, and, before hugging and kissing me, would ask: "Do you think you can take a break from that hunger strike and come out to dinner with me and your sister at Daddy's Restaurant?" As if by magic, my rebelliousness would evaporate. I would get up from my prostration, cover my father in kisses, and ask him, "Why did you take so long to come back?" My happiness was so great that it wouldn't fit inside me. I would get ready and anxiously wait for him to finish resting after his trip.

The three of us would catch the tram in front of our house and head toward the Praça da Sé.[3] Daddy's Restaurant—its name more than perfect—was a popular spot for São Paulo's bohemian set. It never closed and was located in the basement of a building, with wooden stairs with a golden banister. I would descend the stairs feeling very important, holding on to the banister, and there below we were received warmly by the waiter who had been serving my father for decades.

We always sat at the same table and ordered the same food: a mozzarella pizza and poached pears with whipped cream for dessert. Dad would ask if we wanted something different and our answer was always no, which made him laugh. "Children are very traditional in their tastes," he would say. The fact is that he also always ate the same thing: a simple filet of beef washed down with lots of wine—two or three bottles of a good red, preferably Portuguese.

He asked us about school, our reading, the motive for my last hunger strike, and the reason I fought so much with my mother. After a while, he would open up and talk about her. He would say that she was beautiful, but that she had a terrible temper. He complained that she was influenced by her humble family on the farm, good people, but, even so, she would never be able to understand his way of being, living, and working.

For her part, my mother would accuse my father of setting a bad example for us. "Women are born to suffer and you treat them as if life were a big party. I can't wait to see when they get married and dare to invite their husbands to eat lobster in the middle of the night." She could be funny, my mother.

Once he stayed away for a very long time, about two months. My mother didn't say anything when he came back, but, as a punishment, she washed and ironed all his white shirts and hid them in a dresser. When he realized he didn't have any shirts to wear, he became desperate. He was very vain

3 São Paulo's Praça da Sé, or Cathedral Square, is a main landmark in the city center, home to the Metropolitan Cathedral.

and would never go out without donning a suit and an immaculately pressed white shirt. He spent a week walking around the house in his blue pajamas with black trim, passing the nights reading or practicing on a mini roulette wheel he kept at home. We went to sleep to the sound of the pink ball rolling past the numbers. He was so used to living at night that he wasn't able to sleep at a normal time.

I remember one particular day, a Thursday, market day. Mom went out with Gina and I was left alone with my father. I couldn't stand to see him so sad anymore, not knowing what to do at home. So I went to the dresser, grabbed all the shirts, and gave them to him. To my surprise, he refused to accept them and asked me to put them back where they had been, because this was a matter between him and my mother, he said, and one day she would give them back. No, I responded, take your shirts and go out so you can feel better. In the end, my father ended up packing his suitcases, and when my mother came back from the market, he was nowhere to be found.

My mother punished me and hit me, and from then on, whenever I disobeyed or contradicted her, I would hear the same sentence: "It's no use, you are the same as your father!" A sentence that, in fact, she continues to exclaim when the subject at hand is me.

Sometime later, they made up. They went on a trip and we stayed at my aunt's house. On the way home, we found out that my mother was pregnant. In the following months, we lived well; my mother even accepted the impromptu late-night feasts, which were wonderful. She was always in a good mood, playing with us, teaching us how to knit and crochet, and at the same time making little jackets and slippers for the baby.

On the day of my sister's birth, we woke up to go to school and my father prepared our breakfast. He said that he was going to visit my mother in the hospital and, on the way, he would swing by the notary's office and register our newborn sister. In the middle of my mother's pregnancy, Gina and I had bought a book of baby names and their meanings and the four of us had many conversations about what the name of my new sister would be. We chose Thais Helena. My father went to register her, and, for the first time in our lives, we had the opportunity to go to and from school alone. On that day, a drizzling May 31st, we gained not only another sister but also a bit of freedom.

But not long after, my father went away forever. I don't know why he and my mother fought. They never argued in front of us, and we never knew why one of them was angry at the other. I only know that Dad packed his bags, as he had done innumerable times, but this time it was for good. He gave me a hug, and then hugged Gina. He gave Thais a cuddle and said that he wouldn't be back. Off he went to Caxambu and the four of us women were left living alone.[4]

Once in a while Dad would come to São Paulo and meet me and Gina at his sister's house. They were secret visits, as my mother had prohibited us from seeing each other, and my aunt went out of her way to hide it from her. It was a different time; they never considered getting formally separated (divorce wasn't legal yet), so they hammered out the details of the separation themselves.

To his dying day, Dad harbored the hope that one day they would reconcile. It never came to pass, but nor did they get legally separated, which Mom said was foolish: "A woman only has one man in her life. Having a second one is nothing but shamelessness."

Mentioning my father was prohibited at home after his final departure, but we continued to meet up with him and go to Daddy's Restaurant, for old time's sake. But it no longer had the same magic, as my aunt was always with us.

That was how it was until I became a grown woman.

In those days, I saw him many times, each time he came to São Paulo. After these encounters, I would return home so happy that my mother surmised that I had been with him. But she didn't say a word. I only know this because recently I was chatting with her in my yard and she said, "I always knew everything. I didn't say anything because I respected the great love you had for your father." That's how my mother is: loving and tough as nails at the same time!

One Mother-in-Law, Two Faces

My mother is of Indigenous descent, or, as folks say in rural São Paulo, a *cabocla*.[5] During her entire childhood and part of her adolescence she worked on the farm, planting and harvesting coffee. She never went to school, so she only knows how to sign her name, but she knows her way around numbers like nobody else I know. She learned to sew from my grandmother, who was also illiterate but became the most sought-after seamstress for men's attire in the small city of Americana, where my grandparents moved after they gave up working on the farm. Because she sewed so well, my mother had many clients, and that was how, when my father would disappear for months at a time, she was able to keep our household afloat without wanting for anything.

---

4 Caxambu is a small city in the southeastern state of Minas Gerais.

5 A *caboclo* or *cabocla* is a person of mixed Indigenous Brazilian and European ancestry.

The only friend my mother had in those days was my aunt, who was married to my father's brother. Aunt Olinda was a very solitary and quiet woman whose family lived in Portugal. She had come to Brazil to work as a maid in my grandparents' house, where she met my uncle, who was completely addicted to betting on horses.

The two of them were quite the pair: they were both young and pretty, although one was considered an Indian hick and the other an ignorant girl from the old country. They bonded in order to survive the woes caused by my grandmother's contempt.

My *vovó*'s great disgust was having to live with these two women in the big house in Vila Mariana.[6] Dona Olívia, the matriarch of our family, had studied at the Sacré-Coeur school and left to marry a cousin of hers while still a teenager. With her white, nearly translucent skin and her fine hair and mannerisms, she was a genuine aristocrat, intolerant of those she considered beneath her. However, these women were her daughters-in-law, chosen by her beloved sons, whom she spoiled like princes.

With Dad always traveling and my uncle basically autistic, Vovó turned my mother and Aunt Olinda into her servants. It didn't matter that she already employed the services of a cleaning woman and a cook.

Vovó Olívia lived in bed because of a problem with her legs, and her biggest source of entertainment was to yell things like "Mathilde, bring me the bedpan!" or "Olinda, you are a slug and you take so long to bring me my food!" As a girl, I was frightened of her strident screaming.

When my father returned home, she transformed into the epitome of kindness, requesting in a quiet and polite voice, "My dear daughter-in-law, please, would you bring me a cup of coffee?" Because of this, my mother's complaints fell on deaf ears. My father didn't believe that she was mistreated by her mother-in-law. Under these conditions, Mom got pregnant with me and soon after with my sister Gina.

What a bizarre home I had for the first twelve years of my life. When I was born, my grandmother Olívia already had the "strange illness in her legs," as we called it in the family. She lived confined to the ground floor of the house, in the living room that had become her room, surrounded by trinkets, family portraits, numerous notebooks that she kept as diaries, and books, countless books, which she read avidly. No one knew what exactly the problem was with her legs, and, because she never let herself be examined by the family doctor,

6 *Vovó* is the diminutive of the Portuguese word *avó,* meaning "grandmother," and has an affectionate connotation, perhaps used here ironically.

the illness got worse as time marched on. Often she would wake up in the middle of the night, screaming in pain. I never once saw my grandmother walk.

My parents lived in a large room with sizable windows and a balcony that looked out onto Rua Domingos de Moraes.[7] Their heavy furniture of fine, dark wood was a testament to the good taste of my father. He would take refuge there to read his books during the days he spent in São Paulo. And at night, like all the men of the house, he would venture out into the *Paulistana* night.[8]

Mathilde: From Feeble to Feared

There was a giant abandoned garage behind our house, and, as an expression of independence, my mother decided that we would move into it. She was sick of eating, drinking, and doing whatever my grandmother demanded; she was sick of living in a house in which my grandmother was the ultimate sovereign, despite being permanently laid up in bed.

Even though the garage belonged to the main house, Mathilde decreed that that territory would belong to her and her daughters. To get there, we had to descend a car ramp and open a large two-sided gate. She managed to transform the garage into a decent house; with the renovations she undertook, we soon had a living room, a dining room, two bedrooms, a kitchen, a small bathroom, and even a little playroom.

All things considered, it was quite pretty. Dad bought furniture: a beautiful dining set, an attractive red divan, and rugs. My mother, for the first time in her marriage, came to have her own stove, her own pantry, and her own life as a married woman and a mother of two daughters.

With the move, Dona Mathilde, an illiterate Indigenous peasant, signaled to that aristocratic family that she was a strong woman who could take control of her own life. Vovó came to have great respect for my mother's strength; she even came to fear raising her voice in her presence.

Despite having our own house, our playroom, and phenomenal food, our life as children got much harder after the move. My mother turned into a rigid person of few words and repressive looks, personality traits that had thus far not manifested themselves to us with such force. Although I was only ten years old, we already began to experience the alienation that we would live with until the day I left home.

My mother had a stick of quince wood that she had brought from the coun-

7 *Rua* is the Portuguese word for "street."
8 *Paulistana/o* refers to a person or thing from the city of São Paulo.

tryside to "educate us." We got a lot of beatings. To this day, I still have aches and pains from the spankings I received: the quince-wood stick, an iron wire, a leather belt with a buckle. All this made it so that never in my entire life did I lift a hand to hit a child. And when I see a mother hitting her child on the street, I stop and call her out.

On the one hand, I recognize the difficulty of an intransigent girl figuring out her personality. But, on the other, I know how much my mother, because of her own education and her fear of failure, impeded any type of camaraderie between us and never put faith in our dreams.

I know that, just as it was difficult for me, it was also very difficult for her living with a daughter who never agreed with her rules and way of doing things, one who was ashamed of her backwoods ways of speaking and acting.

Rua Domingos de Moraes, number 2026. The strange mansion in Vila Mariana, with its lonely inhabitants isolated in the solitude of their rooms, shaped my life greatly. I frequently recall my time there as a child, remembering how I used to wander through its immense hallways. Behind the doors were people, hidden away in their silences, their monosyllabic dialogues, their aristocratic airs bolstered by classist prejudices.

First Act of Rebellion: For the Right to Chat after School

When Vovó Olívia died, her children decided to sell the big house. With my father's share, my parents bought a house in Jabaquara. In that time, Jabaquara was still a lower-middle-class neighborhood on the periphery of São Paulo, many of its streets unpaved. Our house was large, though, and it had an enormous yard with trees where my mother planted vegetables. We were already in elementary school by that time and later moved on to high school at the Colégio Brasílio Machado, in Vila Mariana.

With these changes, we had achieved a great freedom: going to school alone on the bus. It was very fun and at the same time distressing, because my mother gave us one hour to get home after school, despite the fact that the buses often ran in very infrequent intervals. We would run from school to the bus stop in order to not miss the 12:10 bus so we would arrive at home on time. We never stayed at school chatting with our classmates after class or laughing and playing at the bus stop like everyone else did; instead we always raced home to have lunch at the time my mother designated, every single afternoon.

One day I got sick of this routine and I resolved to confront her. I decided that I wasn't going to run after leaving school, but walk slowly, conversing with my classmates until we reached the bus stop.

Gina grew desperate and couldn't bring herself to stay with me. She ran off crying, and boarded the same bus that we took each day. I stayed and let the second one pass, and the third one, and so on. I only went home when there were no more classmates left with whom I could talk.

I arrived at home late, fearing the reaction of my mother. She didn't hit me. She just yelled, venting all of her distress at the responsibility of caring for three girls on her own. "This house is not an inn that waits for its guests to eat at any old time. This is *my* house and here we eat at the times *I* decide!" That's how she justified the punishment of depriving me of lunch.

This was my first major act of disobedience, and after that there wasn't a single day in which I didn't do something to affront my mother. I had simply lost some of my fear and decided that I would be happy. I was fourteen years old, and I had many dreams and the desire to know what life was all about.

A Job to Forget

It was at that age that I decided I would start working. At that point, my mother worked as a seamstress and my father no longer lived with us. I wanted to have a bit of freedom and, at the same time, as the eldest daughter, help my mother to support the household. That year I would finish junior high, and I really wanted to continue on to a rigorous high school. Of course, my mother's desire was that I go to teachers' college to be a public-school teacher and wait for a fiancé and marriage. My objective, however, was to study literature, because I wanted to know more about books, which kept me company in my solitude.

After finishing junior high, I matriculated in high school. I enrolled in the night session and found a job as a receptionist at a dentist's office during the day. Only after I had arranged everything did I tell my mother. Her reaction was horrible, but I had expected as much. It wasn't so intense that it made me consider changing my mind.

The first day at both the dentist's office and at night school was unforgettable. I considered myself an important, responsible person — a woman, at last. It was a basic job that only paid half the monthly minimum wage to minors. I cleaned the office, washed the tools, scheduled the appointments, and aided in the procedures.

The dentists were two Arab brothers with the last name Abdala, and they had many rich clients, mostly women. One brother worked in the morning and the other in the afternoon. Each day I would bring a packed lunch and heat it up in the bakery next door. One day, I went back up to the office after lunch and one of the brothers was in the office. As I entered, I saw him seated in his chair behind his desk, dressed in his pristine white uniform, legs open, fly down, one of his hands holding his penis. It was the first time I had seen an erect penis, and it gave me quite a fright. I stopped abruptly in the doorway. He continued to stare at me with a lustful gaze and asked: "Do you like it? Isn't it nice?" And he rubbed his huge penis up and down. I didn't know what to do. I was frozen there with my eyes glued to the scene in front of me, feeling disgust but unable to move. I don't know how long I stood there. All I know is that suddenly I came to my senses and said: "Doctor, put that thing back in your pants." I turned around and set about my work, nervous and trembling. He then came up behind me and started rubbing himself on my bottom. I didn't say anything, but I grabbed my purse and ran out to the elevator crying.

I walked around the streets disoriented. I didn't say anything to my colleagues, or to my mother or my sister. That night I didn't sleep, thinking about what I should do. I wanted to keep working there in order to finish out the month to get the full salary. But I was afraid of going back and having him do it again, or even having him fire me because I had run out on him.

When I went back, it was as if nothing had happened. He didn't bring it up and he treated me with the same coldness as always, until one day he approached me again and started rubbing himself. He said that he was going to show me how nice he could be and that I was going to learn to be a woman. When I tried to pull away, he grabbed me with all his strength. I started screaming and at that moment a patient arrived in the waiting room. As soon as he heard the bell ring, he straightened himself up, combed his hair, and, without looking at me, opened the door with a large smile and received his patient. I went to the bathroom, took off my apron, grabbed my purse, and again went out to wander the streets and cry, without knowing what to do.

I decided during my walk that I could no longer work for that horrible man. The following day, I went to the office in the morning, during his brother's shift. I said that I had found another job that would be better for me, received my money, and never saw those men again. I never told my mother what had happened, nor that I had left my job. I simply continued to leave the house every day at the same time and with my packed lunch in my bag. I would buy the newspaper, go downtown, sit in the garden of the municipal library, and there I would stay, looking up receptionist jobs in the classified ads.

School Passions

I loved high school, in part because I had wonderful teachers. Violanda, who taught philosophy, was my favorite. I liked her so much that I imitated her gestures and even her haircut. It was through her that I discovered philosophy, and her class helped me decide to take the entrance exam to study that discipline in university.[9] In those days, I used to tell my friends pompously that I was going to be a philosopher.

At that time, figures in the student movement would appear here and there, like Luís Travassos, so interesting and dead at such a young age; Zé Dirceu, who was a tad foolish but very handsome; and Vladimir Palmeira, who would climb up on lampposts and give wonderful speeches while hanging from them.[10] We were all fairly politically engaged at the public schools, but in front of Vladimir we would turn into silly little kids. When he appeared, the girls would swoon. He was simply the best. Most girls fell in love with Zé, but I nursed a platonic love for Vladimir.

I was very interested in boys. I flirted on the bus and at school, but I didn't have a boyfriend. Boys would look at me, but they didn't approach me. In those days, I was very diligent, obsessed with knowing everything and reading every book I could find. Besides, despite studying at night and arriving home after eleven, my mother didn't let me go to dances. I had an immense curiosity about sex and dreamed constantly of kissing a boy. But that day hadn't yet arrived, and I didn't really give myself the opportunity to explore. I blamed my sister's beauty, secretly imagining that she outshined me.

Gina, eleven months younger than me, had already had a boyfriend, had already held hands, and had kissed by the famous wall at school, and the more

9   In Brazil, high-school students traditionally take an exam, for which they spend a significant amount of time studying, to gain admittance to a particular department in a university.

10 Brazil boasted a robust left-wing student movement in the 1960s both before and after the 1964 coup. The União Nacional dos Estudantes (National Student Union, UNE), founded in the 1930s, was an outspoken critic of the censorship, violation of democratic principles, and social conservatism of the military regime in the late 1960s. Because of this stance, after months of tense protests in 1968 following the death of a secondary school student at the hands of the military police, the regime systematically and violently dismantled the organization, and many of its members entered the underground resistance.

Travassos, Dirceu, and Palmeira were all major figures in the student movement and were imprisoned for their activities in 1968, the beginning of the most repressive phase of the military dictatorship. Zé Dirceu went on to be an important leader in the left-wing Workers' Party.

boys she dated, the more boys wanted to date her. Gina was jovial, happily swinging her ponytail from one side to another in an eternal good humor. I was unhappy. I thought that the world was against me and I felt like I was the longest-suffering and most wronged girl on the planet. Unsurprisingly, the boys stayed away!

My First Boyfriend

At fifteen, I got permission to attend the parties put on by youths of the local neighborhood parish. The bishop was Dom Mauro Morelli, who, before going to Duque de Caxias in the state of Rio de Janeiro, had been in charge of the diocese of Jabaquara. Because he was a modern clergyman, there were many activities in the local churches, especially for young people. Despite my Catholic upbringing, I wasn't interested in these activities, but I started participating because they were my only chance to have fun on the weekends. There was a group of boys who were considered the rebels of the neighborhood, and the church kids, all very proper, detested them.

At the dances on Saturday, whose soundtrack was dominated by the Bee Gees, the rebels arrived with LPs of hard rock. Without asking for permission, they would remove our records from the record player and put theirs on. They danced, kicking up dust and forcing the straight-laced kids to give them a wide berth. That is precisely when I started liking hard rock. I loved those boys, and one of them just happened to become interested in me.

His name was Márcio, and he was my first boyfriend and my first love. My relationship with him made it so that the fights at home became more and more frequent. My mother detested that rebellious boy, who didn't work, cut class constantly, and, worse, smoked pot without hiding it from anyone. I came to be part of his crew, and on the weekends, I would join them in harassing the rest of the kids in the neighborhood, including my sister.

Every day Márcio would come pick me up. When he was alone with me, he wasn't a rebel; on the contrary, he was a boy full of dreams. He wanted to be a pilot, and he read a lot. He taught me how to kiss with tongue. Until then I had thought that kisses were done with the mouth closed. Sometimes I even cut class to kiss Márcio for hours and hours, catching up on all the lost time from my adolescence. Lots of making out and touching against the school's wall, caresses of my breasts, timid strokes of his penis, but nothing more! Between moments of intimacy during the week and a life of teenage rebellion on Saturdays and Sundays, we dated for quite a while, but we never had sex. I was terrified of losing my virginity and getting pregnant.

Years later, I was living alone and ran into Márcio by chance, on the subway in São Paulo. He hadn't managed to become a pilot but was a flight attendant and looked great in his Varig uniform, his cap tucked smartly beneath his arm. We got off at a random station to catch up and ended up sleeping together. We spent the night in a hotel, overcome by a wild passion. I had imagined many times what sex with him would be like, and he didn't disappoint. In the morning, we said goodbye, and I watched that handsome man, cap under his arm, walking down the street without looking back. I never saw him again, but every time I smell pot, I remember him and his rugged yet sweet good looks. I remember his mouth, which was the first one I ever kissed.

Without Heels, Not a Chance!

A while later, I got a temporary job at Partime, a temp agency. I made fairly good money and could afford to stop working during the period of my exams at school. My mother demanded that I give her my entire paycheck because she said that I was too young to administer my own finances. Every day she gave me the exact amount I needed for my transportation. As one might imagine, I grew very angry that I couldn't spend my own money. I wanted to wear beautiful clothes instead of the long dresses my mother made for me. I wanted to acquire lots of shoes, but I couldn't buy them myself.

I used to wear sandals out of the house but carry a pair of classic high heels in a bag. I climbed the hill where we lived in the sandals, which, when it rained, would get heavy, accumulating a thick layer of mud from the unpaved street. When I arrived at the bus stop, I put the sandals in the plastic bag and put on the clean shoes. I proceeded on my way downtown as if I were a girl who lived on a paved street.

I started smoking because I found the image of a woman with perfectly manicured nails, an aura of intelligence, and a cigarette between her fingers supremely elegant. Before long, I took on freelance typing jobs during my lunch hour to have some money for my personal expenses. I dressed like a typical São Paulo secretary, in flared or fitted skirts, blouses with frills or trim, a black or gray blazer, and high heels, preferably Chanel, my favorite brand. Everything was bought in installments in the stores on Rua Direita, in downtown São Paulo. I refused to wear shoes without a heel because of my complex about my height. It was so ingrained in me that, even if I had to go to the bakery next door, I took off the old flip-flops I wore around the house and put on heels. I was addicted to pastel colors, but I also loved black, which was due to the influence of my teacher Violanda. I never wore bright colors;

red only came to be part of my life when I started frequenting samba schools. Sometime after, when I got involved in the trends and fashions of the era, I abandoned the classic style and started dressing like a hippie. I gave all my secretary clothes and shoes to Gina.

Between Machado de Assis and Marx

I finished high school with excellent grades, with the exception of French and English, and I decided to take a preparatory class to help me study for the university entrance exam. There was one course called Objetivo, which was all the rage among university hopefuls at the time, but it was inaccessible to me, because it was so expensive. The fact of the matter was that I didn't really have money for any preparatory course, even the cheapest one.

I discovered that on Rua Consolação there was a course offered called Etapa that operated out of a small house with only two classrooms, one for the sciences and one for the humanities. I summoned all my courage and went in and asked for an appointment with the director. I told him my sob story, and he gave me a test to evaluate my level of schooling. I got an excellent score, and the director, a political guy, considered me a dedicated girl, a victim of Brazil's unfair distribution of wealth, and gave me a full scholarship to the intensive night course. He asked only for my promise that I would study a lot and be one of the highest scorers on the university entrance exam. That was precisely what I wanted to do, of course.

The course brought about the first major change of my life, a radical change—in fact, a shift in everything I had learned about history, geography, and literature, specifically about Brazil. From the very first class I was enraptured, and I decided that everything I had been taught in my seven years at Brasílio Machado School should be thrown in the trash. That was foolish, of course, because, little did I know, as a student in the 1960s I had experienced the best era of public education in Brazil.

All my professors in the Etapa course were Marxists, without exception. It was there that I learned about Sérgio Buarque de Holanda and Gilberto Freyre.[11] It was there that I discovered Machado de Assis, the great love of

11 Sérgio Buarque de Holanda (1902–1982) was one of Brazil's preeminent historians; he was also influential in the founding of the country's left-wing Workers' Party in the early 1980s. Gilberto Freyre (1900–1987) was an important anthropologist and a public intellectual whose writings were greatly influential in theories of Brazilian race relations throughout the twentieth century.

my literature teacher.[12] Yet I struggled to reconcile my great desire to learn with my obligation to work. I spent many hours on the bus, but, much to my chagrin, I couldn't use them to read, because I got nauseous. My enthusiasm for work diminished drastically in the face of office culture, which was filled with timecards and bureaucracy and bosses imposing cruel routines. The only relief was that mine was a temporary job. All I wanted to do was study and pass the university entrance exam. But I also wanted to read Machado de Assis and, after class, go to the snack bar next door and share my nervousness about the exam with my classmates. But, because of my job, I couldn't!

I started confronting my mother more openly, and some days I didn't return home. I stayed at friends' houses who lived closer to work, and I studied at night. I would spend two days at a time without seeing my own bed. Having a boyfriend at that time was unthinkable. Time was too scarce for such things, and the boys were just as sexless as we were as they were also preoccupied with passing the exam.

Finally, the day arrived in which we would find out the exam results. That day I didn't go to work. Two friends and I got up just after dawn and headed to the building where they posted the lists in the lobby. There was my name, on the list of the Faculty of Letters, Philosophy, and Humanities of the University of São Paulo.[13] I passed in second place for the department of philosophy, making good on my promise to the director of the preparatory course.

The three of us went to a bar nearby, one frequented by journalists. We were broke, so we ordered *cachaça* with currant soda, which ended up putting me in the emergency room in need of glucose injections, as I was nearly in an alcoholic coma.[14] It was the end of 1969, the peak of the military dictatorship, the last time I would drink *cachaça*, but the beginning of my life as a university student.

Revolutionaries or Reactionaries?

Receiving the second-best score on the exam was an honor and the result of a superhuman effort, but Dona Mathilde didn't receive the news with joy—quite

---

12 Joaquim Maria Machado de Assis (1839–1908), one of Brazil's most important and beloved novelists, also wrote plays, short stories, poetry, literary criticism, and nonfiction.

13 The University of São Paulo, or USP, is one of Brazil's premier public universities, famous for the quality of its academics and the left-wing activism of its students.

14 *Cachaça* is a widely consumed Brazilian liquor made from sugarcane.

the opposite, in fact. She thought that women didn't need to study so much, and that university, with its communist permissiveness, snatched good girls away from the proper path and made them unbelievers in God's teachings. Her dream was to see her daughters in teachers' college, and, after finishing their studies, she wanted to see them married, fulfilling their obligations as good wives and mothers.

But Oswaldo, when he found out, was thrilled and began introducing me to all his friends as "my daughter, the USP student." Caught between these two diametrically opposed opinions, I entered the vacation period anxious, waiting for classes to start. I continued working for the big company, now as the junior secretary of one of the directors. When my temporary work period ended, I was invited to continue at the company. I accepted because it was close to the university and the salary was good. I needed a calmer professional life so that I could dedicate myself to my studies of philosophy.

If only that had been the case.

I started university the year following the riots on Rua Maria Antônia, when students from USP built barricades and fought with right-wing private university students and with the police.[15] For us, the post–Maria Antônia generation, what remained were stories full of heroism against the dictatorship, which had resulted in the imprisonment of countless students.

After the riots, the Faculty of Humanities had been moved to the University City campus, far from downtown São Paulo. There was only one bus line to transport us, packed in like sardines, as if heading to the end of the earth. When it rained, classes were suspended because of the deafening sound of the water hitting the roof tiles, which were made of asbestos. The only bar, Shake King, located at the exit of University City, served only *cachaça* and shakes. By that point, the end of the 1960s, the great majority of professors had gone into exile out of fear of political persecution. The only good one left

---

15 In October 1968, an infamous violent altercation transpired between left-wing students from the public USP and right-wing students from the private Presbyterian university Mackenzie on Rua Maria Antônia in the São Paulo neighborhood of Consolação. The fight originated in USP students' decision to erect a pedestrian toll on the street, which Mackenzie students did not want to pay, in order to raise funds for the UNE. A Mackenzie student first threw a rotten egg at USP students, but tensions quickly escalated. The weapons soon included rocks, Molotov cocktails, and even guns, leaving one student dead, the street destroyed, and a USP building badly damaged by fire. The police did not intervene during the scuffle, but they used the altercation as a pretense to invade the USP and forcefully dismantle its UNE nucleus.

was Marilena Chaui, who had to teach in a huge auditorium, such was the popularity of her lectures on structuralism.[16]

My first year progressed, and I soon realized that philosophy wasn't my thing. The people were very pedantic. To make matters worse, much of the bibliography was in English or French, and, because I only mastered the basics of these languages, and I didn't have time to take courses to improve my skills, I wasn't able to do the readings.

I changed my direction. I opted for sociology, which was very fashionable at the time, and this went a lot better for me; I even took some classes in the history and literature departments. I had the privilege of being the student of Antonio Candido in literary theory, of Lúcio Kowarick in introduction to sociology, and of the great professor Moraes, with his old-fashioned suits, brusque mannerisms, and tremendous intellectual integrity.[17]

The busiest and most exciting place on the humanities campus was the academic center. Between rounds of ping-pong, students hatched plans for Brazil's socialist revolution. Fights and disagreements between Maoists, Trotskyists, Stalinists, and other "ists" broke out daily, and tensions ran high when we had to decide who would lead the student government. I found all of this banter obnoxious and chose not to participate in training for the armed struggle. Despite my limited knowledge of politics, I intuited that it was just naive student enthusiasm, and, besides, my idealism didn't reach the point of making me willing to accept the imprisonment and torture that befell militants who were captured by the regime. At first I loved hanging out in the academic center, but I soon came to be ignored by all because I didn't fully share their beliefs. I was considered to be the definition of alienation, and, on top of it all, I worked at a multinational corporation. I might even be a spy for the military.

Sex: The Fixation of the Counterculture

One day, as I was traversing Rua Consolação on our famous bus, a classmate invited me to take a walk to Rua Maria Antônia and get a beer at Sem Nome,

16 Marilena de Souza Chaui is a philosophy professor at USP and one of the founders of the Brazilian Workers' Party.

17 Despite my research, I was not able to determine the identity of this "Professor Moraes." Antonio Candido and Lúcio Kowarick were notable leftist intellectuals and professors of literature and sociology, respectively, at USP in the 1960s and 1970s. Many such academics were targeted by the regime for their political convictions and sought refuge abroad during the most repressive phase of the dictatorship.

or No Name bar, the fad of the moment among students who were partial to art and revolution. The architecture students would meet there, the majority of whom were attractive, well-born boys, among them Chico Buarque, who was unanimously adored by the girls.[18] He played the guitar, drank *cachaça*, and sang "Pedro Pedreiro," one of his first hits. I loved the bar, and after that day, I started going every day after class. There I met a group of young people who were cool and totally wild. They, too, spoke of revolution, but the revolution they spoke of was sexual rather than political.

Despite all my pretenses of being hip and modern, I was still a girl from the outskirts of the city who was scared to death of losing my virginity and getting pregnant, the worst fate of all. My new group, however, spoke only of sex, sexuality, and virginity. After No Name, we started going to a place that, according to my friends, was truly home to the hippest crew: Redondo Bar, in Roosevelt Square.

There, in front of the Copan building, amid critiques of religion, I began to feel ashamed of being a virgin. My girlfriends and I, all virgins, tricked the boys with invented stories of our sexual exploits, trying to seem like modern girls. Redondo was located near the famed Arena and Oficina theaters, places frequented by directors, actors, and actresses, all incredibly beautiful and glamorous to our dazzled eyes. We couldn't even begin to imagine that we were part of one of the biggest shifts in culture in Brazilian history. It was a very important period for me and for my discoveries, a dizzying and chaotic moment, difficult to describe in words.

Meanwhile, as sexuality consumed much of our thought, the country was living through the peak years of the dictatorship. On one end of the political spectrum, students were taking up arms, getting arrested, being killed and tortured. On the other, young people from the anti-communist patrol would come into Redondo to distribute flyers that blamed communism for the existence of homosexuals and for the destruction of homes, among other nonsense. They proposed the extermination of all communists, and, for them, we were victims of this plague. Our fear of these young people—with their shaved heads, wearing suits and wielding flags—was immense, which led us to never walk alone through the streets. We moved in a group, constantly looking around us.

18 Chico Buarque (b. 1944) is a composer, novelist, playwright, and singer best known for his popular and socially minded music. He is the son of famed historian Sérgio Buarque de Holanda and was an architecture student at USP in the mid-1960s before dropping out to pursue music.

The founder of a conservative Catholic group constructed an altar near Rua Maria Antônia to honor his mother, whom he considered a new Virgin Mary. Every Tuesday, the youths from this organization, wearing black suits and red capes and waving red flags with black inscriptions, would pass in a line in front of Redondo on their way to the altar to pay homage and pray. Despite our fear, and impelled by the recklessness of youth, we would follow them, making a racket and disturbing their vigil. It was our way of demonstrating our radical convictions and showing, even to ourselves, that we were doing something to change society.

Those years were very difficult. And for a portion of the youth, including myself, it was hard to find spaces where we could express ourselves. At Redondo, I met the playwright Plínio Marcos, who sold his mimeographed books from table to table, stopping at each one to chat.[19] I listened drunkenly to his theories about theater and society and how urgent it was to change the rules of the game to be more free and less attached to the reigning sexual morality. And each day my girlfriends and I concocted new sexual adventures to brag about to whoever would listen. Boyfriends, love, and marriage were linked to conservative values, and fighting against sexual conservatism was our chief goal in life.

False Libertines

Surrounded by so many modern young people, being a virgin began to feel like a burden, yet I continued to conceal my status. My friends from Redondo and I spoke a lot about the wonders of having sex without getting pregnant. In fact, we would tell anyone who listened that we took the miraculous pill. But it was a lie. We hadn't even had sex yet. I needed to change this, fast.

There was a theater director that hung around us named Rodrigo. He was handsome, much older than us, with black hair and a black beard. With the air of a disgruntled intellectual, he bragged about being a great director, in the same vein as the avant-garde master Zé Celso Martinez Corrêa.[20] The dream of all the girls, a gaggle of groupies, was to have sex with this guy. One

19 Plínio Marcos (1935–1999) was a Brazilian writer, actor, and playwright whose theatrical works on themes such as homosexuality and prostitution were censored by the military regime.
20 José Celso Martinez Corrêa (1937–2023) was an avant-garde theater director and one of the founders of Teatro Oficina, a politically charged theater company associated with the 1960s artistic and countercultural movement *tropicalismo*.

day, he deigned to look at me, and we ended up spending the wee hours of the morning chatting. He told me his fantastic stories from the theater. When dawn broke, he invited me to his house, and I felt my stomach go cold. I was the chosen one; despite being short and thinking of myself as the ugliest in the group, he was somehow attracted to me.

On the walk to Avenida São Luís, I went to the moon and back. He talked and talked and I didn't hear a word. I thought about how I would act, about what having sex for the first time would be like, and, worse, about how to acknowledge my lack of experience after having spoken so often about my countless affairs with men.

For the first time, I found myself in the home of a man who lived alone. On the street, he hadn't hugged me or made any gesture of affection, but as soon as the door closed he grabbed me and started to kiss me and pull off my clothes. Feeling a bit suffocated, I asked to turn off the light. It was then that he let go of me and began giving a speech about the modernness of sex out in the open. He said that I was still a conservative girl, a mama's girl, and that all we mama's girls actually wanted was a wedding with a veil and a tiara. Preferably in a Catholic church. Humbly, I told him that I was ashamed to be naked with a man and that it was still difficult for me to accept that sex was something normal. I think that in that moment he lost some of his lust for me, but, because I was already there, he started groping me again and kissing me without any affection, even hurting my mouth with his force. Finally, he took off his pants, right there in the living room, stuck his dick in me, and came. Lying on the floor, he started laughing uproariously and said: "So, this is the girl who has had tons of experience? That is one thing I have never done before, fucking an idiot virgin." After laughing heartily while looking at my stunned face, he showed me the bathroom so I could wash up and then sent me away, saying that he didn't want to get involved with an inexperienced girl.

When I got out onto the street, the sun was fully out and I didn't bother going to work. I walked around, thinking about what had happened. Was that what sex was? People said that the first time hurt, but I didn't feel anything other than the violence of being possessed with coldness and indifference. Afterward, the only thing remaining was that viscous liquid running down my legs. Only that. That was all that I had as a souvenir of my first time.

At night, after walking around for a while, I didn't go to the university; instead I went back to Redondo. When I got there, everyone, from the patrons to the waiters, knew that I had had sex with Rodrigo, and not only that, they knew that I had asked to turn off the light. They knew that I was a virgin and that he had been obligated to perform the unpleasant and dull task of deflowering me. My friends were upset with me because all the men now thought that if it had been that way with me then it would be that way with them, too.

So that was the first time I had sex, and it was with a standard-bearer of the so-called sexual revolution. It was worth the experience, chiefly for the fact that, starting that day, I wouldn't need to lie anymore: I was no longer a virgin! It turned out that I became very disappointed with the crew at Redondo, including my girlfriends, who, instead of sticking by my side, criticized me for what had happened at Rodrigo's house without even asking me how I felt. I was also very embarrassed to have my intimate business discussed by everyone and to be the subject of debauched laughter.

I no longer saw myself as part of the traditional Left. Its social conservatism and lack of courage to stand up to age-old prejudices had become clear to me, and, most importantly, I finally understood its tendency to think in terms of dogma, which made it no better than its rivals.

In my own way, I made my own revolution and moved on.

> The door of truth was open, but only half a person was al-
> lowed to pass through at a time. . . . They broke the door. They
> knocked down the door. They arrived in the luminous place.
> —CARLOS DRUMMOND DE ANDRADE

Samba Invades São Paulo

Disappointments aside, I kept working and eventually became secretary to the director of a large company that sold water coolers.[21] I made fairly good money, and, as a result, life at home improved money-wise, now that Gina also worked and was engaged to her boyfriend, Toninho.

Even though my mother and I still fought, my new job left her a bit calmer regarding her insecurities about her daughters' futures. She had more or less accepted that I was a hopeless case. During my Redondo period, I stayed away from home so many days at a time that she grew tired of worrying about what would come of me and let me be. She eventually realized that it was no use singing the same old tune. When I finally stopped going to Redondo, she was astonished to see me arriving at home every day after class and staying in on the weekends. She didn't ask me anything, but I could tell she was happier, and she even made an effort to chat with me at times.

---

21 Carlos Drummond de Andrade (1902–1987) was perhaps Brazil's most famous modernist poet.

I took advantage of this respite from socializing to study, which I hadn't done in a while, and I dedicated myself more to my job. As for men, no way; I was still quite traumatized from my experience with the theater director, despite denying this to myself.

For the first time, I started paying attention to my coworkers. I hadn't given them a second thought before, only chatting with them superficially from time to time. I had thought of myself as superior to them because I was the only one who was enrolled in university, but in that moment of truce with myself I actually made some friends. One Friday, one of them invited me to go to a party. She told me that her boyfriend was in the samba scene and that we were going to go to one of São Paulo's most authentic bastions of popular music. Such places were unfamiliar to me and I had prejudices about samba that stemmed from my upbringing in a downwardly mobile aristocratic family clinging to its respectability.

We went to one of the most traditional São Paulo clubs, Guaritão, a large dance hall in a square near Avenida Angélica where people from the samba scene gathered. Once inside, I was introduced to a group of handsome and elegant Black men. They were from the group Originais do Samba, which had founded the modern *pagode* genre and introduced it to the middle class.[22] They were all from Rio, temporarily in São Paulo to take advantage of the newfound popularity of samba to make a little money.

All the men flirted with me that night, except one. He stayed in a corner looking at me furtively, without speaking. At daybreak, we left the dance hall as a group and went to a bar on Avenida São João for a nightcap. I was having a lot of fun with all the flirting, but I didn't want to go out with any of the guys. They all made me laugh, and I was quite taken with receiving so much attention from all of them. It was positively heavenly, to be honest. The guy who had been looking at me before—tall, thin, with a large Afro— continued to keep his silence. He wasn't handsome, quite the contrary—he was the ugliest one of the bunch—but I was hypnotized by his gaze and his air of neediness.

When we emerged onto the street, he approached me and asked for my telephone number. I didn't hesitate, writing it down on a piece of paper from my office and passing it to him. On Monday, as soon as I arrived at work, the telephone rang. We scheduled a date. His name was João.

---

22 *Pagode* is a subgenre of samba music that tends to be more commercial; its lyrics almost always are about love and romance. Both samba and *pagode* originated in Rio de Janeiro.

Sex: No Bells and Whistles

João wasn't the man I loved the most. But he was the first man who treated me like a woman; he made me face my prejudices, principally racial ones, and, most importantly, he took me on an unforgettable journey through the fascinating world of samba.

In the beginning, I found myself drawn to João out of pure curiosity. I wanted to know who that man was who just had watched me all night without uttering a word. He picked me up after work one day, and we took a taxi to a bar downtown, on the corner of Rua Aurora and Rua Vitória. I learned that he was a composer, born in the community of Salgueiro, in Rio.[23]

His friends, who were all very funny, practically lived at that bar, drinking beer and playing music. João lived in the building next door, in a small studio apartment above a movie theater that played porn films with a live striptease before each screening. We would have sex to the sound of the songs that came in through the window. Despite my lack of experience, I had found a man who was very patient with me and even made me come. It was probably because of this that I got over the trauma of my first time with Rodrigo. It was simple sex, just penetration, but he was a good lover. He would say that real men didn't mess around with licking or putting their fingers in pussies. A man has to have a hard dick and that's that. The sex tended to be over quickly because the house was always full and, most times, as soon as we would start fooling around the doorbell would ring. It was usually his friends arriving to play guitar or write music. Every day was a party and we would all chip in to go to the store on Aurora to buy food and beer. It was the first time in my life that I saw men cooking enthusiastically.

At night, we would go out together to the samba spots: Camisa Verde e Branco, Nenê da Vila Mathilde, Vai-Vai, wherever there was a guitar and the main event, *partido-alto*.[24] I stopped going home. At times, I even missed work, giving the excuse that I was sick. I felt myself coming alive amid the effervescence of Afro-Brazilian culture and samba. In my wildest dreams, I hadn't imagined that all this beauty existed.

Of João's friends, the person I liked the most was Almir Guineto, a genius at *partido-alto* with an incredible capacity for improvisation, who was responsi-

---

23 Salgueiro, a favela community in Rio de Janeiro, is home to one of the city's most famous samba schools, or large bands, that participate with an entourage of dancers in the annual Carnival parades.

24 *Partido-alto* is a type of samba music that tends to be more improvised and provides an opportunity for spectators to sing along.

ble for the introduction of the banjo to samba. Guineto doled out nicknames with an incredible generosity of spirit and he took to calling me Carneirinho, or "little lamb." To this day that whole crew still calls me that. He said that my politeness and my way of always appreciating everything, combined with my pale skin and curly hair, made me seem like a little lamb. Palmira, his wife, was my best friend during that time, and I believe the first genuine female friend I had in my life. I envied that woman with her cascading curls and incredible body, very self-possessed and always sporting tight pants. She was everything that I wasn't.

The time that I lived with those people was the foundation of everything I know about samba, one of my great passions, and the burial ground of my silly prejudices about Blackness.

Plainly Pregnant

Ironically, the modern woman who wanted to change the world didn't use contraceptives, the development that truly revolutionized the 1970s and female sexuality. I had a lot of sex with João, and I discovered the secrets of my own body, but I never took even one of those magic pills.

So, of course, I got pregnant. I never had been one to go to the doctor much, and my mother, out of shame or lack of habit, had never taken me to the gynecologist, which should be standard practice in adolescence. When I realized I was pregnant I was scared, so scared that even today when I think about it I become upset. I had to act, to do something, but I didn't have the slightest idea of what to do. For the life of me I couldn't bring myself to tell João. Perhaps because I was fearful that he would discover that I was inexperienced and insecure.

I thought about getting an abortion, but it was just a passing thought. My modern ways had limits and were so inconsistent that I didn't even know where to go and who to ask for. Day after day, I woke up and decided to go talk to Palmira. Except that I lost my nerve and the day would come to an end and I'd leave it to the following one. I began distancing myself from João, and little by little I decided that I wouldn't tell him.

And then I disappeared. I started going home to my mother's house every day. It wasn't long before João showed up there when I was at work, but my mother treated him very badly, saying that he should never come back to knock on her door. I only found out about this much later, when I finally saw him again.

I quit the university as well. I didn't tell my mother about the pregnancy, I bought a belt to hide my belly, and I continued living my life, except that now I didn't go out anymore. My routine was home, work, work, home. Nine months of misery. I only managed to distract myself at work, where I became a model employee; it was the best way of forgetting my predicament. Nine months passed in which I didn't speak to one person about the pregnancy. Nine months of total solitude, and, the more time passed, the more painful it became to carry the weight of both my sadness and the baby. I didn't go to the doctor, which meant that I didn't receive any prenatal care. My only happiness came at night, when everyone went to sleep and I could take off the belt, liberating my belly, the baby, and my mind.

I didn't prepare anything for the birth or the arrival of the baby. I didn't even buy a single diaper, out of fear that my mother would find it. It is remarkable to think of the isolation that can exist between people who live under the same roof.

The Not-So-Secret Secret

February 1972. One day, I left for work at six in the morning, not feeling well. It was quite difficult to walk; the belt was uncomfortable, and I was overcome by a deep sadness. I arrived at the office and continued to feel sick. All of a sudden, I felt liquid flowing between my legs. I was shocked and ran to the bathroom to get a rag to clean the floor, not wanting anyone to see what looked to me like urine. But I couldn't make it. I went into my boss's office and told him that I wasn't feeling well and that I needed to go home. He understood that it was serious and called for the company car, asking a work colleague to accompany me home. When we arrived, my colleague left me in the car and knocked on the door. My mother opened the small window of the living room and said: "Take my daughter to the maternity ward immediately." The girl didn't understand; she came back to the car and said that she didn't know why I would have to go to the maternity ward. I responded: "I am going to have a baby."

The driver took off through the streets of São Paulo and dropped me off at Santa Casa Hospital. The baby was already coming out and it didn't take long. In less than an hour along came Alessandra, my first daughter.

I was very moved when they brought me that little doll, beautiful and healthy, weighing 2.9 kilograms and measuring fifty-one centimeters. It was a miracle—I had kept her hidden, concealed by the belt for nine months—but somehow she had emerged perfect, unharmed by all of the missteps of a foolish young woman.

Finally, my mother and I had to confront one another face-to-face. We were both submerged in our fears, our shames, and our prejudices. When she arrived at the hospital with Aunt Olinda, I was so helpless that I didn't know what to do. It was my aunt who broke the tension and said: "Mathilde, look how beautiful your granddaughter is!" My mother looked at Alessandra and immediately fell in love with the little girl. I remember that the nurse came into the room to take the baby to the nursery and my mother didn't want to let her go.

I couldn't nurse Alessandra because I was anemic. When they changed my IV and Dona Mathilde saw the needle in my arm, she said to the nurse: "My poor daughter, she is scared to death of syringes and now she has to get an IV." My mother went to the window of the room and hid her face to cry. It was a brief cry, freighted with embarrassment. Soon she wiped her eyes, grabbed a plastic bag, and showed me what she had bought on Rua Vinte e Cinco de Março: "I ran to the stores, so that the baby wouldn't be born without clothes."

The Pedophile of the Family

As much as she loved me and her new granddaughter, Dona Mathilde was confused and didn't really know how to deal with the situation. She thought that I needed the help of a man, so she called someone to give me advice, a close family member who ended up being the least helpful person imaginable.

The guy worked as a film censor, which meant that he was a federal police officer.[25] He thought of himself as exemplifying all the proper family values, the only person who had the moral authority to answer all manner of difficult questions. But this was a façade that hid his true character as a torturer and hypocrite, the essence of the evil of the military dictatorship for which he was a foot soldier.

He and his wife had a beach house, where once in a while we would spend weekends as kids. What no one knew was that this supposedly dignified man would take us past the surf and touch us inappropriately underneath the water. He did this with me, Gina, and a cousin of ours. We were nine or ten years old, and it left us with emotional scars, so that to this day we are all afraid of the ocean. I still have dark memories of the waves passing over my head,

25 During the military dictatorship, the regime employed bureaucrats to review cultural products and censor any material deemed politically or socially objectionable.

gulping down water, and this man, the supposed guardian of virtue, touching my body.

I, thin and weak, still going over and over in my mind what had happened, was called to the living room to have a "father-daughter" chat with this disgraceful man. I listened politely to him telling me that it was essential that I reveal the name of the child's father, his clichéd speech culminating with the absurd statement that "you have to realize that making a mistake for the first time is only human, but the second time it is nothing but shamelessness. Therefore try, starting now, to be prudent." Despite feeling completely helpless, I told him that he would never pry the father's name out of me, because I was afraid of what he might do as a police officer. I said, looking him in the eye: "I don't trust your intentions and I know very well that you don't have a right to tell me what is moral." I ended the conversation and returned to my room, where I cried until I couldn't cry anymore.

For the first time in my life, I had confronted my enemy. In that moment, I discovered that it is unbearable to keep one's anger and indignation at hypocrisy and wrongdoing inside. It was then that I discovered how wonderful it is to speak out.

Too Fragile to Complain

My mother respected my decision not to reveal Alessandra's father's name. The following day she called a taxi to take us to the notary. We registered Alessandra, and I officially became a single mother. To this day, my daughter believes my decision was unthinkable, but we were in the midst of the effervescent 1970s, and it really was a different time. I was ashamed to tell João about a pregnancy that wasn't planned, nor even fathomed. I did what I thought was best.

After a few days, we had a visit from my boss at the company where I worked. He spoke at length with my mother and told her that I was a great employee, but that, due to what had happened, I couldn't go back to work. It was company policy not to employ women who had children, which, of course, referred mostly to single mothers. The thinking was that they could be a bad influence on the many proper girls who worked there. He gave my mother a check with all the money he owed me plus a severance fee so that, according to him, I could live "without worries" for the next couple of months. He apologized for firing me— "but the rules are the rules" —and upon exiting he advised me to be more careful, which had become a common refrain.

I was under a lot of psychological pressure, so much so that I felt sick, on the verge of depression, and I looked horrible. My hair was a mess and I had no desire to take care of myself. Alessandra, on the other hand, became more and more beautiful every day, and my mother fell more and more in love with her. I believe that Dona Mathilde never took such good care of me as she did during that time: she brought me breakfast in bed and made me *fubá* porridge with cheese so that I got more protein.[26] I had a lot of love and care at home, despite the fact that the neighbors looked at me askance and I was reprimanded by my maternal grandparents and uncles.

To distract myself from my confusion and doubts about the future, I started knitting a dress for Alessandra's baptism, and I invited Gina and my brother-in-law, Toninho, to be her godparents. For two months, I knitted like Penelope wove, and the baptism took place at the Nossa Senhora da Saúde church, in Vila Mariana. It was the same church where we were all baptized and had our first communion, and where Gina got married.

The little girl grew up healthy as can be, constantly flashing the most beautiful smiles. But the time was arriving in which I would need to confront the world again. My mother told me that now that I had responsibilities, I needed to get a steady job. I asked her for a bit of the money that I received from the company to go to the hair salon, and to buy some new clothes. I was so thin that none of my old clothes fit anymore.

Off I went in search of a new job. I ended up getting another temporary gig to fill in for a secretary in the buying department of the Shell warehouse, in São Caetano. It was far from home, but there was a chance that I would be hired full time.

When I arrived home with the big news, my mother sat me down on the living room sofa and, in a very serious tone, made clear what my life would be like starting then. She would take care of Alessandra during the day, and, because I left work at six, I should be home, considering the distance, not a minute after eight. Not a chance of going back to my studies at the university. According to her, everything that had happened to me had to do with the bad company I had kept and the communist ideas that they put in my head in that den of sin. Now that I was a mother I would have to take responsibility for Alessandra. Dona Mathilde, once again, had the formula for my salvation. I was too fragile to contest this or much of anything. I accepted all the rules she laid out and the next day I started work.

26 *Fubá* is cornmeal, a common food native to Brazil.

At the new job, it seemed that all I had to do was dedicate myself to the work to guarantee a long-term contract and benefits. Every day, religiously, I would give Alessandra a kiss and leave home at 5:30 in the morning and I wouldn't return until 7:30 or 8 at night. Sometimes she was already sleeping when I arrived. It was only on the weekends that I was able to spend more time with her; I was glued to her then, washing her clothes and mine and reading a lot. I was crazy about Brazilian literature, which I had discovered in my university preparatory class. That was when I read all the works by José Lins do Rego, Machado de Assis, and Jorge Amado, and I never stopped.[27] Books were my only friends, my only escape valve.

It had been two and a half years since I started university, full of dreams, and in so little time so much had happened! My life had changed completely, and I no longer had any plans for the future. I was carrying the weight and stigma of being a single mother, a fact I had to keep secret out of fear of losing my job. In any case, it was a calm period. For the first time in my life, I was getting along well with my mother and I could pay more attention to my little sister, Thais, who was already a teenager.

The End of the Dilemma

I had been hired to work in a department where all the employees were men. Six buyers, one boss, and me, the only woman in the place.

Every Friday the staff went out for happy hour, and they always invited me. I would give an excuse so as not to have to go, but I was left nursing an intense desire to enjoy myself a bit, which I had already gotten a taste of in the years before. I saw everyone going out happily to the bar, and I would watch them from the bus stop, feeling a longing for the times in which I went out at night, when I had discovered samba and the world around me.

One Friday, fed up with living a monotonous life that was nothing but work and home, I decided to let go of my guardedness and go out with the crew. They were all astonished, because I hadn't gone to a single office party before. We went to one of the bars serving fruit cocktails on Largo do Arouche, and I had fun like I hadn't had in a long time. One beer led to another, and

27 José Lins do Rego (1901–1957), a novelist from Paraíba, Brazil, was a member of a regionalist literary movement that foregrounded the harsh realities of the country's impoverished northeast. Jorge Amado (1912–2001), a Bahian novelist, journalist, and communist politician, is perhaps Brazil's best-known author of the twentieth century. His many works have been widely translated and adapted for the stage and the screen.

the beers led to many conversations, and I ended up staying at the bar until three in the morning. I turned down the offer of a ride from my colleagues and instead walked to Largo de São Francisco, the last stop on the Jabaquara bus line. Only then did I start thinking about what was in store for me at home.

My mother didn't give house keys to any of her daughters, so I had to knock on the door, not ringing the doorbell so as not to wake the baby. It took a while until my mother, looking like she hadn't slept a wink, opened the window and said: "Oh, it's you?" She shut the window, opened the door, and put a suitcase outside: "I warned you that everything had changed since the birth of Alessandra. I don't want a daughter in my house who is the talk of the neighborhood and sets a bad example for her own daughter." And she shut the door in my face.

I sat down and leaned against the fence next to the door, staring at the suitcase for hours. I had two options: I could leave for good, abandoning my daughter, or knock on the door again and ask forgiveness for having had the audacity to have a little bit of fun. I was stuck in this dilemma as the dark sky became blue, then lilac, then red . . . Once the sun had risen, I had made my decision: I left.

My daughter was almost one year old. It was deeply painful to give her up. But at that time, I didn't see any other way out. I was living a lie, and I couldn't bear to think of myself as a woman without a future. Why did I have to renounce my youth and my dreams? At that moment I had lost track of what those dreams even were. I also thought it was better for Alessandra to be rid of me. I decided to go out in search of myself, embracing the egoism and the risks of being a free woman, without knowing for sure what freedom was.

In Search of Unknown Freedom

I took my suitcase and, having nowhere to go nor friends to help me, went to the city bus station. São Paulo's station was horrible, full of colorful plastic ornaments hanging from the ceiling, and it was these ornaments that I looked up at for four nights, trying to sleep while sitting on a hard bench.

In the morning, I would take clean clothes from my suitcase, pay to take a shower, and go to work. After work, I would wander around the city. And after wandering aimlessly, I would return to the hard bench at the station to sleep sitting up. I continued this way until I decided to ask for an advance from my job, allowing me to rent a room in a boardinghouse for women near Avenida São João.

I was soon promoted at Shell and became responsible for the distribution of gas from the warehouse. I stayed all day, and sometimes into the night, sitting inside a security cabin, monitoring the trucks that came to fill their huge tanks. The lines were very long, and I think that I met every single gas truck driver in the city. Despite how tiring it was, it was also fun. I started going to the games of the staff indoor soccer team. I would go out every Friday night to happy hour, and on the weekends I would stay in my room reading my books, falling more and more in love with Machado de Assis and Jorge Amado.

I tried not to think of my house and my daughter, so as not to suffer. I missed João; occasionally I even thought of seeking him out, but I would always give up on the idea. I even missed Redondo bar and the university.

I decided to take up my degree again, reuniting with my classmates and studying hard in order to make up for the lost time. I still went out on Friday nights and to the staff soccer games to cheer on the players, but I played it safe. Despite being hit on a lot, I was afraid of getting involved with someone again.

Plínio Marcos, All Ears

One day, after monitoring an epic line of trucks, I left Shell really late and missed class. I was tired but didn't feel like going home. I decided to return to Redondo to see my old friends again.

So much had happened in my life, but, there, everything was the same as it always had been. The same Rodrigo and the same idle talk about changing society. Like a perfect idiot, he approached my table and told me that I looked very pretty. I laughed in his face and said: "Motherhood made me into a beautiful woman." He turned pale, and I laughed even more. I loved revealing my great secret in that way, as if it were no big deal.

Plínio Marcos was passing by with his mimeographed books, and he stopped to greet me. I invited him to have a beer with me and recounted the trajectory of my life up to that moment. Attentive, deeply interested in his fellow human beings, the great playwright listened to me for hours. It was wonderful, being able to speak without fear or guilt about anything for the first time. Better yet was to hear from Plínio that he didn't regard me as a woman without a future.

I started going to Redondo regularly to speak with more freedom about life and the changes that were taking place around us. I needed new energy and new ideas. I was hungry to understand my upbringing, one based on conservative Catholic values, and for that reason I had a lot to say and many questions to ask. I also wanted to have sex and express my sexuality without guilt. I wanted to hug, kiss, and acquaint myself better with the male body, with all its desires and fantasies. I wanted to be a desirable woman, to wear red lingerie, to feel men against my skin, to have a lot of sex and never be satiated. I didn't want to get married, nor did I want to live with anyone. I just wanted to see and feel many men wanting me. Why couldn't I live like them, who were constantly with different women? Why did we women have to content ourselves with just one man for our entire lives? I wanted to have the sexual freedom that men enjoyed, but I didn't know where to start.

Second Commandment: You shall not kiss on the mouth. Kisses on the mouth signal affection, and you shall only give them to those you like.

Hollywood in the Boca do Luxo

Between the Redondo bar and the luxurious Hilton Hotel, there was an incredibly chic nightclub that also operated as a brothel. It was called La Licorne. It was at its peak in the 1970s and 1980s, when it brought together extremely rich men and the most beautiful prostitutes in all of Brazil. The comings and goings of those women caught my attention. They arrived in the best cars, clad in long, sensual dresses, perfumed and beautifully made up, with an air of Hollywood glamour about them. When they entered the club, I found myself wondering what happened inside.

During that time, I was feeling quite pretty for the first time in my life. I had lost my ugly duckling complex and started to imagine myself like those women, getting out of a car, elegant and fragrant, saying goodbye to my friends at Redondo and entering the nightclub all gussied up to attend to my men.

I realized that, if I wanted to, I could radically change my life.

I kept going to Redondo, but not to meet up with people. I went to observe those women. One day I finally worked up the courage to venture down Rua Major Sertório, home to a lot of nightclubs where prostitutes worked.

I walked up and down several streets before eventually deciding to go into a club called Michel. Dressed as a *Paulistana* secretary in a flared skirt, a white blouse with black polka dots, and a black velvet blazer, I entered the club. No one so much as glanced in my direction. My eyes gradually grew accustomed to the darkness. The music was loud, and there were a number of strippers on small round stages. None of it was really my thing. I hate loud music and dark spaces. I realized that I would never be able to make it in that environment. I left just as I entered, unnoticed.

Back on the street, I felt disappointed, because my first incursion into the world of prostitution had been a failure. I went to a bar and bought some cigarettes. At the door, three men struck up a conversation with me with the classic question: "You new around here?" They thought that I was a prostitute from the Boca do Luxo. Perfect. I told them that I was looking for a place to work and that I hadn't liked Michel.

What I never would have guessed is that one of them was the husband of a brothel owner. The man wrote down an address on a piece of paper and said that if I was interested, I should go meet her the following day and see if I liked the place. At that moment, I felt myself on the verge of letting go of countless things in my life, things that, in truth, didn't really matter to me anymore.

And so I went to 623 Avenida Rio Branco. It was an entire building dedicated to prostitution. A world that I had never even imagined existed. I wondered if my friends from Redondo knew about this building and laughed to myself: compared with what I was seeing, those cerebral guys had their heads in the clouds.

I asked for Dona Elsa on the fifth floor. I said that her husband had sent me and that I was considering turning tricks for the first time. She said, laughing: "They all come here and say the same thing, but it's fine. Each night you pay me a fixed daily fee, regardless of the number of clients that you see. You didn't bring a towel? Grab one from the closet right there and you can go to the door and get to work."

First Client, Second Client, Third, and So On . . .
I went to the door as Dona Elsa had instructed me. I was a bit scared, but I didn't stay that way for long.

My first client, a somewhat bald man, approached. He asked me how much, I named the price, and he said, "Let's go!"

For the first time, I entered one of the rooms where the prostitutes had sex with their clients. Inside, there was a nightstand, a small rug, and a single bed with a threadbare old sheet and a pillow. I learned afterward that the rug was very important; I was told that people shouldn't have sex and then put their feet on the cold floor, as it would increase the risks of contracting a venereal disease. To this day I still don't understand what these two things have to do with one another; I just know that I found rugs on the floor in São Paulo and later in Belo Horizonte. In Rio, because the precariousness of our working conditions didn't permit such luxuries, the most careful girls carried their own rugs under their arms when they entered a room with a client.

I sat on the bed and stared at the man without knowing what to do. He asked me if I was new at the brothel. I explained that it was my first time in the *zona* and that he was my first client.[28] "They all say the same thing," he said, laughing and starting to take his clothes off. I remained seated, not knowing what to do, and it was then that he realized that, in fact, I was totally inexperienced. In his underwear, he sat down next to me and embraced me. Instinctively, I pulled away in disgust and started to cry. By then it was more than clear that I hadn't been lying. He put his clothes back on while looking at me, took some money out of his wallet, gave it to me, and said: "Go home, this isn't a place for you."

This was the first time I heard that sentence, one that I would hear many times in all the cities where I worked. It is one of the biggest fantasies of men who seek out prostitutes: to be with a newbie. A while after, once I was well schooled in the decorum of the place, I started responding: "I'm here just so you can send me home." They laughed, said that I was naughty, and ended up happy that they weren't corrupting a proper young lady.

That first day, I was profoundly moved by the stranger who had expressed concern for me, and I even came to think that maybe he was right, that this wasn't the place for me. He paid me what we had agreed upon and went off to go be with another woman. When I saw the two of them go into a room together, I recomposed myself. I realized that if I just sat on the bed like a silly girl watching a man undress, I would be a lousy prostitute. After all, I was there to have sex, and that was what I had to do. Moreover, I was hardly a virgin anymore. I dried my tears and returned to the door, back to the crowd of men coming up and down the stairs as the women beckoned to them, saying things like, "Come here, my darling."

The second client, a young guy, was easier. We decided on a price and off I went through the hallways with him behind me. In the room, I started taking off my clothes and putting on the air of a woman with a lot of experience. I invited the guy to lie down next to me, and he started caressing me. I repressed the initial disgust that I felt at being with a stranger, and he got on top of me and came. Afterward, he paid me but he said that he hadn't liked it, that I was

---

28 The Portuguese word *zona* means "zone," or "district," and is used as shorthand to refer to the red-light districts in Brazilian cities.

really cold and hadn't come. My God, how was I supposed to come from sex with the fattest man I had ever seen and whose name I didn't even know? I had discovered that it was hard being a whore; it wasn't as if you could just open your legs and take care of things easily. Far from it. There was a lot I needed to learn. I just didn't know how, mostly because none of the other women had taken the time to educate me in the tricks of the trade.

In the middle of the day, I received my first compliment from a client, who said that I was very affectionate; unlike the other women, I kissed on the mouth. I said goodbye to him, but I remained puzzled by what he had said. Now, if no one else kissed on the mouth, why was I putting in so much effort? Something was wrong, and I definitely had a lot to learn.

It is a rare thing for a prostitute to teach others her trade secrets. This lack of frank instruction stems from the assumption that everyone knows what prostitution involves and how to do it. Plus, teaching someone else your tricks means potentially losing clients, and the world of prostitution is extremely competitive.

In any case, that day I returned to the boardinghouse on Amaral Gurgel with a nice chunk of change. I had made more in one day than I made in a month working at Shell. It would cover a lot more than the rent that I had been owing.

The Boca do Luxo and the Boca do Lixo

The red-light district in São Paulo is divided in two: the Boca do Luxo and the Boca do Lixo, which were polar opposites.[29] While the former slept during the day and shone at night, the latter was open during the day and closed its doors at night. I chose never to work in the Boca do Luxo. I don't like nightclubs—the loud music, the darkness, none of it. Not for working, at least. I liked that stuff in my free time, for my own entertainment. And the two districts were right next to each other, so I could go back and forth on foot.

Those were the golden days in the central *Paulistana* neighborhood of Bixiga, with its countless music halls filled with good musicians. Until 1968, the neighborhood was home to the Faculty of Philosophy, Humanities, and Literature of the University of São Paulo and the School of Sociology and Poli-

---

29 The Boca do Luxo and the Boca do Lixo were the two red-light districts in São Paulo, the former catering to affluent men and the latter geared toward a working-class clientele. The nomenclature creates a clever pun in Portuguese, because *lixo* means "trash" and *luxo* means "luxury."

tics, a private university through which a lot of great people passed. In other words, everything happened there. Late at night on Fridays, all types of people gathered for *feijoada* at Eduardo's.[30] There were so many people that you couldn't even walk around inside. São Paulo of the late 1960s and early 1970s was incredible! Maybe even the best era of bohemian São Paulo. Compared to all that, the city today is a drag.

A Dog-Eat-Dog World

Despite my eagerness to work in prostitution, I was plagued by doubt and ambivalence. It was very difficult to fully grasp the meaning of my radical life choice. I still felt lost, not knowing if I should keep going or not. As a result, I was confronted by my own prejudices and stigmas. Despite making a lot of money, I felt dirty and ashamed of what I was doing.

The building didn't help, either; instead it reinforced my bad spirits. Number 623 Avenida Rio Branco teetered on the margins: there were girls there who had been chewed up and spit out by life, lots of drugs, and pimps, a crew of cowards who only knew how to steal money from women and pretend to be tough guys.

The building had a security guard—in fact, he was an extreme caricature of a security guard. If a woman greeted him in the hallway, he would say: "What are you looking at, you good-for-nothing slut? I already told you to lower your head and not dare to look at me when I pass by. I hate sluts!"

He was only good for restraining men who tried to get away without paying or women who wanted to create a scandal. He hit the deadbeats and stripped them of their clothes, leaving them in their underwear. He then made those unfortunate guys go out onto the street, saying that he would only return their clothing if they came back with the money they owed. I was always curious to know how they got home in their skivvies.

The madams were in the habit of observing the notorious "PP," or payment to the police. But sometimes Rota, a special officer from São Paulo, entered the building under the pretext of hunting criminals, or so he said. He would detain the working-class guys who had come to the building just to get some sexual satisfaction, and take all their money, calling them "suckers" and worse.

The clients in the building used to go up to the top floor in the elevator, then go down via the stairs so they could get a look at all the different options

30 *Feijoada* is a traditional bean and pork stew.

as they descended. The prostitutes, in turn, grabbed the men and practically dragged them to their rooms, especially on days with slower business. At times the men fought with them and sometimes even hit them, which would cause the security guard to appear out of nowhere, leaving the guy in question bloodied. Every day something like this happened, and I started getting tired of it all, even thinking I might return to my sheltered life as a secretary, leaving behind that dog-eat-dog world.

In those days, there was a guy in a suit and tie who frequented our building. He greeted all the girls and stopped to speak to one and then another, always very genteel. One day, he stopped to talk to me and introduced himself as "The Português." He said that he was a longtime client and that he loved prostitutes. He wanted to know what such a sweet young girl as myself was doing in that place, such a dirty building, and with so little business. I didn't pay him much mind, but he kept talking to me and said that he could recommend a much better brothel, one that would be worthy of my beauty. I thanked him for the compliment and the offer but I didn't give it a second thought, mostly because I suspected he might be an agent for the madams. I was doubtful; could it be that a man his age lived off of prostitution? In any case, I kept his offer in the back of my mind in case it might come in useful in the future.

A Big and Painful Favor

One morning, I arrived at the building and the line of men waiting for the elevator was enormous, snaking all the way out onto the street. I walked past the men and went for the door, but the doorman came over and, without saying anything, gestured to the end of the line. I became furious and told him that if it weren't for us women, there wouldn't even be a line and therefore no prostitute should have to wait her turn. All the men in line agreed with me, but the doorman, again without a word, slapped me in the face. He then said that he would punish me for having talked back by not letting me go in to work but charging me my daily fee regardless.

Ultimately, I realized that the doorman had done me a huge favor. He closed the door permanently on my time at 623 Avenida Rio Branco. After I was sent packing, I walked to a bar on the corner of Rua Vitória, where the local shady characters liked to hang out. I decided to wait for the so-called Português, who frequented that very spot, and accept his offer of introducing me to another establishment.

I didn't have great expectations, but I also couldn't bring myself to believe that prostitution in São Paulo was limited to my experience in that first building. After all, I had spent months observing the ease and grace of the women from La Licorne.

Same Job, Different Address

Before long, I saw The Português walking by in his usual suit, impeccable yet out of place in those parts. He looked like a character from a different world. I got up and ran after him, telling him that I wanted to accept his offer to introduce me to another spot. He looked me up and down and said: "Let's go, then."

I walked alongside that man, who was possessed of a kind of dated elegance, perfumed with a lavender scent that reminded me of my old grandfather Juquita. As we walked, taking shortcuts through the streets and alleys of the Boca do Lixo, he said little but greeted everyone we came upon. We walked past striptease cinemas, prostitutes, and bars full of men, until we arrived at 134 Rua Barão de Limeira, a building with an imposing entrance in the architectural style of the 1920s. At the door, a kindly Black man was introduced to me as "Senhor Antenor." We took the elevator to the third floor to meet with Dona Cecília, the second madam whom I met in my career as a prostitute.

I entered a spacious apartment, in which everything was very clean and tidy. The Português introduced me to Cecília, a beautiful Black woman in her late fifties, supremely elegant in a silk dress that didn't go unnoticed, my eyes well accustomed to seeing fine fabrics.

She invited me to sit, and The Português told her where we had met. Cecília nodded her head, proffering a cryptic aphorism: "The paths taken by an inexperienced girl are undefined and sometimes offer no way back." I confess that I felt a degree of fear at this enigmatic ritual, but she soon abandoned her formal tone and started explaining the trivialities I was expecting: "Very well, the daily fee is fifty cruzeiros. I don't like unkempt women who don't wear makeup. In my house, there will be no hard drugs. Drinking at work is prohibited, and I don't like to see my girls sitting at the bar on the corner after their shifts. The minimum price for any service is thirty cruzeiros but you can, once in the room, negotiate for more, never less, because then the clients develop bad habits."

I accepted all her rules, changed into my leotard, and when I came out of the bathroom, The Português said that he wanted to sleep with me and that I couldn't refuse, because it had been him who had introduced me to Cecília. He also said that he considered himself a sort of amulet and that he would bring me good luck in my new workplace.

Off I went, thinking that I would have to have sex for free, as a courtesy to him. I took a look at The Português and decided that he wasn't even one of the worst men I had had to sleep with. He just wanted a quick fuck without any bells and whistles, but he did try to be affectionate and seductive. The problem was that he was really full of himself; he thought he was a great expert on women's sexuality, and he said various times that I was lucky, that all of the women of the Boca do Lixo dreamed of sleeping with him. But he was selective, he said, and I was the chosen one of the moment. I listened to everything he said politely, figuring that, after all, he had helped me to escape that hole where I had been working, and that, in light of that, I should treat him well.

Afterward, he took money out of his pocket and paid me. I almost didn't accept it, but then I told myself to act like a professional. What would Cecília say if she found out that my first fuck in her apartment had been for free?

Third Commandment: You shall not have a pimp. You shall not fall into that trap or else you will end up in the gutter.

Criminals, but Not Really

Contrary to what you may think, the pimp doesn't have much in common with the so-called madam, who should more accurately be called a "prostitution entrepreneur." The pimp essentially has no practical function. Decades ago, he reigned like a type of parasite, taking advantage of the fragility, fear, and isolation of women of the night in order to exploit them. In exchange for "protection"—very much in quotes—women ended up supporting these men financially. In truth, most of the money these women made they didn't end up keeping. They were only allowed to keep enough for their expenses.

The fact is that today the prostitute is commonly seduced into having a pimp, mostly because the prejudice that they are subjected to leaves them vulnerable to his overtures. Many girls spend years and years working in prostitution and end up with nothing because of their pimps.

The prostitute herself isn't mentioned in the Brazilian Penal Code. However, prostitution is one of the activities that suffers most from discrimination and police repression. Working as a third-party exploiter is criminalized, which includes the pimp, the ostensible protector, and the madam, the owner of a brothel or massage parlor. If a group of prostitutes forms a cooperative, automatically it would be classified by the Penal Code as exploitation, and those women would be considered criminals. But in theory, when a prostitute exercises her profession, no charges can be brought against her—I repeat, in theory.

The Brazilian Penal Code is very old, and it hasn't undergone substantial changes since it was written, in 1940. The articles pertaining to prostitution were originally created to protect the whore. They have had the opposite effect, unfortunately. The prostitute ended up completely marginalized because those who surround her are considered criminals, and, in a way, they transfer that condition to her. The madam, even one who works in the most low-end prostitution, spends tons of money on bribes, pays all her expenses, and still ends up making a lot of money. Money that the prostitute will never see.[31]

From Puta *to Property*

I had problems with a pimp myself, as you might have gathered, and it was precisely during the time of Cecília and the building at number 134. In that brothel, there were two apartments per floor, and women waited for clients by the windows, in the hallways, and on the sofas. The first day, in my black leotard and high heels, I went to the door and had barely leaned against it when a client approached me. From that moment on I didn't stop working. At ten o'clock each night, when the building closed—religiously, as demanded by the police—I would have a nice chunk of change in my wallet. I was always starving and somewhat dazed after all that had happened over the course of the day.

At the end of my first day, The Português appeared in front of me, smiling from ear to ear, asking if I liked Cecília's house. He invited me to dinner, extending the invitation to Cecília as well. He sat on the sofa waiting for us to get ready and, before leaving, asked me very seriously where I was keeping the money I made. I grabbed my wallet and showed him a bunch of bills, proud as I was of my first day at number 134. Cecília commented that I was a promising woman of the night, and off we went, laughing and chatting, to the restaurant, Filé do Moraes, right near Praça Julio Mesquita.

At dinner, Cecília and The Português recounted many stories from the Boca do Lixo. After a while, The Português told me that it was very dangerous to walk around with so much money in my wallet. He advised me to leave it with him so that he could keep it in a safe place until I had enough money to open a bank account, which at that time required a minimum amount to

---

31 This is still the case in Brazil today, despite decades of efforts on the part of the sex-worker movement to fully decriminalize the profession.

make an initial deposit. Cecília observed all this unspeaking, and, although I was initially distrustful, I eventually convinced myself that it was safe. I gave nearly all my money to him, leaving myself only enough for the taxi ride home and the one back to work the following day. Cecília just looked at me, silently.

I said goodbye to the two of them at the door of Moraes, and I went to sleep with mixed emotions, unsure if I had done the right thing.

Back at the brothel, I soon got over the initial shock of having sex with strangers, and I went about perfecting my skills with clients. Cecília was happy with me, and she started giving me small tips on how to comport myself, but without meddling too much.

Occasionally, The Português would appear for his little visits, always paying and inviting me to have dinner after at Moraes or sometimes at Tabu, on Rua Vitória. Invariably, at dinner he would get out a little notebook and write down the day's total, add up how much money I had made up until that point, and put it back in the pocket of his blazer.

Almost a month had passed since my arrival at number 134 and I wasn't sleeping well, preoccupied about why I had given my money to a stranger for safekeeping. I decided that it was time to put an end to that.

One day, The Português dropped by to take me to dinner, and when we arrived at the restaurant, I brought up the topic. He looked at me, chuckled, and asked if I actually believed that he was keeping the money for me. After hearing those few words, I realized that I had a pimp and that I had buried my head in the sand and pretended not to know. To say that I didn't know is to be very complacent with myself; of course I knew, or at least I knew that I didn't trust him, but because of some sort of magic, or maybe even the sensation of safety that a well-dressed man transmitted, I had been seduced by his sleight of hand. Perhaps it was his lavender scent.

I became livid and began shouting in the middle of the restaurant. He kept it cool and didn't open his mouth during my outburst. He simply took a small revolver out of the same blazer pocket where each day he had put my money and placed it on top of the table. The few other guests in the restaurant, and even the waiter, pretended not to notice.

Calmly, he explained that, upon seeking him out to get an introduction to number 134, I had automatically become his whore, and, therefore, the money that I made was his, except a small amount for my personal expenses. He made it clear that for all the dinners, and even the times he slept with me, it was me who was paying and that these outings were merely a courtesy that wouldn't happen again. The following day, he said, he would go to the brothel to pick up his money around nine at night, and what I made from then until ten I could keep, for whatever foolishness I spent money on. If I didn't agree, I should disappear from the building or my mother would end up crying at my grave.

After dinner, I didn't go home. I hid and watched my executioner walk calmly toward Avenida São João. When he was far away, I went to the brothel and started screaming for Cecília from the middle of the street. She appeared on the balcony, then came down and invited me in. She explained everything. She said that she couldn't say anything to me at the time because if she did, she would lose her apartment. She explained that The Português was a famous pimp in the Boca do Lixo, and that he pimped out about ten women on that block alone.

I was destroyed, thinking that the only thing left to do was to leave and forget that I had ever wanted to be a prostitute. The learning curve was too steep. I don't know what came over Cecília then; either she felt some inkling of sympathy for me or she didn't want to lose a good tenant. She asked me if I wanted to keep working, and I said that I did. Under the condition that I would keep her assistance a secret, she offered to help me figure out a scheme to stay permanently at the brothel. She asked if I was woman enough to take on the challenge, and I told her that I was.

I slept in Cecília's apartment that night and spent the entire following day locked in her room, without being seen by anyone, not even by the women of the house. At night, The Português dropped by to collect my money and Cecília told him that I hadn't showed up to work. "She'll be back," he commented.

A Solution Named Velvet

That same night, a Black man appeared at the building, dressed in the typical elegance of a São Paulo gangster: a silk shirt, tailored pants, kid-skin shoes, and a giant gold watch engraved with a single word: *Veludo* (Velvet).

A civil police officer from the vice squad, he was a friend of the madams in the Boca do Lixo and did favors for them from time to time. His nickname was Velvet because he spoke gently and was extremely polite. But he had the reputation of being a tough cop.

With the doors locked, Cecília called me into the living room and asked me to tell him the story of my troubles with The Português, without omitting any details. Velvet listened to me attentively. When I finished, he asked me one question: "Are you, like the rest of these silly girls, in love with him?" I said no, not at all. Quite the contrary, in fact; what I felt was rage toward him. Velvet told me that, starting at that moment, I should be seen at restaurants and in the vicinity of Boca do Lixo in his company.

On Rua Major Sertório, near the brothel, there was a dance hall named Som de Cristal. It doesn't exist anymore; at some point a while back it became a church. Back then, on Monday nights it filled up with pimps, prostitutes, police officers, and *malandros*, because the following day was our day off, to this day a tradition in those parts.[32] Of course, the *zonas* are still open on Tuesdays, but usually business is pretty weak. Sunday is great for prostitution, because the weekend hasn't ended yet, and Monday is the day of choice for married men. Tuesday is very light, and then on Wednesday the week starts up again.

I was no devotee of Som de Cristal, but now that it was part of the plan, on the following Monday Velvet and I showed up and put on our little show. Velvet knew that if The Português saw us together, he would certainly leave me alone. It was part of the deal, of course, that I would pay for our dinners, and at the end, when The Português left me in peace, Velvet would get one day's wages. A fair bargain.

The brothel closed at ten, and each day that week Velvet came by to take me to dinner at Moraes or Tabu. We would stay late, drinking beer and whatnot. Boca do Lixo was like a small town, where everyone knew everyone else's business, and so The Português soon found out that I was going all around town with Velvet.

I started working by the door again, and for three days The Português didn't come by. On the fourth day, he appeared. He didn't even look at me, he just went directly to Cecília and asked to speak with her. Afterward, Cecília told me that he had asked if I was having an affair with Velvet. She responded that he shouldn't pry into the lives of his women. The Português walked past me and said: "Snitch, you know what happens with snitches." I kept quiet, but I laughed inside and felt avenged.

Walking around with Velvet wasn't half bad. He wasn't vulgar, he didn't openly carry his gun, and he treated me really well. The funny thing is that I never had anything romantic or sexual with him. A long time later, we ran into each other at Som de Cristal and danced together. We had become friends, in a certain sense.

When Monday arrived, we went to the dance, as planned. We rented a table, everything paid for by me, and waited it out, drinking beer and dancing,

32 The *malandro* was an infamous figure in urban spaces in Brazil in the twentieth century, frequently associated with petty crime, swindling, gambling, and samba music. Despite being linked to delinquency, vagrancy, and urban marginality, the *malandro* is also a cherished cultural figure and a mainstay of Brazilian bohemia.

as if we were a couple. Finally, The Português showed up. Velvet called him over, invited him to sit down, and said: "I know that you were wanting this lady to be your property. But you don't have a chance anymore, because she is with me." Velvet made it very clear that if The Português bothered me, he would go to jail. He even ordered that, if he walked by me in the hallways of number 134, he should lower his eyes. The Português laughed ironically and eventually said: "Is that all you wanted to say?" Velvet responded: "That's it." The Português got up, looked at Velvet, and offered: "Make good use of her money. That woman will give you a lot of trouble."

Our little show had worked out. The Português never bothered me again, even though I saw him constantly hanging around the buildings and bars of the neighborhood. As Velvet had demanded, he didn't even look me in the eye. The most he did was tell people that I was a snitch, and that I palled around with cops.

Today, a guy like The Português is almost a museum piece; they don't make them like that anymore. These days, women have more freedom to work on their own.

The Swansong of Pimps

In those days, there was a very famous pimp named João Branco. Once, I went out to dinner at Tabu and there he was, sitting at a table in the back. He was a real bastard, a specialist in pimping out very young girls whom he would bring from the backwoods of the state of Minas Gerais. Right there in the Art Palácio building he had four or five apartments full of girls that basically lived as slaves. In fact, he and his girls had a monopoly on all of Avenida São João. With the money he earned from prostitution, he had become a gentleman farmer in the Minas countryside. From my table, I could see him surrounded by other men, all of them dripping in gold watches and drinking whiskey. All of a sudden, the federal police came in and arrested them all. The arrest of João Branco signaled the beginning of the end for pimps in São Paulo.

Legend has it that the pimps of the old *zona* of Mangue would sit outside the door of a brothel with two boxes of matches, one on each leg.[33] One box

33 Mangue was the red-light district in Rio de Janeiro from the nineteenth century until the late 1970s, when it was dismantled to construct the subway system and a complex of municipal buildings. Until the mid-1990s, the district was located in another region in downtown Rio de Janeiro before finally being moved to present-day Vila Mimosa. Mangue was famous for its vibrant social life and bohemian, eclectic clientele.

was full and the other empty. For each man who entered the brothel with a whore, he would take one match from the full box and put it in the empty one. At the end of the workday, he would count all the matches in the second box and determine how much the whore should pay him. During that time, there was no such thing as a prostitute without a pimp. He would even go so far as to determine how many clients a woman should have per night.

The episode with the Português was an important learning experience, and I never again fell into the hands of a pimp. That was the first and only time that I made that mistake.

Fourth Commandment: You shall not reveal the fantasies of others. The fantasies of your clients are secret and their identities shall never be disclosed.

Fantasies: An Antidote

There are some regulars in the red-light district who come to be well known to the women who work there. Most of these guys have very particular fantasies.

There was a really good-looking kid whose thing was to have a woman wear sky-high stiletto heels. We didn't tend to wear such shoes to work because they tired us out. But when that guy arrived at the door of the brothel, word would spread, and within five minutes there would be a squad of high-heeled women awaiting him. After all, he was very polite, and he paid well. He didn't even put us to work, really, because he didn't want to have sex. His ritual was as follows: he would go in the room with a woman who was wearing heels and ask her to walk from one side to the other. Afterward, she would place her foot on his belly, and then the interview would start: "Where did you buy those shoes? How tall is the heel? Are they comfortable?" And then the guy would come, happy as a clam. That was it. Such are the mysteries of desire.

I had a client who always showed up in the *zona* with a bag draped over his shoulder. He would enter the room, open the bag, and take out nothing less than a yellow négligée. He would put it on and parade around like a little nymph, with as much elegance as he could muster, despite the big belly adorning his silhouette. Then he would ask sweetly: "Do you think I'm pretty?" With the utmost professionalism, I would answer: "Pretty? You're gorgeous!," making an incredible effort not to laugh. "What color lipstick do you think goes with my complexion?" he would ask, and I would respond, "Light pink." After this preamble, we would have sex while he said in my ear: "You are shameless! You love having sex with another woman!" And I had to agree — "Yes, I love it!" — or else he couldn't come.

Often these men are married and spend their whole lives with women who don't know this other side of their personality. Many times, I would ask them: "Do you do these things with your wife?" And they always responded: "No, my wife is the mother of my children. I respect her." The relationship between a man and woman, especially the old-fashioned kind, can become an expanse of loneliness. And the world of fantasies, which is immense, can be an antidote to the problem. It's a shame that many couples don't share that.

There are prostitutes, mostly high end, who specialize in certain fantasies. Sadomasochism is one of them. In Europe, there are even courses in this practice, because it can be dangerous; if it isn't done skillfully, it can even be fatal. One must be careful. This phenomenon reveals an uncontested truth: there are a lot of people who like to be hit, who only come if they are knocked around. In low-end prostitution, which is my scene, it's very common.

I must confess that this was always a professional limitation of mine. If there is one thing I don't know how to do, it is to hit someone. Trauma from my childhood, I think. If they ask for it, even jokingly, I don't know how to deliver. I suffer; it just doesn't sit right with me. So I refuse.

The Marginalization of Difference

Once I was at the door of a brothel when a Black man with severe physical handicaps got out of the elevator. His arms were contorted and paralyzed. He walked very slowly, dragging his feet, and he spoke with difficulty. I immediately quoted him a very high price, much higher than usual, so that he wouldn't want me, but he accepted. We entered the room, and I was overcome with dread; I didn't want to sleep with him. I felt disgusted and kept thinking about how I could get out of the situation when I realized that he couldn't take off his own clothing. He tried many different ways, but he couldn't do it by himself. I stood there watching him until he very humbly asked for help, and, in that moment, I felt a knot in my chest. Tears rolled down my cheeks. I understood how prejudiced I had been.

I took off his clothes, trying to hide my tears. I was crying for many different reasons: out of anger toward myself, shame for having charged so much, and still more shame for being repulsed. I realized that this guy was a person with feelings. And I asked myself: "My God, what type of woman am I?"

Having sex with him was really difficult. He didn't have muscle coordination, he struggled to get an erection, and he couldn't control his weight when he got on top of me. But he ended up becoming a very important person in my life. I never would have had an experience like that if I hadn't been a prostitute. The guy became my regular client, and we would always talk a lot. I told him all that had gone through my head that first time, and he told me that he had picked up on everything.

After him I had other clients with physical handicaps. Blind men, guys paralyzed from the waist down that couldn't have erections but still had desire. Every prostitute has clients like this, and they become very important to us. Not all prostitutes understand that this is a privilege of our profession, that it is one of its most noble aspects—this learned solidarity, the breaking of prejudices that are so embedded in society, forces that worship beauty and marginalize difference.

A Trick Corresponds to How Many Bricks?

In my years as a prostitute I had three great friends: Helena, Vera, and Lourdes. It's really difficult to make friends in the *zona*, actually, especially because the girls are always thinking about making the most money possible while spending the least. In other words, they basically don't have any fun.

The chief goal of all prostitutes is to buy a house, preferably far from work, normally on the outskirts of town. And it has to be a big house. The prostitute spends years counting bricks to build this house, and each man represents a quantity of bricks. It's a professional compulsion.

I once had a colleague, Marilene, who spent years obsessed with buying a house. She would go to our NGO meetings and all of a sudden say things like "Ah, I need to get back to work because I need to buy cement." Well, she was finally able to finish that house—large, beautiful, out in Jacarepagúa, on the outskirts of Rio de Janeiro. But suddenly she became unsatisfied with it, because she discovered that the area was controlled by organized crime and it was unsafe for her children. Unfortunately, she only realized this after the house was finished. She didn't hesitate, however: she sold the house and bought a plot in Maricá, in the state of Rio. And then she started the whole affair over again. When I see her these days, she is still very concerned with buying bricks and cement.

At Home in the Zona

Because I didn't feel like furnishing an apartment, I lived in a boardinghouse on Rua Albuquerque Lins. I wasn't interested in anything that might tie me down. I would go out in the morning, head to the Boca do Lixo, and after work I'd have dinner at a restaurant called Rice and Beans, located in front of the boardinghouse. I repeated this routine until I grew tired of living there. The owner was rude, and that was enough to push me out.

In São Paulo, we paid a daily fee in the brothels. Even if you don't go to work, you have to pay to keep your spot, just like taxi drivers, who are in debt as soon as they leave home in the morning. If you are sick, on your period, or whatever, it doesn't matter; you still have to pay, whether you show up or not. I got to thinking that I shouldn't have to spend that money twice over. The local police station obligated all the brothels to close at ten P.M. and open at eight A.M, so why didn't I just live there? I wouldn't have to pay any extra to do so.

Cecília, like any self-respecting madam, was very serious and organized. She carefully selected the girls who would live in her building; after all, there wasn't room for everyone. She ran a whorehouse, yes, but she didn't want things getting out of hand. And not because she was my friend, but because I was one of her most profitable girls, she accepted my request.

As strange as it seems, life there was calm—quite peaceful, in fact. I would wake up in the morning and read the newspaper. At night, I would have dinner at Moraes or Tabu. The thing I liked the most was to sit around in restaurants, thinking, flirting, and drinking beer. I read a lot and pondered the stories I was living firsthand; I was the leading actress in the film of my life. I felt good, very free. Life was good.

These moments compensated for my intense work routine, the comings and goings, the pills, the Coca-Cola by the liter, the police, who always showed up demanding money. At ten P.M., when business stopped, a silence would descend upon the place. There would be only a couple of women who lived in the building left. I would sit in Largo do Arouche or at Redondo bar and think a lot about what had happened since my mother had kicked me out. Once or twice I skipped work to go to her house to try to see my daughter. But my mother had walled me off from Alessandra, and as time went on I started to give up.

I loved going to Mappin. That huge department store with its green lettered sign was a fixture of downtown São Paulo. Brought to Brazil by the English in 1913 and located right near the Municipal Theater, Mappin had a very pleasant café, where women liked to sit before or after going shoe shopping. I would buy at least one item of clothing per week for my outings to the dances at Som de Cristal.

In the Crosshairs of the Dictatorship

In the late 1970s, Brazil was still living under a military dictatorship. During that time, the police instituted a curfew in the Boca do Lixo: prostitutes weren't allowed to stay on the street past ten P.M. Either the girls would leave the brothel and run to catch the bus just before then or they would leave after and risk being arrested and beaten up in the police van, whether or not they were on the clock. In fact, any woman, if she was in the area after curfew, would be considered a prostitute and would get arrested. We couldn't even sit down at a restaurant to have dinner. We had to flee and hide like criminals, constantly running the risk of falling into the clutches of the police.

During the day, the situation was no less complicated. Police officers entered the buildings, demanded identification from the clients, and beat the hell out of anyone who crossed their path. This caused a crisis. What man would enter a brothel with two police cars parked out front? The situation got worse and worse; every day police would fill up their van with people. They took money from the women and the *travestis* and beat them up.[34] The girls would get in the van, and when they came back, they would be in a sorry state.

In my case, I got the doorman to buy food for me because I didn't dare set foot outside the building. We could only leave during the day, and, even then, there was a risk that we would come across a police car on our way back and it would lead to a scene.

In late 1979, two girls disappeared. They got in the back of a police van and they were never seen again. One of them was pregnant. I was convinced that we had to do something, that the people of São Paulo needed to know what was going on. But because of their extremely low self-esteem, my prostitute colleagues thought that what had happened was relatively normal: What can we do? We are just prostitutes, after all.

---

34 These instances of police brutality also served as a catalyst for a burgeoning gay rights movement in São Paulo, which had been energized by the formation of Somos: Grupo de Afirmação Homossexual in 1978 and by the founding of its associated newspaper, *O Lampião da Esquina*, the same year. *Lampião* reported extensively on issues prostitutes faced, including forced displacement from Rio's red-light district after its destruction as part of an urban renewal project in the 1970s.

But we decided to stage a protest in the Praça da Sé. We organized ourselves by area, each person tasked with informing a different subset of the community. To the neighborhood *malandros*, who spent all day scratching their balls on the street corner, we assigned the task of going to the headquarters of the *Folha de São Paulo*, which was located on the same street as our building, and informing the journalists.[35] It was left to me to write up a flier explaining that two of our colleagues had disappeared two weeks prior after being loaded onto a police van. We took up a collection and convinced the madams to pitch in; the protest was in their interest as well. With that money, we made thousands of mimeographed copies of the flier and distributed them widely.

The support came immediately. Everyone was suffering from the mess with the police, and it is in times like these that people are able to stand up—never before, only after they are beaten down. The news spread quickly by word of mouth. Owners of bars, waiters, madams, *malandros, travestis,* all of the Boca do Lixo and the Boca do Luxo came together on behalf of the prostitutes.

The big day arrived. Of course, the police already knew what to expect. But the protest was a success; the newspapers all showed up after the brilliant invitations of our impromptu press liaisons. There were hundreds and hundreds of people in the Praça da Sé, their presence sending shockwaves through the city. And the repression was even more intense afterward, as the police immediately ordered the shuttering of the brothels. But the press and the local artists—who, despite sharing the neighborhood, had never approached us before—became our greatest allies.

Ruth Escobar went personally to one brothel closed by the police to offer us her theater, which bore her name, for a public meeting with the press.[36] It would be up to us to bring as many victims as we could so that they could give their testimonies to the public. That, at least, was easy to pull off. In times of suffering, people magically let go of their shame and speak out.

On the one hand, the protest had been a success, because now everyone knew about our problem. On the other hand, the cops kept squeezing us, and we knew we needed to stage another event to keep the momentum going. We immediately accepted Ruth's idea to have a meeting. It was an incredible moment, one that brought together all types of people united against the re-

35 *Folha de São Paulo* is the largest newspaper in São Paulo and one of Brazil's newspapers of record.
36 Ruth Escobar was an actress and politician and an important figure in Brazil's nascent feminist movement in the late 1970s. She went on to be the first president of the National Council on the Rights of Women (Conselho Nacional dos Direitos da Mulher), a state organ founded in 1985.

pression. But, again, the repercussions were immediate. The police officers denied their abuses, despite the witnesses' testimonies and the fact that the two girls they had taken away hadn't reappeared. However, before long, one of the police chiefs was fired, and life went back to normal in the Boca do Lixo.

Many years later, people used to see that same ex-chief downing whiskey at a bar right near where the *travestis* worked. One late night, a bunch of them got together and beat him up. They left him lying there on the curb and no one ever heard of him again.

After life went back to normal, for better or for worse, the prostitutes retreated. They closed their mouths and stayed silent. With this retreat, they affirmed once again that the prostitute doesn't have to speak up: after all, she is just a prostitute. It was that way for many of us but not for me. For me it was different—I was certain that speaking out was very important. It was yet another confirmation of the path I knew I needed to follow. Eight years later we would organize the First National Meeting of Prostitutes in Rio de Janeiro. Despite the years that had passed, the theme would be the same: violence.

Fifth and Most Important Commandment of All:
You shall not fall in love with your client.

The Prince Turned into a Frog

There was a certain guy in the neighborhood who made custom jewelry for the girls. Gold was their preference, and it happened to be his specialty. This young goldsmith, an elegantly dressed Black man, was the brother of Leontina, the madam of another brothel in the vicinity. But at the time I didn't know this.

The goldsmith made a lot of money attending to the vanity of the women of the *zona*. He was very nice with his clients, and even dated a couple of them. A guy from Casa Verde Alta, a middle-class Black neighborhood in São Paulo, he had that characteristic pride of the Black man. He was ascending the socioeconomic ladder by means of his talent for jewelry, which was prodigious. An employee of H. Stern, he also kept a small workshop in his house where he created made-to-order pieces, which the prostitutes would pay for in easy monthly installments.[37] He ended up becoming a regular in the *zona,* as he was always having to pick up money from someone or another.

37 H. Stern is a luxury jewelry brand founded in 1945 in Brazil.

I had a soft spot for the Volkswagen Karmann Ghia sportscar, but at the time the Brasília was all the rage, and the goldsmith had one, yellow and all decked out. It was basically an egg yolk with four wheels, which were made of magnesium. The guy would spend all weekend stroking it like a baby, and at night he'd parade around in it, leaving a trail of broken hearts in his wake.

At first, I wasn't attracted to him. He flirted with me, but I didn't pay him much attention. He was just nice to have around. We would drink beer together, and he was a fun partner for the outings I loved most: going to dance samba. He was a fan of the Mocidade Alegre samba group, and I had always been a fan of Camisa Verde e Branco—a vestige of my time spent with João, who was one of its composers.[38] As time passed, I became smitten with the goldsmith, and we started dating. There was a calmness that did me good in the routines of that honest worker, who was so dutiful that he even took his mother out to dance samba. Perhaps calm was what had always been missing in my life.

As much as I enjoyed being with him during that time, I always knew that we didn't have much in common. To marry a guy like that, a woman would have to be willing to lead the life of a traditional wife, living with her mother-in-law while her husband indulged in his favorite sport: sleeping with everyone in sight. He was the most traditional type that I dated in my entire life.

I felt jealous of him and his roving eye, but I never really fell in love with him. I had experienced a very difficult situation with my pregnancy with Alessandra, and I had already made two serious decisions in my life as a woman. One was to not get married. The other was to not have any more children.

Once in a while we spent a couple of days at a beach house in São Vicente, taking a break from work together, and on one of these trips it happened. I got pregnant. My first reaction was to go directly to an abortion clinic, but for some reason I couldn't get past the door, and I gave up. It wasn't a moral objection per se, but perhaps the effect of my Catholic education was too profound for me to go through with it alone. Naively, I had underestimated the importance of bringing a friend along to give me moral support.

Whether I wanted to or not, I had become an expert at hiding my growing belly. As I thought about what to do, I waited months to tell the goldsmith what was happening. When I finally told him, he completely lost his tactful veneer. He became a frog; in fact, deep down, I had never fully believed that

38 Mocidade Alegre (Happy youth) and Camisa Verde e Branco (Green and white shirt) are two São Paulo–based samba schools, or large clubs, centered around music and dancing in the annual Carnival festivities.

that frog was a prince. Then the frog said the following phrase that has stayed with me ever since: "My child? Yeah, right! The child of a whore has no face." As luck would have it, of course, our child was born with none other than his face, complete with the little chin dimple that was his most notable feature. But he only came to know this long after, because he disappeared from building 134 after our conversation. He started sending a messenger to collect his payments and was nowhere to be found, afraid of having problems with the other girls because of his relationship with me.

A Happy Present

As my pregnancy advanced, I stopped working as much as I had been. Cecília even released me from paying my daily fee. She was a tough cookie, but when push came to shove, she helped me hold things together. Between seeing a handful of clients and lots of crocheting, I had a pretty calm pregnancy and was very well cared for by the other girls.

After the protests in 1979 and '80, I had become really popular in the *zona*. At times, it seemed like all my friends were worried about my situation except me. I preferred to embrace the current moment rather than get upset thinking about a future I couldn't control. My friend Helena told me that when the baby was born I should go live with her in the small city of Barra Mansa and find work around there, and eventually buy a little white house with a porch in the countryside, near hers. It was a possibility, but nothing that I took especially seriously.

Until my water broke, that is. It was total chaos in the *zona*. At dawn one morning, amid a furor of happiness and panic, it seemed like the baby would be born right then and there, to the euphoria of all those present. But she didn't come. I was whisked away to Santa Casa de Misericórdia, after a quick fight between taxi drivers. Afterward came the party. That night, a lot of alcohol was consumed at the bar on the corner, in homage to my baby. She was a child of the city's underbelly and belonged to all of us whores. Everyone had lived through and cared for my pregnancy with such devotion that no one emerged unmoved by that remarkable moment.

If happiness depends on my daughter having luck in her life, she's all set. The birth was normal; I proved myself to be an exemplary obstetric patient. And, differently than my first daughter, the second was born practically rich, with so many clothes and toys.

Affection Times Three

When I was released from the hospital, Cecília was there to pick me up, and I arrived home in the middle of another party at building 134. But I knew that raising a baby in the *zona* wasn't going to work out. It was then that Ana Maria —to this day someone I like very much—entered the picture. She was a manicurist to the girls, and very beloved, a great friend of mine. She lived with another woman, a fully out lesbian. Like many gay couples, they felt the melancholy of not having children. So Ana made me a proposal. I should go to their house that same day, stay there during my recovery, and her wife Terezinha would help me to take care of the baby. Then I would go back to work.

I accepted. I soon joined them in their house on the periphery of São Paulo, in a neighborhood called Brasilândia. I spent some wonderful days with my two friends in that house, where we would often stay up all night talking. At that time, the child of a single mother bore a profound stigma, and I was still holding out hope that the illustrious gentleman goldsmith would acknowledge that he was the father of that child. Even without an official registration at the notary's office, the three of us chose the baby's name together: Cristina.

One day, while giving manicures, Ana came across the goldsmith in the brothel. She pulled him into a corner and said to him: "Your daughter is beautiful." He became enraged, denying it, saying that he didn't have a daughter. I became even more pissed off than he was when I heard about their interaction. Who ever heard of such a thing? I decided that, as soon as I recovered, I would go to the notary and register my daughter with my name only. I had no use for him, as everything was going perfectly fine without him.

Yet, to my horror, one day the famous yellow Brasília sportscar stopped at the door of Ana and Terezinha's house. It was him. I couldn't bring myself to see him face-to-face. Because the house was spacious, typical of the outskirts of São Paulo, I stayed in the living room while he went in the bedroom to see the baby. Then came the grand drama: the goldsmith cried. On his knees in front of the girl, he wept. It wasn't unfounded—the girl was beautiful. Even though she had her father's face.

From that moment on, he became a very devoted father. He brought presents and left money "for the necessities," which I accepted, for our daughter's sake. After all, that's what a father should do. My way of dealing with things between us was to not speak to him; I didn't even say hello or good night. I was able to rise above the fray because I was in a state of grace, without the slightest interest in fighting.

When my recovery was over, I went back to the *zona*. My daughter continued living with Ana and Terezinha, and that was a big relief for me. Those two loved the little girl, and they treated her with so much love and care that I wasn't worried at all. Twice a week I would stop by the supermarket, stock up on dozens of Nestlé products, and traverse all of São Paulo by bus to get to Brasilândia.

I left downtown at 10:30 at night, and by 12:30 I would arrive at their house. We would spend all night chatting, them telling me stories about my daughter, the visits of the goldsmith, and everything else. The following day, I would go back to the *zona*.

Sixth Commandment: You shall not leave the *zona* to live with a client, lest you run the risk of his lording it over you during your first fight ("It was me who took you out of that place!")—in which case you will go back to the *zona* with your tail between your legs.

A Tempting Folly

I emerged from my two pregnancies slender and beautiful. One day the goldsmith dropped by and asked me out to dinner. He was very nice and agreeable— uncharacteristically so, in fact. He told me that he was so taken with his daughter and so forth. To this day she is the apple of his eye. Despite the stable of women he kept, she was his first daughter, whom he would spoil and cherish his whole life. Sometimes it was even a bit over the top.

The goldsmith confessed that he admired my grit and poise in taking the pregnancy so well and then made me an astonishing proposal. It was very simple, at least according to him. The first step was to go live with him. And with his mother, evidently, whose side the guy would never leave. If I were to accept this proposal, I would then have to leave the *zona* for good. Once I left the *zona*, I would have to definitively forget my past, erasing the stain that was the last few years of my life. And I would never, ever again speak of it with anyone at all. Only if I took these steps would I win the prize of becoming a respectable woman, his wife, and the mother of his child.

Yes, it was preposterous. But, on the other hand, everyone dreams of having someone, of building a life together, of having a happy family. On top of that, his proposal offered me the real possibility of changing my life and thus obtaining the forgiveness of my mother in order to get my older daughter back.

I took to dreaming about all this, and eventually I accepted. I happily accepted his proposal, like Cinderella. Every woman has a Cinderella moment in her life; it is difficult to always resist those cultural forces. And so I began packing up my things, a myriad of books and trinkets that had accumulated in my little room. I called my sister and asked her to tell my mother about my decision. And I dreamed and dreamed. Like the poor mortal that I was, I believed that I was the happiest woman in the world. I even started attending luncheons at his mother's house. Not attend, exactly—more like I confronted those luncheons at his mother's house. I say *confront* because she didn't much like the Cinderella that her son had secured for himself. But he and I would go on outings to dance samba and eat in restaurants, reconstructing the relationship that had been interrupted when he found out about the pregnancy. It was a way of reliving my best moments. I was immersed in the bohemia of the *zona*, but I needed to prepare myself because, once again, my life was about to change radically.

Cinderella, Crashed and Burned

One night I invited the goldsmith to go to Brasilândia with me to see our baby. It was a Friday, and he, being a staunch *umbandista* of the kind that wore sacred necklaces and all that, said that he had to go to the temple.[39] Besides, he said, he had ritually cleansed his car with smoke and didn't want anyone to get inside. Cleansing his car was part of his routine, a ritual that dispelled the envy and greed that was surely directed at that sensational yellow Brasília. Fine, then, I thought. We said goodbye and each went our own way.

It was drizzling that night. As for Ana Terra, a character in a novel by Érico Verissimo in which the famous southwesterly winds blew when something was about to happen, it would always drizzle when something important was coming my way.[40] Or perhaps not—at that time it drizzled a lot in São Paulo, and here I am trying to make literature out of it. In any case, it was

39 *Umbanda* is a syncretic Afro-Brazilian religion that contains elements of both West African and Roman Catholic religious practices, as well as some Indigenous traditions. It was formalized as a religious faith in the early twentieth century and generally involves the worship of *orixás*, or deities, that roughly correspond to Catholic saints. Its practitioners are called *umbandistas*.

40 Érico Verissimo (1905–1975) was the author of many novels, including the trilogy *O Tempo e o Vento* (*Time and the Wind*), which tells the story of frontier life in southern Brazil during the colonial period. Ana Terra, a Brazilian woman who has a child with an Indigenous man, is one of the protagonists in this series.

indeed drizzling that night. A thick fog settled over the building where the goldsmith's sister worked, extending all the way to the bus stop to Brasilândia. If the Brasília wasn't egg-yolk yellow, I wouldn't have seen it. But it was the only one of its kind and it was impossible to miss. There it was, the goldsmith's yellow Brasília. Needless to say, he wasn't at the temple.

I stood there looking at the car in the cold drizzle, bags of Nestlé products in my hands, and I decided to cross the street to check the license plate and the magnesium wheels to know for sure that the good-for-nothing bastard who had just asked me to marry him was in fact deceiving me.

I went back to the bus stop. I let one bus pass by, and another. No sign of the goldsmith. But I wasn't going to budge. If necessary, I would spend the whole night waiting. There was nothing else to do. Finally, he emerged on the street all cozied up against a beautiful *mulata,* a woman I knew. The gentleman even opened the car door for her. Then he went to the driver's side, got in, and turned on the ignition. I took in all the details. He backed up and passed me by, not noticing me standing there. That was the last time that I saw the goldsmith and his yellow Brasília.

I caught the bus, and that day the long expanse to Brasilândia came in handy. I could cry as much as I needed. After letting out my emotions, I had the opportunity to reflect quite a bit. When I arrived at my destination, I had a plan.

Barra Mansa was too small, and I couldn't see myself living in a town in the countryside, so Helena's suggestion was out. Leaving São Paulo was the obvious choice. At least for a time. Rio had always been a dream of mine, but it would have been biting off more than I could chew at that moment. Belo Horizonte, in the neighboring state of Minas Gerais, was perfect. The girls, especially Helena, spoke a lot about BH, saying that you could make good money there, that there was a lot of business, and that it was a nice city. While it was a bit farther away from São Paulo than Rio, it seemed closer to my speed; I preferred a smaller challenge to start off with. As for my baby, Ana and Terezinha would keep her. They could contact me when they needed to, but they were to keep my address a secret. I would send money regularly to help with the expenses for the three of them, and I would visit at least once a month. That was the plan.

The following morning, I packed my suitcase, left some things with a peeved Cecília, and, when night fell, I got on a bus bound for Belo Horizonte. I cried a river all the way from the São Paulo bus station to the one in BH. I wept about all that had happened to me over the course of my life, and it became clear that, along the way, swallowed up by the mountains of Minas Gerais, I would emerge from that journey forever changed.

Seventh Commandment: You shall maintain an ethic of professionalism. You shall never mix fun and work, but you shall enjoy both separately.

In the Footsteps of Hilda Furacão

Leaving São Paulo was like severing an umbilical cord. It wasn't that BH was so different. The south of Minas is very similar to São Paulo: it has a similar culture, and the accent is even the same. In that sense, Minas was basically an extension of São Paulo.

But it was a new situation. And, for me, that trip was a journey into the unknown, crossing the mountains that are the emblem of Minas itself. The crossing, with its thousands of curves, always leaves me dizzy.

The bus station where I arrived in the early 1980s is the same one that exists today. I got there while it was still dark, and only after getting off the bus did I realize that I didn't know where to go; I had forgotten to ask my colleagues. Getting away had been more important than going anywhere in particular. I only knew the name of the *zona* in Belo Horizonte, Zona Boêmia—a perfect name for the place.

The Zona Boêmia is where the famous Hilda Furacão supposedly lived.[41] I say *supposedly* because there are people who say that she never existed. In any case, legend has it that Hilda was a fixture in the golden age of the Zona Boêmia. And the image of her is so iconic that it has taken root in the minds of the people who work there and frequent the place. Hilda Furacão and the *travesti* Cintura Fina, or Slim Waist, will always be the great symbols of the Zona Boêmia.[42]

41 Hilda Maia Valentim (1930–2014), or Hilda Furacão (Hurricane Hilda), was a famous Brazilian prostitute and the subject of a novel and a television series.

42 Cintura Fina (1933–1995) was a migrant from the northeastern state of Ceará and a *travesti* who was a fixture in the bohemian spaces of Belo Horizonte from the 1950s to the 1980s. The constant target of police repression, she took to carrying a dagger to defend herself, and she taught others to do so as well.

My first moment of culture shock came at breakfast in the bus station. In Belo Horizonte, people don't eat bread and butter for breakfast; they eat a plump, delicious cheesy bun and a fried manioc wafer, equally as big. The coffee, that famous Mineiro brew, is weak. After eating, I asked the guy working the breakfast counter where the *zona* was. He responded with that old question that I, at nearly sixty years old, continue to receive, one that I was asked at least three times per week during the duration of my professional life: "But what would a nice girl like you do in the *zona*?" Because I was well versed at answering this question, I didn't falter: "Work," I said. When I became an activist, people would say to me, "But you aren't a normal prostitute, you went to university, you are white." I got used to it, and I would swiftly disabuse them of their preconceptions.

Prostitution in Belo Horizonte is wild; there isn't anything like it in all of Brazil. It's where I broke my record. When a whore from São Paulo or Rio needs to make a bit of extra money, she goes to Belo Horizonte, where there is always demand. The quantity of men is extraordinary.

In that time, like today, the *zona* comprised just two streets: Guaicurus and Avenida São Paulo. Where there was once the Cabaré da Olímpia, Montanhês Dancing, and Chantecler, famed nightlife destinations frequented by names like Juscelino Kubitschek, and Noel Rosa, there was a long corridor of stores selling construction materials.[43] It was exceedingly discreet—so discreet, in fact, that I thought I was in the wrong place when I showed up in the early 1980s. There were no signs of prostitution anywhere to be seen. Door after door just led to cement, bricks, pipes, and so forth. But when I raised my eyes, I came across a whole other sight. Mounted above the storefronts of the cement shops, there were dozens of illuminated hotel signs. And I mean dozens, all in a row. It was as if they had divided the street in two, one part on the street level and the other above. So, I decided to just choose one of the names in lights. Hotel Maravilhoso, Hotel Caliente, Hotel Brilhante . . .

Capital of the Missionary Position

There was one sign in red lettering, not illuminated but written in red: Hotel Lírio. I liked the name. At that point, my sadness had dissipated, and I was full of adrenaline. I went up the stairs and caught a whiff of seasoned beans,

43 Juscelino Kubitschek (1902–1976), president of Brazil from 1956–1961, was responsible for the building of the new capital city, Brasília. Noel Rosa (1910–1937) was a samba musician and composer.

Minas style. I passed by dozens of doors and all the way at the end there was an open one, leading to a kitchen. A very old woman was making not only beans but also a full traditional Minas-style lunch. It was Dona Ruth, the proprietor of Hotel Lírio.

I later learned that she would start cooking lunch early in the day for the girls who worked for her. They paid, of course, but it was a meal with no equal. I never ate so well in my life. And Dona Ruth, a completely different type of madam from those in São Paulo, made dinner as well as lunch, honoring the Minas tradition of culinary abundance. In Minas, even the madam was a cook. Upon entering the kitchen, I said, "Good morning," and she responded, "Where are you coming from, Rio or São Paulo?" The old lady seemed pissed. I was taken aback and said, "São Paulo," as if I had been caught in the act of doing something wrong. "You want a room to work, right?" And then she launched into the whole spiel: the daily fee is this much, lunch is provided but it is paid separately from the daily fee, and so on and so forth. The daily fee was very high, but it allowed me to live there in addition to working.

She showed me a big room with a double bed. The main problem of Lírio was that the bathroom was communal and located outside the room. In the room, there was only a sink and a basin. If you wanted to wash up, you had to make do with a sponge bath. But everything was very clean. Minas is like that: immaculate sheets, furniture, sink, floor, everything in order. It was just that there were no individual bathrooms.

I spent a number of months at Ruth's place and she grew to like me. I have always been lucky with madams; I never had a shady one, and when they aren't shady, they generally treat the girls with respect. You just can't be too blunt with them, and you have to take it easy, without causing a commotion. I always kept to myself; the worst I ever behaved was that scene I made at the elevator, when I was hopped up on pills. Madams don't tolerate women who cause trouble, a common phenomenon in the world of prostitution.

In Belo Horizonte, in one week of work, a woman can earn the equivalent of a month's wages in São Paulo. That is even after paying a high daily fee. If a prostitute is willing to work a lot, she can see fifty, even sixty clients in one day. Whereas in São Paulo, the norm is five and in the old Vila Mimosa in Rio, ten at the most.

At the end of the workday, the hotels of BH fill up with so many people that you can barely move. But each girl has her own room where only she can work. She chooses if she wants to wait in the hallway, in her doorway, or on her bed, doing crosswords, for example. There are always long lines at the doors of certain women. But there are enough men to go around.

Men from Minas are crazy, and I mean crazy, for quickies. Belo Horizonte is the land of the missionary position. Nothing fancy, just the basics. No so-phistication involved, usually not even a special request. Mineiro guys don't want any fuss, and they don't talk much. Around those parts, Freud would die of boredom. I was used to having little chats with my clients in São Paulo and found this new way very strange. In Rio, not only do you chat with your client, but you also drink beers with him, you know about his whole life; it's basically a relationship. In Belo Horizonte, it's more like a factory. That's why women like to work there, because of its efficiency. But those who go there can't stand it for very long. A woman has got to be in the mindset of making a lot of money, motivated by ambition. The prices are low, but the demand is high.

Politics: an Aphrodisiac

In 1982, Tancredo Neves, a politician from the opposition movement, was running for governor of Minas Gerais, and Belo Horizonte was really politi-cized.[44] On the day of the election, the *zona*, which was already full, was out of control. Tancredo's victory left guys with an extraordinary appetite for sex. I thought to myself: Gabriela, today is your day! And I worked without stopping until the evening. When I left the *zona* that night, I had reached the unbelievable sum of seventy-eight men. I went to have a beer at the bar with sore legs, as if I had just run a race.

Sometime later, I met up with a friend from the gay movement who said to me, "Look, Gabriela, I admire your work a lot, but I think you get car-ried away. Seventy-eight clients in one day? That is outrageous!" At a certain point, there are so many men, so many dicks, that you can't see straight. But it's just like being overworked at any other job.

On Rua São Paulo, which ran parallel to Guaicurus, was the Hotel Catete, considered the finest whorehouse in the area. It was where girls were treated the best, and to work there you had to get in line. So I signed up. It took more than a month for them to call me, but it was worth the wait. Hotel Catete was a whole different beast. Each girl had a huge, beautiful room, and a maid came to clean each day. The only thing missing was Ruth's lunch.

The men who frequented Catete had more purchasing power; they were from the upper middle class. But Irene, the boss, was a terrible madam. She

44 Here, Gabriela is referring to the opposition bloc to the military regime, which began push-ing for regime change more publicly in the late 1970s.

is alive to this day. She was never my friend, but she wasn't really a friend to anyone, come to think of it.

More Fun than Work

Besides the Hotel Catete, Irene kept a large house in a fancy neighborhood of Belo Horizonte where she lived with all her girls. The daily fee at the brothel paid for a room in the big house as well. So that we could take care of ourselves, we had a kitchen where we could make our own food, and there was a gym and pool as well. It was a luxurious place, but it wasn't luxury prostitution, exactly—just well maintained and well managed.

Irene was a modern madam; she knew how to manage her business. Her prostitutes had everything they needed, and all of it was of top quality. They paid for it, of course—that quality didn't just fall from the sky. For example, for a fee, a kid would deliver your lunch to the hotel. We worked all day there, but the evenings were when things really heated up.

Irene operated a small clandestine casino out of her house, a gambling setup that went late into the night. Just card games, but the stakes were high, really high. It was there that I secured my nest egg. The men who played were rich, and they paid a lot as clients, a lot more than we charged at the hotel. If a session at the hotel cost fifteen reals, at the casino it was five hundred. It was the first time that I had worked in high-end prostitution. During the day I worked at the hotel and at night in the casino. Once in a while I took a day off to rest, but this was rare. I worked hard, because I knew I wouldn't get more opportunities like that. But it wasn't just me putting in long hours. Belo Horizonte was the land of ambition. Everyone there wanted to make a lot of money. And, for real, I had never had so much money in my life. I even bought a plot of land during that time.

I understood everything about the casino environment. My father, who was an excellent croupier, had taught me everything he knew. But I hated playing for money. For me, the maxim of the game is as follows: "If you are afraid of losing money, then don't play. Because you are going to lose." I never put my money in the game, but I did enjoy the ambiance, and it was wonderful to spend those late nights at the casino.

My clients were very refined men, and, because I understood cards, I loved giving them little tips here and there when they played poker. When I told them that my father was a croupier, they liked me even more. The work was more fun than it was work. Twelve-year-old whiskey flowing, interesting conversations . . . Those late nights in Belo Horizonte inside that nineteenth-century mansion were straight out of a television show. After working all day in the *zona* with poor men, it was thrilling to bathe and get all gussied up to go to the casino.

Love (and Prostitution) among Equals

When a woman went to live in Irene's house, she could rent an individual or a double room. And there is a detail I must mention: all the girls were lesbians. I had never seen so many lesbian prostitutes in my life. Being straight, I was completely outside the ordinary there. Even Irene had a girlfriend. But I didn't feel even a bit different or uncomfortable. I got along great with everyone.

In the house, there were couples who were really in love. And they had a wonderful agreement between them: love with women, sex with men. They didn't get jealous over what was simply the exercise of our profession. Love is love, work is work. What was forbidden was cheating on each other with other women. If someone got with the girlfriend of another, that would cause a problem. But when the men arrived, they were able to share their girlfriends with total ease. The men didn't know about any of it. It was a house secret and everyone was really discreet. But, of course, when men wanted a threesome, it was perfect for them, because they could have sex with their girlfriends while they worked. Needless to say, this they did especially well.

When there was no gambling, we all would go to a lesbian club. The only guy at the club was the waiter, and I would flirt with him all night long. The girls teased me: "Gabriela, will you ever stop with that nonsense of liking men?" I never stopped. I loved to dance with my girlfriends; it was an interesting sensation to have a woman guiding me. I, on the other hand, could never figure out how to guide another woman. In partner dances, the great thing is the woman being guided by the man, so it was interesting to invert that dynamic. But I never fell in love. And none of those girls ever fell in love with me.

When I first arrived at Irene's house, I didn't know about any of that. I went in search of comfort; I was attracted to that beautiful house with all its amenities, where I knew I could make good money. But I loved cohabiting with those girls. Lesbians generally aren't competitive like straight women; they don't claim men for themselves. As a result, the coexistence is much calmer. It didn't change my desires, however. I continued loving men, despite enjoying my new environment.

Irene, for her part, wasn't dumb. She made money every which way, even selling fine clothes to the women. They say that she is still working to this day.

She was pretty and modern, with a stylish short haircut. She was the chicest madam I ever had.

I've heard that the Hotel Catete isn't the same today. I'd be afraid to see it. I want to maintain my memories of the most glamorous phase of my life. That is more or less the story of my time in Minas.

I can't really say that I made a conscious choice to leave Belo Horizonte, because I didn't have a plan to leave or even to say a proper goodbye. After a year of working there, my friend Suzana, who lived in Rio but worked in Belo Horizonte every so often, invited me to spend a couple of days at her house in Rio. I accepted her invitation and off I went.

Arrival, Rio-Style

I have the impression now that going to Rio was the secret objective of my entire life. Since I was a girl, when I saw my father's postcards, something told me that that's where my future would lead me.

My sheltered life had been spent almost exclusively in São Paulo, with not even one year in Belo Horizonte. More than a place, Rio was a state of mind, an ideal, one that I had not yet reached in my thirty years.

That's why my arrival was such a big deal. Driving down through the Petrópolis mountain range, my *Paulista* eyes were intent on seeing the ocean.[45] But the mountains took it upon themselves to delay that moment, interrupting the trip like giant sentinels who made me believe that I would never arrive.

Crossing Avenida Brasil—the first of many times I would do so—countless feelings washed over me. Rio was supposed to be beautiful, and because I was sure of that, the chaotic avenue that confronted me made no sense. It was a miserable and inadequate entry point to the paradise I was expecting.

It was February 1982, just after Carnival.[46] I got off the bus at the Novo Rio station at seven at night. I was overwhelmed by the unbearable heat, by the people of different races and colors coming and going at a frenetic pace. I found a full row of public telephones and called Suzana. She lived in Copacabana, on the legendary Rua Prado Júnior. All the whores of Copa live on that street. The yellow taxis fought over me, and when I chose a driver, he

45 *Paulista* refers to someone or something from the state of São Paulo.
46 This was more likely 1983, as Gabriela was in Belo Horizonte for Tancredo Neves's election as governor in 1982.

ended up being a typical Carioca, as people from Rio are called, talkative and extroverted.[47]

I had yet to meet a Carioca who wasn't like that guy, the kind who in your first conversation treats you like a relative. His friendliness didn't stop him from scamming me, however. He practically drove into Madureira, in the distant suburbs, to get to Copacabana, in the South Zone. But he gave me the pleasure of talking as much as I wanted, and I was able to let go of both my anxiety and my euphoria at having finally arrived in the Marvelous City, if you will forgive me the cliché.

"Why haven't I seen the beach yet?" I asked naively. The guy just laughed at my provincialism. At thirty-one, I was a bit like Sleeping Beauty, and my congenial guide took advantage of this, charging me a fortune. That's Rio for you.

Copacabana at Last

My friend was very happy to receive me in her tiny studio apartment. She had dinner ready for me when I arrived, and we chatted a lot that first night, about our lives in Belo Horizonte, our bosses, and a guy I had been dating whose name was Benvindo. But I couldn't imagine that I would be leaving all that behind, without ever looking back. I had left everything from my clothes to a plot of land; I even had a deed. Little did I know, I would soon abandon my plan of living out the rest of my days in Belo Horizonte, but on that night, I was in Rio just to spend a few days and get to know the city. After that, I planned to go back to my life in the Zona Boêmia and start construction on my house, the fulfillment of every prostitute's greatest dream.

Trying to hide my eagerness, I asked Suzana: "Did you know that I still haven't seen Copacabana Beach?" Suzana immediately got up and said: "That's unacceptable. Let's go right now." It was midnight the first time I glimpsed that monumental curve of shoreline, designed by the compass of some genius, whoever he may be. To this day it is the beach that I love most. Even without the ridiculous streetlights, we were able to see the delicate white froth of the waves crashing on the sand. The scent of the tide washed over me, and it was

47 A national stereotype posits that people from Rio are by nature gregarious, fun-loving, welcoming, and, depending on who one consults, also sly and perhaps a bit lazy. This characterization is often articulated in opposition to the typical *Paulistano*, or person from São Paulo, who is said to be cosmopolitan, hardworking, and, according to some Caricoas, uptight.

more heavenly than I could have ever imagined. The people at the bars and on the sidewalk smiled and laughed, conveying the impression that everything was all right, in this life and in this world.

It wasn't as if I had never seen the ocean. When I was a girl, my mother would take me and my sister on trips to Santos, a region of beaches in the state of São Paulo. Besides this, my aunt had a beach house in Itanhaém, on the southern coast of São Paulo, as I already mentioned. But those places were very different. In Copacabana, the ocean has a sense of freedom that mirrors the very spirit of the city. This spirit made me grow, made me more like myself. And in that moment, if not completely shackled, I was still not fully free. Looking out at Copacabana, I couldn't even imagine that the place would come to represent a watershed in my life.

I didn't sleep well that night. By six in the morning it was already really hot, so I put on my bikini and went to the beach. Lots of people were walking on the sidewalk and sunbathing on the sand. I promised myself that I would buy a new bikini that very day. It was completely unacceptable to go to Leme Beach in my ancient bathing suit from São Paulo.[48] I didn't give a thought to work! The task at hand was getting a tan and observing the beachgoers. I was dying to get into the water, but I was afraid. To this day I still don't know how to swim, and I can't seem to get over the fear. I stayed on the sand, envious of the boys and girls who went running into the water and dunked their heads into that blue expanse, swimming out with a heroic bravura that I could never muster.

Suzana took a nap. After our outing, she went to the club to work. She was a gorgeous Black woman, and she did well for herself. I had met her in Belo Horizonte, where we worked in the same hotel for a good while until she came back to Rio. She was a Rio native, from Madureira—the community of Serrinha, to be exact. She turned tricks for many years, always in Copacabana, and when she needed to make more money she would go to Belo Horizonte.

After a week in Rio, I got very tan. I all but roasted myself in the sun. I went to the beach every day, from morning until sundown. I ate sandwiches and manioc crackers and drank delicious lemonade sold by the snack vendors who dressed all in white. How I miss that lemonade that you just can't find anymore. It is my version of Proust's madeleine.

At the end of the afternoon came cold beer and conversations, endless conversations, with people I had met on the beach. Suzana never came with me. She never went to the beach or the bar, or anywhere, really. She just worked

48 Leme is the northeastern end of Copacabana Beach.

and worked, often well into the night. She is yet another example of a prostitute who doesn't have any fun, which never made sense to me. During all those years I worked in prostitution, I always went to the bar and talked with my friends, as I do to this day. I also like to cook and invent recipes, as well as replicate ones from good restaurants. In other words, I like to have fun. When I asked Suzana about her feverish work regimen, she told me: "Listen, Gabi, we are already called shameless whores, so the least we can do is to make lots of money. Having that reputation while making a pittance? Now, that would be really stupid." Her greatest pleasure was going to her mother's house, bringing her some money to help out with expenses, having lunch, and playing cards with her family. She had a heart of gold, that Suzana.

He Didn't Like Whores, at Least Not to Date

On a very hot Sunday, I went with Suzana to meet her family. It was the first time that I had been on a bus in Rio in the fifteen days since I arrived. I saw Avenida Brasil again, but now with different eyes. I realized that all the ugliness I had observed on my arrival wasn't really that different from what São Paulo looked like upon arriving. I even thought it might be better because Avenida Brasil doesn't have the Tietê River, which is utterly destroyed by pollution and gives off a dizzyingly bad smell.

That day, we went to a favela community called Baixa do Sapateiro.[49] I had such a good time there! I ate a spectacular *feijoada*, and after lunch we sat around in a bar—Suzana, her boyfriend, her brother, and me—playing cards and drinking beer until late at night. It was back in the day when you could go to a favela and enjoy yourself without the fear of getting shot by a drug dealer or the police. I love the word *favela,* by the way. I think it is beautiful and sonorous. It says a lot about what it is, or at least about what it was before it became the tragedy it is today.[50]

49 The *favela*, the Brazilian term for "slum," is famous in Rio (and all over Brazil) as a bastion of popular music such as samba and Carioca funk. Favelas are also known as territories that lack adequate public services for their populations and struggle with high levels of crime and violence, often incited by fights between criminal factions and the police.
50 Gangs formed in Rio's favelas in the 1990s now control drug trafficking in the city, which has led to an increase in violent altercations with the police and rival factions. Despite the state government's attempts to "pacify" the city's favelas, most are governed by gangs or so-called militias, groups led by retired police officers who extort local business owners and rule with an iron fist.

Over card games and beer, Suzana's brother and I started to flirt. It was that delicious sort of flirting when you exchange glances and brush your legs up against one another. That night, we kissed at the bus stop when saying goodbye, but nothing more. Suzana told me that he had liked me a lot, but that he didn't want to get involved with a woman who lived so far away and on top of that, one who liked being a prostitute. Men are like that: full of contradictions! So fragile in their convictions, which is precisely why they are so wonderfully charming.

I started my explorations of Rio de Janeiro in Copacabana, constantly wandering around alone and meeting new people. I had been there for a month, and my daily life consisted of getting up early, going to the bar on the corner to have breakfast, and crossing both Avenida Nossa Senhora de Copacabana and Avenida Atlântica to arrive at Leme Beach. At night, I would go to the bars on Rua Prado Júnior. I had no boyfriend to speak of. Men kept their distance when I told them what I did for a living. They all seek out prostitutes, but not to date them, of course. Suzana told me that I was crazy for speaking out left and right about my job: "It's not written on your forehead, so why go around talking about it?" I got really angry at her, but then I realized that I had spent eleven years as a prostitute, without really leaving that world. I had isolated myself in the *zona*, and, of course, everyone there knew what I did for a living. I went to bars, restaurants, and *gafieira* dances, but always to places that were frequented by prostitutes and the men who liked them.[51] I grasped that, for the first time in my life as a prostitute, I was on vacation and the people with whom I spoke and drank beer on the beach belonged to the normal world, a world from which I had cut myself off. And I realized that it had been more than a month since I had left Belo Horizonte. It was time to go back to my little world, to work, and to my boyfriend, whom I hadn't called once during all that time. I had left a good deal of my life's plans on hold back there and I needed to return, but it was very difficult to think about doing so.

During all the time that I stayed with Suzana, I only experienced Leme Beach, Rua Prado Júnior, tuna sandwiches at the fast-food joint Bob's, a bar called Beco da Fome, or Hunger Alley, and the community of Baixa do Sapateiro. However, I had already fallen in love with the city and didn't want to leave. At a certain point, I could no longer delay my departure. *OK*, I would think to myself, *I'll go tomorrow*. And tomorrow never arrived.

51 *Gafieira* refers to a style of partnered dance done to a samba rhythm but can also mean a dance hall where one goes to dance in this style.

In Search of Locals

I was baking in the sun one day when I decided to stay and work in Rio permanently. I went back to Suzana's house immediately and told her my decision, informing her that, since this was the case, there was no reason to keep invading her privacy. I needed to find my own place. She recommended an apartment nearby that rented out rooms to prostitutes, and off I went, that same day, bags packed and ready for my new life.

I hated the place. Allotted to me in that dump of an apartment was a bunk bed, two drawers in a dresser, use of the bathroom — and the company of cockroaches, of course. A battalion of small roaches roamed up the walls and across the floor and even marched through the kitchen, which, it was just as well, I wasn't allowed to use. No matter, I thought. I will stay here for a while until I find a place to work and make enough money to rent a studio like Suzana's — ideally, one without cockroaches.

Suzana invited me to try my luck at a nightclub called the Pussy Cat, where she worked. That day, for the first time in two months, I got all gussied up like a proper whore and went to work. But the bouncer stopped me at the door, telling me that he couldn't let white women in. "Our clients prefer Black and mixed women, so we specialize in those types," the gentleman explained to me. Suzana hadn't been aware that this was a rule; for her, the fact that there were only Black women in the club was just a coincidence.

Back to square one, I had to find somewhere to work. I left Suzana at the club and from there went to Beco da Fome, on Rua Prado Júnior, to think about what to do. Could it be that there is nowhere else to work in Rio other than Copacabana? *That can't be!* I thought to myself. I must have taken on the single-mindedness of the local women, who think that the only place to work is in the clubs of Copa. There are tons of tourists around those parts, who, besides being more polite and handsome than Brazilian men, pay in dollars. But, in reality, Copacabana was a ghetto. A ghetto with an ocean view, but a ghetto nonetheless.

I asked myself: "I wonder if Rio has a *zona* for locals?" I had always worked in the low-end red-light districts, which, despite the horrible name that lawmakers invented for them, were the places I liked the most, with their working-class men: factory laborers, street vendors, taxi drivers, and truckers — men from all over Brazil who are struggling to survive. A place like that had to exist in Rio. I then remembered the stories I had heard about the famous Zona do Mangue, which is said to be the oldest red-light district in all of Brazil.

The next day I went to the beach while I waited for Suzana to wake up so I could ask her how to get to Mangue. Upon hearing my question, she was horrified. "What are you talking about, Gabi? You're crazy for wanting to go to that dangerous place! It isn't a place for women like us. There are only cheap whores and criminals there." I responded: "What is the difference between the *zona* in Belo Horizonte and the one here? A *zona* is a *zona,* no matter the city." Suzana looked at me like I was from outer space. But, as I was already regarded by my colleagues, including her, as a little bit nuts, she yielded and told me that Mangue, which had been displaced several years before, was now located in the neighborhood of Estácio.

Eighth Commandment: You shall always charge. Within the *zona*, you shall never receive a client who does not pay you for your services.

If I Must Die, Let It Be in Estácio

I went to catch no. 433, the bus that passed through Estácio. It was big and red and looked more like a fire truck. It was my first time taking a bus by myself in Rio, and I was a bit afraid, but whenever that happens I try to forget my fears and think about other things. I sat close to the window and, looking out at the city as it passed by, reflected on the days I had spent in Copa thus far. I thought about the wonderful snacks that I ate at Bob's almost every day at the beach. In that time, neither São Paulo nor Belo Horizonte had Bob's sandwich shops, so when people spoke of the marvels of Rio, Bob's was undoubtedly one of them for me. To my delight, I immediately noticed there was a Bob's near Suzana's apartment. I discovered their tuna sandwich, which I had never eaten before, and their orange juice tasted like it was homemade, just like the one my mother used to make for me. Beco da Fome, where I drank beer, was another favorite spot of mine. There were the curbside bars as well, real hole-in-the-wall joints, where there was never anything decent to eat. Despite this shortcoming, they were wonderful, with their aura of storied Carioca nightlife. I would always wonder in which bar Elis Regina had sung; only later would I find out that it hadn't been in Beco da Fome, but in Beco das Garrafas on Rua Duvivier.[52] I had seen the live show of her album *Falso Brilhante*

---

52 Elis Regina (1945–1982) was a beloved singer of bossa nova and other popular styles.

eight times, and I was dying to meet Elis, who was so charming with her dramatically arched eyebrows.[53] Unfortunately, that never happened.

Bus no. 433 went along Botafogo Beach at top speed, and then, all of a sudden, the magnificent Sugarloaf Mountain appeared before me. I was ecstatic; I had never seen anything remotely resembling that dramatic landscape. I had the impression that the bus was taking the scenic route through the whole city just for my sake.

I asked the bus driver where Vila Mimosa was. What a beautiful name, I thought, so sweet! According to Suzana, it was the new name for the Mangue district once it had been relocated in the late 1970s. His response hardly came as a surprise: "What are you going to do there? That isn't a place for proper girls like yourself." Oh, men and their contradictions. I would wager that, whenever he has a bit of extra money, that driver makes a beeline to Vila Mimosa. And I, being the brazen woman I have always been, replied: "I asked you where Vila Mimosa is. I didn't ask for advice." He shrugged and told me that he would let me know when we arrived. The other passengers pretended as if they hadn't heard. I could feel their eyes observing me as I got off no. 433 at Vila Mimosa.

I stepped out on the sidewalk and I couldn't believe what I saw. The place was very ugly, nothing about it was *mimoso,* or sweet and graceful. I looked around trying to understand what this place could possibly be. In the surrounding area, there were a number of houses that were nearly falling down, a subway station, which I hadn't even known that Rio had, and an immense empty plot of land at the center. There was a ramshackle bakery with a large group of men drinking out front, and next to it a building that resembled one of São Paulo's most dilapidated and crime-ridden structures. I came upon an alley full of people but I was afraid to enter. I went forward, but then retreated to the bakery. I summoned my courage and asked a guy where the Vila Mimosa was. In contrast to the bus driver, he didn't miss a beat and gave me directions that started precisely from the alley that had given me such pause.

I started walking along a dirt road that had only one house on it and trees on either side. Suddenly, another world appeared before me. A narrow street materialized, with many old houses on either side and lots—and I mean lots—of people. There were men, walking by or standing around, all of them looking at the many women dressed in bikinis, low-cut leotards, bras and

---

53 Regina released the album *Falso Brilhante* (False brilliant) in 1976 to great critical acclaim.

panties. And, of course, there was a soundtrack to accompany all of this. Each of the houses had a jukebox, one more beautiful than the next, all playing different styles. The melding of music on the narrow street created another sound altogether, strange and magical.

My first impression of Vila Mimosa was that it was a place to party, a festive spot that seemed as if it were in a small backwater city. It strikes me as curious that a city like Rio was, until fairly recently, able to maintain a traditional red-light district. It could have easily been included in the country's list of cultural heritage sites.

I walked around Vila Mimosa completely hypnotized, knowing immediately that I wanted to work there. The *zona* was only about one street long, and the entrance was marked by a large gate with the lettering "Vila Mimoza—Welcome," the name of the place misspelled, with a Z instead of an S. I walked back and forth several times. Local underworld fixtures were playing cards, some squatting while others stood, all of them looking around nervously while focusing on the cards strewn atop a newspaper that was covering the dirt ground. I soon discovered that the nervous glances were due to the threat of police entering the *zona*. The guys posted a lookout at the entrance to see if a squad car was trying to enter, which it did with great difficulty, owing to the narrow streets. Sometimes the cops would enter on foot from the other side, catching the criminals red handed and unsuspecting. That was generally the start of a cat-and-mouse game in which the police ended up with money in their pockets, and the *malandros* were left without their cards. Before long, the newspaper was laid out on the ground again and a new game would commence. To this day, I can't for the life of me understand why they would choose such an exposed place for their card games. My theory is that they liked the adrenaline that came from the police's imminent arrival. Without it, the game would become monotonous and pointless.

As I walked through the *zona* that first day, the women teased me: "Hey, cutie, you looking for pussy?" I decided it was best not to leave only to come back later in an attempt to secure a job. I gathered my courage about me and entered a small house near the entrance gate. Behind the counter, a guy answered my query in the affirmative: yes, there was room for me to work. He asked me where I was from and how old I was and gave me a rundown of the basics: "The terms of employment are the following—for every client you bring in, you pay the house five cruzeiros.[54] Bring a towel, soap, and work

---

54 The cruzeiro, the currency of Brazil from 1942 to 1986, was adjusted several times to account for inflation.

clothes with you tomorrow, but if you want to start now just to see if you like it, feel free."

I had yet to learn that in the *zona* you don't have to come ahead of time to see if you get the job. You just show up, pick a spot, and start working, but I always forgot to bring my own towel and work outfit on the first day. The manager of the brothel lent me a towel, and, with that, I headed to the door of the house to start my career in Vila Mimosa.

One Never Forgets One's First Carioca

That day, I was wearing a pair of very tight jeans and a cropped summer blouse. I had barely parked myself by the door when a client showed up. My very first client was a Carioca, a taxi driver. We settled on a price and ascended a spiral staircase to the second floor, where there were a series of so-called rooms. In reality, these rooms were tiny wooden cubicles with such low ceilings that the clients generally had to crouch down so as to avoid hitting their heads. Inside, there was a single bed covered with a dirty sheet, the heat so oppressive that I felt like I would melt. The guy was nice, he just wanted a basic fuck in missionary position. Despite his simple request, I indulged him a bit and took my time.

As I was having sex with this man, I got to thinking, did I really want to work in this glorified shack masquerading as a brothel? In any case, when the session was over, I said goodbye to the client, paid the house what I owed, and directed myself toward what the manager called the bathroom. Inside, there was a bidet without a faucet and a large plastic jug of water with a plastic mug floating in it.

I hated all of it, but I knew I couldn't go back home with just the money from one puny session. I returned to the door and scored my second client, and then another, and then one more. Four clients later, I had pocketed some decent money. I freshened up as much as I could and went out to catch the bus back to my bunk bed in Copacabana. I stopped at a restaurant to have dinner and reckoned that, all in all, my first day of work in Rio had been pretty good, and lucrative. I decided happily that I would go back to the Vila the following day, and, now that I was a bit more familiar with the place, I would look for a better place to work.

The next day, before arriving at work, I went downtown to buy a couple of towels, soap, and a roll of good-quality toilet paper. In my bag I carried my black leotard, which was my work uniform and my armor.

This time, I observed the area more closely. Estácio Square was no more than a name on a plaque on the corner of Rua Joaquim Palhares. There was no square to speak of, just the Rua Estácio de Sá. On the other side of the road, there was the entrance to the São Carlos favela, and, surrounding the path up the hill, there were people selling all kinds of things: vegetables, sandals, clothes, rice and beans in bulk, live chickens that women would carry up the hill upside-down, holding on to their feet. When the women would stop to speak to an acquaintance, the hideous birds were left hanging there wide-eyed and frightened. I sat at the bar next to the path up the hill, taking it all in. How could the modern, urban side of Rio coexist with a space like this, one that seemed right out of a small town? Everything was strange and beautiful to me. So different from São Paulo and Belo Horizonte.

I entered the Vila by way of the narrow dirt road and once again became enraptured with the festive atmosphere of the place. Full of energy, I walked around methodically assessing the different brothels. At a certain point the alley became wider, forming a sort of small square, and there on the left was a large old house, its double doors opening onto a staircase with a beautiful— albeit rusted—banister surrounded by many windows.

I had already decided to work in a different brothel, having resolved to walk into whichever one struck me as better than where I had worked the previous day. Once inside, I saw a number of women standing on the staircase. Through another door there was a bar with a long counter, and, seated on a high stool, holding on to a cane, was a Black gentleman of a certain age, looking like a deity from the *Umbanda* religion. Behind him, hanging on the wall, was a painting of none other than the man himself, depicted with a pipe between his lips. With so many people in the bar, many of them looking at me curiously, I don't know why I decided that it was him with whom I should speak. I got closer and asked if there was room for me to work. He smiled and, without speaking, pointed to a woman who was seated on a large antique armchair on the other side of the room.

Dona Isaura, "Isaurinha" to her close friends, was a woman who could only have existed in Vila Mimosa. Originally from the old Mangue zone, she had been working for more than forty years in the business of prostitution—or, to put it in less politically correct terms, more than forty years pimping women out. She had lived most of her lifetime in that world.

In those days, the veteran madams loved to tell the story of how Vila Mimosa came to be. In the late 1970s, after decades of trying, Rio city officials expelled the red-light district from Avenida President Vargas and its two surrounding streets with the excuse of building the subway, leaving the city temporarily without an urban space dedicated to prostitution. Dona Neuza, who was a madam in Mangue, was living in one of the mansions of the Vila at the time and knew that the majority of them were empty. She proposed that the prostitution businesses set up shop in Vila Mimosa, which already went by that name. And that's how Vila Mimosa was born. It was, in principle, an arrangement intended to last until they found a better situation, but it was successful and remained in that spot from 1979 until the middle of the 1990s.

Isaurinha was a petite woman who, in the 1980s when I worked in the Vila, was approaching seventy. On that hot summer day, which seemed like it would never end, I approached her and asked if there was a position for me in her brothel. She laughed and said that no one had ever asked about a position, because what she offered wasn't work per se, but a quick fix for women who didn't have anywhere else to go. She told me about the workings of the house, and that there were only two rules: no drugs and no fighting. She wrapped up with the classic question: "Do you have a towel?" This time I was able to say, "Yes, I do!"

Isaurinha, unlike all the other madams I had met, introduced me to the other girls who worked in her brothel and showed me first the rooms where the business happened, and then the bathroom, which wasn't much different from the other spot, with its plastic jug of water and floating mug, except that this one had a shower—cold water, of course, but a real shower nonetheless. She brought me back down to the bar and introduced me to the older gentleman with whom I had spoken at the entrance. He was her business partner and he managed the bar.

The man was known in the *zona* as "Thousand and One Night"—just like that, not plural. I don't think that anyone knew his real name. Fondly called "Thousand and One," or sometimes "Midnight," legend had it that he appeared in Mangue when he was still a boy, having been kicked out of his house because he was gay. And there he lived his entire life, always accompanied by handsome young men who lived with him in the first house past the entrance to the Vila, right next to the gate. Thousand and One's house was the last one to be destroyed after the demise of the Vila was formalized in a legal suit in 1995. Until the middle of 2005, the lone house could be seen in the middle of a barren plot of land, as if Thousand and One were still there, looking back into the past, recalling stories from his life and reminding everyone that that small place had been home to people who had lived and dreamed, people who had together made up a community: homosexuals, *malandros*, samba musicians, whores, and their johns.

Thus Spoke Vera

I went out to stand by the door on what was my second day in the Vila but what I actually consider to be my first. The previous day had merely served to give me a lay of the land, and only then was I really starting to fully inhabit that world.

Right off the bat I met Vera, who would become my best friend of all time. Unfriendly at first, she was tall, blonde, elegant, and talkative. She was from the south of Brazil, near the border with Uruguay, and she spoke with a very distinctive accent. Itaqui was her hometown and also the bane of her existence. She despised that place, along with all men from the south, whom she considered to be prejudiced and misogynist. She never forgave her countrymen, who had treated her with such scorn for being a prostitute from an early age. She gave off the impression of being harsh, but in reality she was just a strong woman and a good friend, one who reserved sentimentality for her reading. An avid reader of romance novels, she made a point of saying that she only read books of that genre and watched films that told tales of great love. She used to say that in fact life was saturated with reality, and that's why she would read the newspapers every day, in order to learn about what real life had in store for people. No, reality was not to be found in Vila Mimosa. In the Vila we lived lives right out of a play, and it was enough just to step outside its gates to see how "normal" people were different from us.

Every *zona* is unique. Having grown accustomed to the Boca do Lixo and the Zona Boêmia in Belo Horizonte, I needed to get to know the ins and outs of Vila Mimosa, which, for me, seemed straight out of a different era. Luckily, Vera passed along her work tips. "Don't stand around nearly naked like that woman over there. Pay attention—you'll see that men don't care for women who show everything. If he's already seen it all, why pay?" Another one: "Take your wallet with you everywhere, and when you enter a room with a client, place it under the bed, within reach." And still more: "Never leave a man alone in the room, or else you run the risk of him leaving without paying and Isaurinha won't even notice. Do the deed, get the money you agreed on, and leave the room with him, covered up by a towel with your wallet in hand, and only once he's gone go get cleaned up." And finally: "Don't pay any mind to the *malandros* who gamble in the street. I don't even give them the time of day so they don't start flirting with me. There are a ton of good-for-nothing guys around here who are just looking for a woman to provide their daily bread. They're worthless. All they do is snort coke and lose money gambling." I received this advice and a lot more as the days passed in the *zona*. Some of it I followed strictly, some not so much.

I returned to Copacabana that day with a respectable sum of money, feeling open to relocating permanently to Rio. I decided then that I would move to the *zona*. Isaurinha didn't mind when women who had moved from out of town lived there, and I had a good reason to leave Copa. Suzana, my local friend, had cooled on me because of my decision to work in the Vila. Sharing a room with five women who considered themselves superior because they turned tricks in Copacabana and who scorned me because I worked in the poor part of the city wasn't any fun at all. Moreover, sleeping alongside a battalion of repulsive cockroaches and paying a high rent was no longer appealing to me—not that it ever had been. Considering all this, living in the *zona* was blissful. And, because I turned a good profit for the brothel, they didn't charge me anything extra to live there. Isaurinha really liked women like me who didn't dawdle, which made us highly productive. And so I packed my bags and said goodbye to Copacabana and to my vacation.

> Ninth Commandment: You shall remain wary of madams.
> As much as the lady of the house may seem sweet, don't
> let yourself get under her thumb. You shall show her,
> with all due respect, that you can be clever as well.

Isaurinha's Little Sins

Saturdays in the Vila were nuts. Starting early, the *zona* got so packed that the men could barely make their way through the crowds. The ten rooms of Isaurinha's brothel could hardly handle the business, especially because more women worked on Saturdays. Vera and I didn't have any trouble, though. Because we were there throughout the week and we saw a lot of clients, two of the rooms were reserved especially for us.

I had my own sheets and pillowcases, and a bottle of lavender perfume that I always sprayed so that the room smelled good. The men loved my little indulgences and always came back wanting more. At some point the other women started saying that they came back to me because I was the daughter of Iemanjá, a deity of the Afro-Brazilian religion partial to lavender, which gave me good luck. I don't know about that; I neither believe nor disbelieve it. I only know that in my career as a whore I always treated my clients very well, and I always kept my room clean and fragrant. The working-class red-light district isn't synonymous with filth, and the prostitutes who work there, whether they're rich or not, should always be well dressed and sweet smelling.

On Saturdays, Isaurinha brought her sister, Carmem, to help her with managing the flow of women and clients so that no one would pull the wool over the old lady's eyes. One of them sat in each corner of the brothel in their immense armchairs, wearing an apron with a pocket full of cash in small bills.

Carmem, who was much older than Isaura, used a cane, had poor vision, and could barely get around, but she was more clever than her sister. On Saturdays, Isaurinha would get agitated and have difficulty sitting still. She would pace from one side of the room to the other, knocking on doors, telling clients that their time was up, that there were others waiting in line for the rooms. She was desperate to prevent a potential client from giving up and going elsewhere, meaning that she would lose money, which she worshipped. Vera and I were entertained by the old ladies' agitation and sometimes would even have a bit of fun with them.

One of our pranks was the following: we would leave the room, heading toward the bathroom, wrapped up in a towel. On the way back, without fail, one of them, if not both of them, would say: "My money?!" And I would respond: "Are you nuts? I paid you on my way to the bathroom! Just because it's Saturday doesn't mean you can charge me twice!" With that they would become confused, but they distrusted their own memory instead of us and let us pass by. Vera and I laughed a lot and used the money to have a couple of beers, happy to have tricked the madams.

It was on Saturdays as well that Isaurinha took advantage of the chaos to commit her little sins. She would pass through a hidden, narrow hallway at the back of the house and disappear. One day we discovered that she had bored a hole in the wooden wall. Through the hole, Isaurinha spied on the couples having sex and masturbated. At many points during the day, she would disappear and we knew that she was in the dark hallway, spying and relieving herself of her tension. The women of the house would sometimes cover the hole with a towel just to mess with her. She would get furious then and, without naming anyone in particular, would start talking about how times had changed, that prostitutes didn't respect madams anymore, that if we were living in a different time, not a single whore would have the courage to mess with the lady of the house. She would pace back and forth, saying that she was going to kick the whole lot of us out. When she returned to the hallway, the girls would remove the towel and uncover the hole. She would come back as happy as a clam, having forgotten all of her curses against us.

Isaurinha was a real character who deserves to have her story told in both prose and verse. She owned an apartment building in Penha and a very nice house, where she lived with her sister, a niece, and Jorge, the greatest love of her life. Jorge, who was younger than forty, was a tall, handsome Black man who treated the two old ladies with a lot of affection. Every day he brought his wife to the *zona* in his white Opala, which truly had a life of its own. Because he couldn't manage to squeeze any money out of Isaura for himself, each week he invented some problem with the car that meant he had to bring it to the garage. All he had to do was park the Opala in front of the brothel and get out carrying a piece of paper for Isaura to know that he was asking for money. She'd look at me and say, "Here he comes again." In fact, Jorge had a friend who ran a garage in Penha who would draw up phony invoices so that he could get Isaura to cough up some money. Often he would show up with his invoices in search of money and Isaurinha wouldn't have cash on hand. Vera, always Vera, came to his aid and lent it to him—charging interest, of course.

Jorge didn't work. The most he did was drive the two old ladies to the *zona* and play cards with the other layabouts. He never so much as cast a glance at other women in the *zona*, however. In fact, I never heard of him having an affair with another woman within the district. "What the eyes don't see the heart can't feel," goes a wise and popular saying that certain men heed. One of these men was Jorge, who knew full well what kind of woman he had as a wife. Isaurinha loved him and was completely under his spell when he kissed her and told her that he would pick her up at ten. And he would always add: "Use good judgment, no flirting with other men while I'm gone." And, according to local gossip, off he went in his white Opala to rendezvous with Isaura's niece, who was his secret lover.

It was assumed throughout the *zona* that once Isaurinha and Carmem died, their niece, a nurse at the Hospital dos Servidores and their only heir, would marry Jorge and they would live happily ever after. If someone had bet on this outcome, alas, they would have been sorely disappointed. Jorge, against all predictions, was at his friend's garage one day and, upon getting into his car, suffered a serious heart attack. He fell dead onto the seat of his beloved white Opala before his fortieth birthday, and Isaurinha, firm and strong, lived a lot longer. She reached ninety and died at home, alone, most likely thinking of Jorge, her great love, and the *zona*, her lifelong passion.

Samba with No Strings Attached

After seeing a great number of clients, most of whom just wanted the missionary position, a handful who requested oral sex, and usually an obnoxious drunk who took a long time to come—finally, around eleven at night—it was time to call it a day. That's when I would bathe, put on a cute outfit (never the same one, of course), and head out in search of some fun.

Saturday nights were dedicated to samba at Estácio de Sá.[55] All I had to do was grab my bag and walk about one hundred meters, turn right, and there I was. I always went alone. Vera, my friend, hated samba. "Think about it," she would say. "If I can go home, listen to Frank Sinatra, or even watch a movie on TV, why would I stick around listening to noise that is truly a poor excuse for music?" My other colleagues, as much as I insisted that they join, rarely accepted my invitations to go out. They had their debts to pay and nursed the eternal fixation of every whore, that of buying bricks. I, on the other hand, spent all the money I earned on beautiful clothes, high heels, French perfume, and beer.

I didn't mind going alone. Once I stepped onto the court where the musicians played, I felt drunk from the energy of Cariocas anticipating a samba show. In those days, very few people from the middle class frequented samba shows, in large part because of the association between samba and criminality. Estácio de Sá was especially shady, because it was located next to the most famous working-class red-light district in the city. For those reasons, the people who regularly attended the samba shows tended to be residents of the slums of São Carlos, Mineira, and other communities, the whores, and the local *malandros*.

I would stay and listen to the music until sunrise. Occasionally I would leave in the company of some guy, but, most of the time, I would go to the bakery alone to have breakfast before sleeping until noon. I was in a phase of life in which I wasn't interested in falling in love; I couldn't be bothered to put the work in to maintain a relationship and commit to someone. I had just arrived in Rio and I just wanted to enjoy myself, chat with people, and observe the city around me.

---

55 Estácio de Sá is an important samba school located in the Rio neighborhood of Estácio, known as the "cradle of samba."

Lover and Friend

But one day, my peaceful solitude and contemplativeness went out the window. I fell in love. I was waiting at the door of the brothel in search of clients when a man walked past. He was around thirty, short, bald, wearing jeans and sneakers, a rare sight among the local guys who made a point of wearing formal shoes and tailored pants. He passed by once, twice, three times, walking back and forth while making eyes at me. Without hesitating Vera told me that he was Pantomime Carlinhos, nicknamed so because he talked in an exaggerated fashion and bragged about himself.

Carlinhos was indeed a real talker, but he wasn't boastful. He was a guy with a lot of unrealized ideas whose greatest dream was to become rich and have a house with a pool on the Ilha do Governador, where he was born and where he lives to this day.[56]

That day, he walked into Thousand and One's bar, probably to find out who I was. Within minutes he approached me and invited me to have a beer with him. At first, I found him ugly and too short. He was only a bit taller than me, and that's not saying much, as I am barely five feet tall. But, as the conversation flowed, I started to see that he was a kind man, with a beautiful smile and a wonderful way of speaking. He invited me out to dinner and I accepted. Carlinhos drove a taxi, and we went to a bar-restaurant in the Praça da Cruz Vermelha where the taxi drivers would take breaks to eat late at night. According to Carlinhos, the spot had the best roast chicken in the whole city, and, in fact, it was indeed delicious, seasoned with something special.

He had a very specific way of compensating for his short stature: when he entered an establishment, he would speak very loudly and greet everyone, his charisma taking up a lot of space. That first night, we arrived at one in the morning and the bar was packed. Carlinhos introduced me to all of his colleagues as his girlfriend who had arrived from São Paulo not long ago. "It's true what they say, my friends, not everyone can handle a girl from São Paulo," he announced to the crowd.

We stayed at the bar until the sun came up, eating snacks, drinking beer, and talking. We talked about everything: prostitution in other cities, politics, cinema, family, and, of course, Dona Anita, his mother and the greatest love of his life. Carlinhos was the only child of a single mother in a time when that was still quite stigmatized, and he lived his entire life with her in her house on

---

56 The Ilha do Governador is an island in Guanabara Bay belonging to the city of Rio de Janeiro. It is home to the city's international airport and a number of working-class neighborhoods.

the Ilha do Governador. He was always surrounded by women, and when he thought that he was in love with one in particular, he would bring her home to live with him and his mother. He never married, and, according to Dona Anita, there was a long string of women whom she had patiently received in her home.

He never took me to live on the island. He only invited me to have lunch with his mother a couple of times. I wasn't his favorite; that designation belonged to Lídia, mother of his only child, who was fed up with him pursuing multiple women and not being able to sit still. He never loved me, but it was clear that he liked me a lot and respected me. He keenly perceived that I wasn't the type of woman to live the life of a housewife; Lídia was better suited to that.

The first night we went out together, he invited me to sleep in a hotel nearby, on Avenida Mem de Sá, and we spent the whole next day in the dark room having sex. Every so often we would get hungry and he would leave to pick up some food: always roast chicken and a Coke. Exhausted, we finally crashed around seven that night. When I woke up in the wee hours of the following morning with a terrible hangover, Carlinhos was nowhere to be found. He had departed silently but left a note with a brief message: "I'll see you in the *zona*. I loved being with you. A kiss." And that's how my long relationship with him began.

I left the hotel, my eyes struggling to get used to the daylight, and I flagged down my trusty 433 bus headed toward the *zona*. I laughed to myself at Carlinhos's behavior. When I arrived in the *zona*, I discovered that Vera and the other girls had been worried about me. I had disappeared the previous day without sending word that I was all right, and I barely knew the city at that point. It was nice to know that even though I had been in Rio for such a short time, many people cared about me and my safety. When the girls found out who I was with, they made a thousand jokes about Carlinhos's sweet dick, and thus began the gossip. All of them, without exception, insisted that he couldn't offer a future to anyone, that he was a womanizer and didn't have two pennies to rub together, and that everyone knew he had a woman whom he would never leave. I grew annoyed with the girls and told them that I didn't want them meddling in my life. I had left the security and comfort of my mother's orbit precisely so I could rule my own life and make my own decisions!

I kept going out with Carlinhos, but we never made plans ahead of time. Suddenly, when I least expected it, he would appear out of nowhere. Always loud and energetic, he would shout from out on the street, "Mil, put some beers on ice because here I come!" I could be in a room with a client or at the door, but when I heard his voice, I knew that I was about to have a couple of days of pure bliss, excellent conversation, and wonderful companionship.

Until then, with the exception of João, all of the men I had been with would only seek me out to have sex. I didn't mind this, as sex was always a priority in my life. It's just that I came to resent not having a companion to accompany me to the movies or to the theater, someone to join me in my favorite pastime of shooting the breeze at the bar—until Carlinhos came along, that is. He loved to go out and introduce me to his friends, who were all taxi drivers. It was with him that I first got to know the city. He was born and bred in his beloved Rio, and he took great pride in being my guide. According to him, everything in Rio was better than in any other city in the country, which he only knew about from books and photos, as he had never traveled further than the suburbs of his hometown.

Because Rio was his world, he felt he didn't need to go anywhere else. One place he showed me was the Motinha shoe store, which was located on Avenida Mem de Sá. As we stood in front of its glass window displays, he said: "This is a traditional and well-known place in Rio. It is where real men get their shoes made. I don't like it much, though, I prefer my sneakers. I'm modern, but I'm telling you, never trust a man who doesn't wear Motinha shoes or at least high-quality sneakers. Men who wear any old thing on their feet lack imagination."

Side by side we circulated through the streets, me laughing at his colorful philosophy of life. We went to Vila Verde, also on Mem de Sá: "Here, Gabriela, is where you can find the best green cabbage soup in the city. You've never truly had cabbage soup until you've tried this one." The green cabbage soup of Vila Verde was indeed delicious, but for Carlinhos everything was the best in the world and one would never find anything better. I would keep going back to Vila Verde for many years, even when Carlinhos and I were no longer together. It was a corner bar across from a hotel where prostitutes worked. At the end of the night, after work, I would sit on one of the chairs placed out on the sidewalk and order the peerless cabbage soup, chatting with the prostitutes and the other regular customers. I loved Carlinhos. There was a sense of friendship between us that I hadn't experienced with other men. Despite his electric personality, our relationship was quite calm. We were honest with one another, and we knew what each of us truly wanted.

Closed Doors

Once in a while I would go to São Paulo to see if a miracle had transpired, meaning that I hoped that my mother would change her opinion about whether I could see my daughter. I would go to my sister Gina's house, and she would tell me that it did no good to insist, my mother didn't even want to hear my name said out loud. Alessandra was growing up and had started going to school, and I was missing that entire period of her life. Depressed, I swore that I would never return to Guarulhos, the suburb of São Paulo where my family had moved.

All this trouble came from people not accepting my way of life and my profession. It was always the same excuse: that I was setting a poor example for my child, that I didn't have good judgment, and that I lived the life of a promiscuous and shameless woman. I don't accept the moralistic view that a woman is only good if she is faithful to one man and passes her days demurely caring for her children.

Anyway, after moving around between Guarulhos and Vila Formoza, I would drop by the Boca do Lixo to see my friends in an attempt to stave off my depression. At night I used to go to the dance hall with Cecília, and the following day I'd return to Rio. Just as the bus reached the highway that led to the Marvelous City, I would promise myself that I would never go back to São Paulo. Those visits brought me down. In any case, they were promises in vain, because I kept going back and having the same experience.

Yet all it took was for the bus to arrive in Rio for my spirits to lift. I would return to the Vila and carry on with my life, attending to my clients, making money, and enjoying myself with my friends and with Carlinhos. Vera, in all her seriousness and sensitivity, perceived that every time I returned from São Paulo I wasn't in good shape and would invite me to unwind at her cottage in Santo Aleixo, in a rural part of the state of Rio.

That cottage in the countryside was my friend's great pride. It had a little garden, a dog, chickens, a large patio, and a river lined with stones that flanked the house. We would stay there a couple of days, always during the week, eating, chatting, and sleeping a lot. At night, we would go dance *forró* with the local guys in the nearest town until the sun came up.[57] Vera loved to

---

57 *Forró* is a traditional musical style and dance from northeastern Brazil, now widely popular across the country due to the diaspora of northeastern migrants that began settling in more affluent regions of the country in the mid-twentieth century. The music is played with an accordion, a large Afro-Brazilian drum called a *zabumba,* and a triangle.

dance and drink whiskey and caipirinhas. She hated beer; according to her, it was only good for making you fat, and it never left people feeling happy. Vera and I would return to Rio, with her driving her Volkswagen Brasília and telling me that, despite considering me a bit of a nut, she envied my way of being, my optimistic way of only seeing the beautiful things in life.

Vera wasn't totally right. I don't only see the beautiful things in life, but I try not to see the world as full of evil. Sometimes, of course, I find myself in dangerous situations that I am only able to recognize after everything is said and done. I also have never cared about saving money. I like money, but I like it for spending on what I want and for paying my bills. I hate loans. I think it's cruel and painful to live with debt, although I haven't always been able to avoid it. At times, however, I come upon hard times because of my financial habits. I often need money and don't have it on hand. But these momentary difficulties are compensated by the pleasure of living the way I like. Vera, on the other hand, was so squared away that she had the nickname "Madame." She liked having her life perfectly organized, with her car, two apartments near downtown Rio, and cottage, besides having nice clothes and shoes. It was difficult for her to understand my lifestyle, but I think that it was precisely because we were so different that we became such good friends.

A Feasible Dream or Utopia?

On our trips to Vera's cottage, I could finally discuss an idea that had been percolating in my mind since my time in São Paulo. I had been thinking of finding a way to politically organize the prostitutes to fight against stigma, police violence, poor treatment by madams, and the many other issues that affect our profession. Vera listened attentively, but she didn't take my idea seriously; she said I was a dreamer and that it would be impossible to change the natural order of things. According to her, the whore has been the scum of the earth since the beginning of time, and there was nothing we could do to change that. She would say: "I work in this profession because I like sex and also because I could never have all that I have doing something else, but I know that as far as society is concerned I am just a good-for-nothing woman." That was how she understood our predicament, and invariably she would end our conversations with the following sentence: "To believe anything else is like Don Quixote battling windmills." Once in a while, Vera would lose her patience with that particular topic of conversation. In fact, she had fairly conservative and contradictory thoughts when it came to sexual ethics and women's role in society. But that never impeded our interminable conversations.

Vera had a husband named Danilo. She used to say that, a number of years prior, when he was still a boy, he had appeared in the *zona* hand in hand with Mil e Uma (Thousand and One). Danilo was a street kid who had run away from home and never gone back. He lived with Thousand and One, who loved kids, and circulated around the *zona*, collecting tips from the girls who would send him to pick up things at the bakery, the pharmacy, and so forth. Vera said, with a chuckle, that she had taken him in to raise him. She took him to her home and started taking care of him and one thing led to another. She lived with him until the end of her life, when cancer took her away. They fought a lot, and she was terribly jealous of Danilo, who was tall and handsome and always involved with some woman or another. One day she found out that he had shacked up with some woman in a distant neighborhood and that he had even had a son with her. Vera turned into a beast and kicked him out of the house, and for many months they remained separated—for such a long time that she found another boyfriend.

But, eventually, my friend showed up to work all happy and carefree, reporting that they had made up and that he didn't care anymore about that other woman. She preferred to close her eyes and live a lie rather than live without Danilo's company.

Danilo, who is now an older guy, works as a park ranger in Campo de Santana, and we have maintained a friendship to this day. Because the public garden is also a cruising spot for prostitution, he always makes a point of informing the women who work there about the advances of our struggle and has even convinced the manager of the park to let us have meetings in one of the buildings.

Vera and I had a mutual client: Ataíde. He was a tall and elegant guy, manager of a building in the downtown Rio neighborhood of Cinelândia, near the Odeon cinema. I never had sex with him, but I call him my client because he used to pay me to chat with him.

Technically, Ataíde was Vera's client. She introduced us and we arranged a date. But we didn't make it to the sex part, because he wasn't able to, a fact he was perfectly aware of. Rather, he paid me to sit, drink, chat, and listen to his stories. He described himself as a bona fide neurotic and told me that he went to a support group called Neurotics Anonymous. He was a very cultured and solitary guy who read anything you put in front of him, without any preconceived notions. When we met up, he would talk more than he would listen, but he was great company nonetheless. Sometimes he'd take us to have dinner at the classic restaurant Amarelinho in Cinelândia and we'd stay until it closed, when he paid the bill and put us in a cab home. We would leave him there, standing on the side of Rua Senador Dantas, waving goodbye and saying: "Until we meet again, my *chéries*."

Doomed Love

On winter nights Dona Vilma would show up in the *zona* with her cauldron of vegetable soup, bowls, and spoons in a plastic bag. "I've got hot soup! Just one cruzeiro for a bowl!" And what a soup it was! The recipe called for an entire scarlet eggplant. If nostalgia for the Vila could have a flavor, it would be the taste of Vilma's vegetable soup. I ate it every single day in the winter. I got so hooked on the eggplant in the soup that if there wasn't any more left, I would ask Vilma to go home and put more in. I learned to appreciate that vegetable in the *zona*, as well as oxtail with watercress.

Dona Vilma was a classic figure of the Brazilian red-light district. She had been a prostitute for many years, before achieving the dream harbored by nine out of ten prostitutes: she had become the proprietor of her own brothel in the old Mangue district. Yet, as is the case with so many others, a pimp caused her downfall. She ended up shit out of luck after shacking up with a *malandro* who was bad news. He would appear every day when Vilma finished work, and, in addition to taking almost all of her money to buy cocaine, he would invite all his friends to snort it at her establishment, which was the source of her livelihood. The more serious working girls got sick of this and went elsewhere and then the only ones that were left were the ones who liked to get coked out as well. Vilma eventually had to close the brothel.

When she was well into her sixties, she decided to start over, selling sandwiches and soup to the prostitutes. She rented a room in a tenement house nearby and became the best cook in the *zona*. Many times, when there was some kind of party, it was Dona Vilma who was hired to make the beans, the oxtail with watercress, and other specialties of Rio's Black cuisine. She was still with the same guy that had snorted all her money away, but at least when she got old he helped her wash pots and bowls, as he was still dependent on her. When she died, from a stroke that left her in a coma in Souza Aguiar Hospital, he stuck around the *zona*, panhandling, living off of odd jobs, or acting as a messenger for the girls.

Vilma was yet another person who took with her the rich history of Mangue, as no one had the curiosity and good sense to interview her before she died. It is often said that to this day the history of Mangue, the city's oldest and most important prostitution district, has never been compiled and written down.

A Big Dick but an Even Bigger Nose

I also had a boyfriend who loved coke. Those guys always cause trouble. Once this *malandro* won a huge package of coke in a game of cards. It looked like a box of Ferrero Rocher chocolates. Afraid that he would get stopped by the police and have to turn over the drugs, he asked me to keep it safe for him. He knew that because the madams dutifully paid their bribes, the police didn't bother us inside the *zona*. I said no, I didn't want that around me, and I wouldn't hold it for him under any circumstances. He insisted and put the package in my bag. To that I said: "Oh, that's how it's going to be? OK then."

As soon as he left, I went to the bathroom and poured all the coke into the toilet. When he came back to get it, I said: "What coke? I don't have it anymore, I flushed it down the toilet. I already told you that I will not have that crap in my possession."

The guy went nuts. He hit his head against the wall and generally behaved very badly. But hit me he didn't dare. The law of the land in the *zona* is taken extremely seriously, meaning that no one hits the prostitutes. That didn't stop him from crying and screaming that he would get his revenge, however. "You see this incredible dick right here? This huge dick? You will never have it again!" It's true that his dick was huge, but what he didn't know is that huge dicks are not everything they're cracked up to be. It was so large that sex was uncomfortable, and because he was such an idiot, he thought that sex was just sticking his dick in and nothing more. I told him: "You know what, good thing you like your dick so much because I don't!"

In the Hands of the Fearsome Men in White

It was a Saturday night. I was getting ready to go out to a samba concert when suddenly I felt a sharp pain that left me unable to move my legs. Within minutes I felt paralyzed. When I realized I wasn't able to walk, I started screaming for help. Vera had already gone home for the day but there were others around, and they called a taxi.

I was taken to the emergency room at Souza Aguiar Hospital. Once I got there, I was put in a wheelchair, and a bad-tempered doctor, without exchanging a word with me, examined me and immediately summoned a nurse to put in an IV. He left and I spent the entire night in that wheelchair, an IV in my arm, watching people arrive in worse states than I was in, dying of disease, accidents, or gunshots, then left in stretchers to await care. Screams and moans emanated from every direction, and the nurses walked around looking pissed off. I had discovered hell.

Once in a while I asked if the doctor was going to come back and tell me what was wrong with me, but the nurses told me I just had to wait for the shift change at five in the morning. The doctor was tired and needed to rest, they said.

The hours passed excruciatingly slowly and the nurses only replenished my IV because I screamed at the top of my lungs when I saw that the tubes were empty. At five A.M. a doctor showed up and asked me what was going on. I told him my story and was informed that as soon as there was a place available in the hospital I was going to be admitted. "What do I have?" I asked. He replied: "I'm not a fortune teller. We have to wait until you are admitted to run some tests." My patience had run out by that point. I yanked the needle out of my arm, threw it on the floor, and said that I wanted to leave that very moment. The nurse, without reacting, summoned the doctor, who gave me a slip of paper that I had to sign, attesting to the fact that I was leaving against medical advice. All I had to do was sign it. I tried to stand up out of the wheel-chair but I couldn't. I asked them to wheel me to the exit so that I could hail a taxi, but they refused. "You want to leave, so go on, do it yourself." I asked, begged, and pleaded, but to no avail. A kid who had been waiting with his father since the previous day wheeled me to the exit.

I took a taxi back to the *zona*, but I couldn't even get out of the car. I was completely paralyzed from the waist down. I asked the taxi driver to do me the massive favor of going to Isaurinha's house to let people know that I needed help. I don't even recall who took me, but the next thing I remember was that I was at Miguel Couto Hospital. I believe the taxi drivers who worked in the *zona* decided that a public hospital in the wealthy part of the city would provide better care. I was admitted immediately upon arriving.

At first the doctors couldn't figure out what had caused my paralysis. After nearly a month in the hospital and countless exams, they arrived at the conclusion that I had gallstones. They decided they needed to operate. The surgery was scheduled for a Monday, and on the Sunday before, Carlinhos and Vera came to the hospital and helped me walk to the patio on my ward to get a bit of sun. At that moment, the doctor on duty walked past, greeted us, and then stopped suddenly, as if he had seen something strange. Immediately he approached us and asked that I put my face into the sunlight so he could examine my eyes. In a worried tone, he said that as soon as my visitors left, I should undergo some additional tests. Carlinhos asked what was going on, but the doctor seemed reluctant to say. Carlinhos made a scene, saying that he wouldn't leave until we found out what was wrong with me. Once the tests were completed, it turns out I had hepatitis A, the result of an infection I had gotten in the hospital.

Thus began a new phase in the long saga of my illness. The surgery was postponed, and I began treatment for the infection. I spent more than four months watching patients be admitted and released, and I got to know all the doctors and hospital staff, even trading magazines with other patients. I think I memorized all the horses and jockeys of the Jockey Club, because the hospital had a view of Rio's most famous racetrack. I would sit out on the patio and watch them train, and the coaches took to waving at me when they left the track. Carlinhos, whenever he would drive a passenger to Gávea, where the hospital was located, would drop by and say to whoever reminded him that it wasn't an official visiting day: "My girlfriend has an infection because of the conditions of this hospital, and I have every right to come and oversee her treatment." Dona Anita, his mother, would send along bottles upon bottles of a special herbal tea that helped cure hepatitis, as well as candied chestnuts to provide the sugar that my body needed.

Visits were permitted on Tuesdays and Sundays, and Vera and Carlinhos would invariably appear with the magazine of the week, fruit, clean sheets, towels, and lots of affection. One Sunday they brought basically the whole crew from the Vila to visit me. Only Thousand and One didn't show up, because he almost never left his little world. Isaurinha, her sister, and seven or eight women who worked in the brothel with me brought flowers in a vase that they placed on my headboard. That day I wept with happiness because I knew I wasn't alone and that I could count on the love and care of people that I hadn't even known for very long.

Once I recovered from hepatitis, I had to undergo the gallstone surgery. I only remember that they placed me on a stretcher, and I was brought into a very cold room, with air conditioning on the maximum setting. When I awoke, twenty hours had passed since the operation and I was told that I had almost died. I was in a hospital bed with tubes in all my orifices. As a bitter reminder, I have a crooked scar that starts just below my breasts and goes all the way to my lower abdomen—testament to a botched surgery, I'm sure. I never wore a bikini again.

Eventually, I was released from the hospital, but I was scared to leave. I stepped out onto the sidewalk, not knowing where to go, and there waiting for me were Danilo and Vera in the beige Brasília that she loved so much. They had come to pick me up and bring me back to their house. Every time I remember that day, I think of the huge palm trees that line the main street of the Jardim Botânico neighborhood. I had never seen them before, and Danilo, on our way home, decided to take that route. After months in the hospital, those beautiful palm trees, all identical and standing in a row, gave me the certainty that I was alive and ready to return to all the things that I loved to do.

Vera took care of me during my convalescence. Before I was able to work, I would still go with her to the Vila. I'd sit around, reading my book and waiting for her to finish work. My former clients would pass by and see me sitting there reading at the back of the room, and they would approach me and ask how I was. Some brought me chocolate, others gave me money to "help out with medications," and others brought me flowers. When the day was over, we would go back to Vera's house, where she would busy herself preparing food for us. Sometimes she would take me out to her cottage in Santo Aleixo. "The air of the countryside will help you get better quickly," she used to say.

Once I recovered completely, I went back to work, but Vera didn't want me to return to living in the *zona*, so I continued to live with her and Danilo for a couple of years. It was during those years that I began thinking more concretely about my dream of organizing our community. Vera still believed that prostitutes would never come together on behalf of a common goal. She thought that the stigma ensured that the community would remain divided and indifferent. Once we achieved a few victories, like founding the Vila Mimosa Professional Association, she started believing in us a bit more, but she still didn't want to actively participate in the movement. She stayed in the background, helping me with things, listening to my ideas and defending me from the gossip that followed me wherever I went.

As my mother would say: all things, both bad and good, eventually come to an end. I went back to work, having to explain to my clients the origin of my huge scar. They always assumed it was from a stab wound. Of course they did, because whores don't get sick, they only get venereal diseases and injured in fights. That's how people think; the stigma persists.

The Prostitute Speaks

In the early 1980s, Rio had just elected Brazil's first Black city councilwoman, Benedita da Silva.[58] In 1983, she went personally to Vila Mimosa together with Maria Alice, president of the residents' association of Cidade Nova, to invite

---

58 Benedita da Silva (b. 1942) was born into poverty in a Carioca slum and eventually became a city councilwoman, a senator, and the first female and Afro-Brazilian governor of the state of Rio de Janeiro. She was an influential member of the feminist contingent of the Constituent Assembly that drafted a new constitution in 1988 and has been a steadfast ally of the domestic-workers' movement since entering politics in the 1980s. Da Silva was elected to Rio's city council in 1982, the year Brazil resumed gubernatorial elections for the first time since the 1964 coup, and opposition parties performed notably well.

us to participate in the first Conference for Women from the Favelas and Urban Periphery. I accepted her invitation immediately.

Carlinhos had a sign made bearing the phrase "Prostitutes Are Also Women." He gave it to me and off we went, walking down Rua Miguel de Frias, holding that sign. Once in a while I looked behind me, only to see Carlinhos grinning and waving. Little did I know that I was about to begin a new phase of my life.

The first Conference for Women from the Favelas and Urban Periphery took place in a huge warehouse in the Centro de Convivência do Metrô, which was right next to Vila Mimosa. There we found about five hundred women who had been convened by Benedita. There was the progressive state representative Lúcia Arruda and the now-deceased Ângela Borba, a supremely competent feminist, widely recognized and admired to this day.[59] The meeting was also attended by Beth Lobo, who had a radio program geared toward women that was multimedia in a time before we even knew what that was.

At the time, however, I didn't know any of those figures. I was just there to listen, and that is precisely what I did. I spent one whole day listening to women of diverse backgrounds speaking about their living conditions. There were women from the favelas, who lived without sanitation services or basic conditions for survival, completely abandoned by the state. There were domestic workers there, too, who had just started to organize themselves politically. There were agricultural workers from the Baixada Fluminense, and many more.[60] We were an army of poor and suffering women from Rio de Janeiro, not much different from the women of São Paulo's periphery, whom I knew well.

Benedita made the biggest impression on me. She was an attractive woman, tall and slim, and she spoke very well. She knew how to take up space, and she struck me as a perfect representative of Rio, a city I was still getting to know. She also happened to be married to the man who most caught my attention. He was a large Black man, known as Bola, with a carefree and happy outlook on life. He was the only person who came over to our corner

---

59 Lúcia Arruda was elected state representative in 1982 as an explicitly feminist candidate. She was responsible for a short-lived bill to regulate legal abortion services in the state of Rio de Janeiro. She also helped create Delegacias da Mulher, a network of police stations that continues to attend to female victims of domestic violence.

Ângela Borba (1953–1998) was an important Brazilian feminist, cofounder of the feminist periodical *Brasil Mulher*, and an early and influential member of the Workers' Party. She also served as Lúcia Arruda's aide during the latter's tenure as state representative.
60 The Baixada Fluminense is a region in the greater Rio metropolitan area.

of the room to speak with us. The women at the meeting kept their distance, which, of course, we expected.

In fact, it had been surprising that Maria Alice invited us to participate in the meeting in the first place. She lived nearby, in Estácio, and she had a certain understanding of the *zona* that helped dispel our negative image among the women. She said that it was the whores who brought happiness to Estácio. At the very end of the conference, in the final session, Ângela Borba approached us and asked us if we wanted to speak. My two colleagues from the *zona* didn't feel comfortable, but I, on a whim, without knowing that this would be only the first of thousands of speeches, got up and went to the front of the room, quaking in my boots, of course.

"My name is Gabriela," I said, "and I am a prostitute from the Vila Mimosa. [*Pause*] Right next door."

I caused a commotion. The prostitute had spoken! It seems unbelievable, but the taboo persisted even there, among politicized women: prostitutes shouldn't speak up. But I had spoken. Following the model set by the other women, I explained what working conditions were like for prostitutes in the Vila, our hardships, the problems we routinely faced. But I didn't say too much and finished up quickly.

After the conference, Beth Lobo immediately invited me to go on her radio program, and I began answering the same questions that I have been responding to for over twenty years. Why did you go into that line of work? Were you abandoned by your family? Did you go into prostitution out of economic necessity? And the best of all, a nasty little ambush: What would you think if your daughter was a whore? That one is sure to surface, sooner or later. Not long ago, I gave a lecture at a university and I almost got through the whole thing without anyone asking that question. At the very end, when I was about to say goodbye to the crowd, a very young, timid girl piped up all the way at the back of the room. She put her finger up to ask a question and let loose that gem. The conservatism of today's youth gives me the chills. I wonder, where will this take us?

There were a lot of people at that event, the conference where I first spoke, including many journalists from the country's premier media outlets. Benedita was the sensation of the moment. A Black woman, and from the favela, no less. A harbinger of the Lula era to come.[61]

61 Luiz Inácio Lula da Silva served as president of Brazil from 2003 to 2011 and was reelected in 2022. After ascending to prominence as a charismatic leader of the metal-workers' union in the industrial regions surrounding São Paulo, he helped found the Workers' Party in 1980. He was a key figure in the redemocratization movement that began in the late 1970s and continued to be consolidated throughout the 1990s.

A Touch of Media

As it turned out, all I had to do was start talking to discover that many people wanted to hear what I had to say. Many more people than I had ever imagined. Immediately following my little speech at Benedita's meeting, lots of people started seeking me out to give interviews, mainly the radio stations: Rádio Guanabara, Rádio MEC, Bandeirantes, Roquette Pinto.

A popular television program from Rio called *Noites Cariocas*, hosted by Nelsinho Motta e Scarlet Moon, sought me out in the *zona*.[62] I agreed to appear on the program, and twice we arranged everything, but at the last minute I disappeared and the production team couldn't find me. I was scared—of what, exactly, I'm still not sure.

The third time, they arranged to pick me up in the *zona*, and they parked their car and refused to leave until they found me. They practically had to kidnap me to get me to go with them. I had started this whole affair, and now that it was up and running, I couldn't possibly jump ship.

Vera decided that if I was going to be on TV, I would have to be extraordinarily elegant. She dressed me in an incredibly chic green skirt suit, made of some light and airy fabric, probably silk, an outfit that justified her nickname, "Madame." She hemmed the skirt because she is taller than I am, and it turned out great. The only thing that didn't match were my shoes, which were completely incongruous with the elegant suit. They had a high heel with gold detailing, with black varnish and gold stripes. There was no way they would go unnoticed.

After the recording, all of us in the *zona* got together to watch the program at Isaurinha's house. Of course, the camera panned from my head all the way to my shoes, and back up again. No one seemed interested in Vera's chic skirt suit. All the focus was directed toward the shoes, which had caused quite a stir.

Nonetheless, the program was a success. I was treated very respectfully by Nelsinho and Scarlet. They asked the classic questions, but their respect for me was very clear. I have since done interviews in which people with a lot less interest in me treated me very poorly. Those two, however, are top-notch people. I didn't know Scarlet beforehand, but I had admired Nelsinho for a long time because of a song he produced that aired in a festival on TV, called "O Cantador," which Elis Regina, at the beginning of her career, sang in a strapless white dress alongside Dori Caymmi, bravely facing the heckling of

62 The television talk show *Noites Cariocas* (Carioca nights) ran on the Rede Record channel in the 1980s.

the audience.[63] The song wasn't a hit, but it never left my head, and I always sing it when we have singalongs. I told him this on air and he was shocked. I used to watch all the music festivals on TV back in the day; they were my intoxicants in the 1970s.

During the interview, the audience numbers spiked. The program was kind of niche, and it only aired in Rio. But, according to Scarlet, who told me this many years later, viewers requested a rerun of the interview and the production team deferred to the guy in charge of the channel. Silvio Santos, the boss, didn't want to run the interview again and, in retribution for its popularity, he canceled the program. This was around 1983 or 1984, and it was about that time that I started to become well known. I became the spokeswoman for prostitutes, answering the same questions always.

Sometimes Love Means Letting Go

My younger daughter was about five or six by that time. I had stopped going to São Paulo, but my friends Terezinha and Ana Maria would send me news about her regularly. One day, while I was at work, I received a summons to appear before a judge back home. When I arrived there, I found my two friends with their eyes swollen from crying. My daughter's father had hired a lawyer to compile a dossier of newspaper clippings and interviews that I had done in which I publicly admitted to being a prostitute, and he was suing me for custody.

The judge called us before him one by one, each person who was involved in the situation. I already knew that I was going to lose custody, and I told the judge that I thought my friends should be the ones to end up as my daughter's guardians. They deserved custody because they loved her so much and had become completely anguished thinking of the possibility of losing her. I told him that my friends had helped me a lot and taken care of her with so much love for so long. When the judge summoned us before him to announce his decision, he said that custody would go to her father, but Terezinha, Ana Maria, and I would all have rights to see her and even spend weekends with her.

He ended by saying that he hoped the girl's father loved her as much as the three of us did. He even recognized my love for her, which was the sort of love that knows when to let go.

63 Dorival Caymmi (1914–2008), a popular musician and songwriter from the northeastern state of Bahia, was one of the originators of the genres of bossa nova and *música popular brasileira* (Brazilian popular music, or MPB).

The Beginning of Yet Another Battle

During the summer, it would get infernally hot in Estácio, such that the rooms of the *zona* turned into veritable ovens. I still wasn't used to the heat, so I couldn't work during the day, because the men would sweat so much and drip all over me. I hated getting all wet from their sweat, and I would have to bathe constantly. So I decided to figure out an alternative.

There are men who like to drop by the *zona* before work—not many, but there are also very few women working at that time, so the competition is minimal. I had a colleague who would start working at six in the morning and by noon she was on her way home. When I discovered this alternative schedule, I decided to do the same. I would get to work really early and stop by lunchtime. If I didn't get enough business in the mornings, I would work at night.

Vila Mimosa never closed. It was the first *zona* I worked in that was open twenty-four hours a day. But I liked to reserve the evenings for my own leisure: drinking beer and chatting with people. I made a point of never mixing work with leisure. This is a delicate matter, and many women meet their professional end by making this mistake. My father would always say: "When you're out at night, you've got to be clever." This rule I learned firsthand. While I was at work, I worked. After lunch, I was free and could do whatever I wanted.

In the area surrounding the Vila, there were a lot of kids who played in the streets—little kids, most of them the children of prostitutes who lived in an abandoned building near the Vila. It was not a nice place, but the women had nowhere else to live with their children. One day, I decided to play with the kids. Right near the Vila there was a little empty lot with some trees that provided shade from the sun. I bought watercolors, paper, and pencils and took the children to the lot.

We started spending our afternoons there playing. The kids painted beautiful watercolors that depicted their feelings and their day-to-day lives. It was obvious that with every page they painted they got better and better, and not just at painting. Just a little bit of time dedicated to them helped build their self-esteem, their sense of self.

I have a friend, Carmem, who at the time was a little girl and played with us. She worked for a while for the NGO Davida that I would found several years later, and she always remembered those days fondly. Without even realizing what I was doing I had started a social outreach project. Over time, I got to know the children better, and I would also chat with their mothers. Most of them weren't even in school, so I would try to convince the mothers that studying would help them secure a better future, but few of them believed me.

Near the empty lot there was an outpost of the Banco da Providência, a social outreach project of the Archdiocese of Rio. Because it belonged to the Church, it was quite conservative, but for a while they had been running a service that provided prostitutes with medical care.

One of the guys who worked there would always pass by the lot where I was playing with the kids. After I had appeared on television and everything, I was the most well-known person in the neighborhood. One day he stopped to talk to me, wanting to know what I was doing with the kids. I responded that it wasn't a big deal, just that I preferred to have them play with me rather than eating dirt in the *zona*. He told me that the Banco da Providência had a room with school supplies, but that they weren't using it because they had no staff members available to work with the kids. He invited me to take advantage of the free space, and I accepted immediately. It would be much better for the kids to be inside than to have to draw while sitting on the hard ground.

It wouldn't end well; this much was obvious. I'm not sure why I thought that I could handle it easily. I nearly couldn't at all.

Not Even Jesus Christ Saves

Sure enough, before long the Catholic women who worked at the Banco da Providência began objecting to my presence there. They said, unsurprisingly, that because I was a prostitute I was a bad example for the children. Needless to say they themselves didn't lift a finger for the kids. On top of that situation, there was a woman who insisted on offering classes to the prostitutes on craft production, but no one wanted to take it. Her great idea was to teach the women to paint flowers on Hellmann's mayonnaise jars and put a frill on the orange lid. And they seemed to think this would be an alternative source of income for us whores! They operated under the assumption that prostitutes were victims that had never had any opportunities in life, not even to paint mayonnaise jars.

Nilton Guedes was the name of the guy who had approached us in the lot. On that fateful day, he entered my life to stay. A beautiful Black man, incredibly intelligent, he was a great friend of mine. A public-school teacher, he helped me out a lot with the kids. Nilton was responsible for getting me involved in anti-AIDS work later on in the 1980s. He got the virus right when it reached Brazil, when people suffered and died quickly, before there were medications to treat it.

I started going to Nilton's house. He shared an apartment on Botafogo Beach with a friend named Maurício, also from Campo Grande. I would ask him: "Why did you bring me into that lion's den?" and he would tell me all the gossip that he couldn't divulge at the Banco da Providência, all the details about its internal politics and the staff's issues with me in particular.

One day I gave an interview to a chic magazine that was based in Rio, a major interview, with beautiful photos, in which I spoke of my pride in being a prostitute. When the issue came out, there were serious repercussions. I was immediately kicked out of the Banco da Providência and prohibited from playing with the kids under the accusation that I was an apologist for prostitution. To make matters worse, I was threatened: if I insisted on seeing the kids, even outside the Banco in the lot, where we had started out, they would throw me in jail for grooming children! A serious threat, one I couldn't take lightly.

At that moment, I came to regret my decision to associate myself with those people. I started experiencing fits of rage. My relationship with people from outside the *zona* became difficult—hostile, even. I was always on the defensive, ready to retaliate.

Divided Territory

Before leaving the Banco da Providência and once I was already well known around those parts, I was sought out by Leonardo Boff.[64] He showed up in Vila Mimosa in a little Volkswagen Beetle bearing an offering of food to prepare a Last Supper with the prostitutes.

Those were the days of liberation theology, and the Church was creating many different ministries to bring it closer to the poor. The Ministry for Marginalized Women (their euphemism for prostitutes) was one of them.[65] It advocates for the end of prostitution and preaches that the prostitute is a victim of a misogynist society. It is still quite active in some cities in Brazil, but in Rio it never really took off.

In 1984, the ministry was going to hold a meeting in Salvador, Bahia, and Boff's purpose in coming to the *zona* was to invite me. I said that I would go—another mistake that led to a definitive turning point in my life. The

64 Leonardo Boff (b. 1938) is a Brazilian leftist theologian and priest famous for his criticisms of the Vatican and support of Latin American liberation theology.

65 The Pastoral da Mulher Marginalizada (Ministry for Marginalized Women) was founded in 1974 by clergy from the Conferência Nacional dos Bispos do Brasil and informed by liberation theology. It encouraged the development of self-esteem in prostitutes and espoused a vision of empowerment beyond mere charitable endeavors.

meeting was a disaster, but there I met Lourdes Barreto, my great partner in activism to this day.[66] Lourdes is utterly unlike anyone else I know. Together with Helena and Vera, Lourdes was and still is one of my greatest friends. We are very similar, in that we don't accept belligerence from anyone, and we both choose the curbside bar as the ideal place to sit and chat. She must be about sixty by now, and we have phenomenal stories about our antics together.

After I accepted Boff's invitation, he beckoned me closer and gave me some money: "To pay for your bus ticket to Salvador." And off I went. I spent twenty-two hours in a normal bus seat, not even one that reclined into a bed. I arrived in Salvador feeling completely destroyed. The prostitutes from Belém, Juazeiro, from all over Brazil, arrived as broken as I did. However, the entire ministry staff arrived in good humor, with airline stickers on their luggage. At that moment, it was clear where the lines were drawn.

I didn't even really know what the ministry was before arriving at the meeting. Despite my upbringing, I don't observe the Catholic faith. Back when my friend Nilton of the Banco da Providência died, I went to his wake and burial. Afterward, some friends and I went to get a beer. When we moved to pour the bottle into our glasses, one glass turned over, all on its own. We perceived at that moment that something strange was going on, so we decided to leave the bar and drink at home, bringing along a bag with some bottles of beer inside. When one of the guys went to put the bottles in the fridge, the bag fell to the ground and the bottles broke. Not one was left intact! I called out to Nilton: "My friend, follow your path forward, we will always love you. Now, let us drink our beers!" After my little tribute, we drank in honor of Nilton until dawn.

My faith in my ancestors must come from my maternal grandmother. She was Indigenous and spoke Tupí-Guaraní.[67] My mother, her daughter, left the farm where she had grown up only to marry my father. In my childhood, there are certain words that my mother would use that are not used in Brazilian

66 Lourdes Barreto (b. 1943), born into a family of eleven children, was raised on a farm in the impoverished northeastern state of Paraíba before migrating first to Campina Grande and later to southern Pará to work as a prostitute in the gold mines that employed thousands of men in the 1970s and 1980s. By the time she and Gabriela met, she had been involved in the Ministry for Marginalized Women for a number of years; in fact, ministry agents taught her how to read and write as an adult as she had abandoned her studies at a young age when she left home to start working. Gabriela and Lourdes's friendship and ideological affinity would last until Leite's death in 2013 and bear many fruits, including the founding of the Rede Brasileira de Prostitutas in 1987.

67 Tupí-Guaraní is a family of Indigenous languages spoken in Brazil, Argentina, Paraguay, Bolivia, Venezuela, French Guyana, and Peru.

Portuguese. For example, when I was going to work every day, my mother used to pack me lunch, and she would say: "Don't forget your *picuá*." It was only years later that I discovered that *picuá* is a Tupí-Guaraní word for a bag for carrying food.

The Christian God, the inaccessible one, he who judges and condemns, has never made the slightest sense to me. For me, God is found in nature and in our ancestors. I believe in people, in the things that they reveal when one coexists with them.

About ten years ago a friend took me to a Candomblé temple way out in São Gonçalo.[68] There I was told that I am a daughter of Iemanjá, just as my colleagues from Vila Mimosa had suspected.[69] I believe in Iemanjá—in fact, I have had long talks with her. But I don't believe in that stereotypical image of her as white and skinny like a Barbie. My Iemanjá is Black, she is strong, she is a mother. When I started frequenting the temple, an invitation soon came to dedicate my time as an *equede*, a sort of caretaker of the *orixás*, the deities of Candomblé. I thanked them for the offer but said: "Look, I prefer to show up here when I feel the need, is that all right?" I think the *orixás* accepted my proposal because I feel as if I am protected by them. Especially by Iemanjá, because whenever I'm sad or have to make an important decision, I look to her and say: "My friend . . ."

The Forbidden Word

The opening of the ministry meeting in Salvador took place in a packed Teatro Castro Alves. The bishop of Juazeiro do Norte, Dom José Rodrigues, presided over a panel that included several nuns; Leonardo Boff, an acquaintance from Minas Gerais; two other prostitutes; and me. I was still quite rough around the edges and didn't grasp the nuances of social movement politics. My friend from Minas, who spoke before me, introduced herself in the following way: "Good evening, my name is Suely and I am a girl from Uberaba." Girl? I turned to Boff and said: "Why is she saying that she is a girl?" Boff replied: "The ministry thinks it is too harsh to use the term *prostitute* and decided to create an affectionate nickname instead. *Girl* is what they came up with." To this day they still use that term. Soon enough it was my turn to speak: "My name is

68 Candomblé is an Afro-Brazilian syncretic religious tradition that involves Catholic and Yoruba beliefs and practices.
69 Iemanjá is an important *orixá*, or Afro-Brazilian deity, considered to be the goddess of the ocean and the protector of women.

Gabriela and, unlike my colleague from Uberaba, I am a prostitute and I currently live in Rio de Janeiro."

Later, during the open discussion period, the auditorium was packed, and everyone wanted to know why the woman from Minas had said *girl* while I had said *prostitute*. Thus began my long fight against politically correct terms, one of the most important aspects of my work to this day. I told the audience: "I think it is because people are ashamed of the word *prostitute*." That caused quite a commotion.

Across the board, I was treated quite poorly at that meeting. Lourdes was the only person there who defended me. We were housed in a large convent where she and I shared a room. At night, we would talk for hours on end about all the absurd things that had gone on during the day. It was there that we began thinking about creating an autonomous movement of prostitutes. I dreamed of one that would be free from the tutelage of the Church, that could exist without anyone watching over us. Yet Lourdes, unlike me, came from a long trajectory inside the Church. She didn't agree with a lot of its teachings, but she couldn't imagine any other possible path. I could imagine one, but I knew I would need to do a lot more research and preparation.

Around the time of this meeting, I started to realize that my time cooperating with the Church and with the Workers' Party Catholics who came as part of a package deal had lasted too long.[70] Creating an autonomous movement for our community had become an urgent matter. The objective of the ministry was to get me to take on the discourse of the victimized whore, and that would never happen. I believe that if you consider a person to be a victim, you have already established a relationship of dominance over her. On this particular point, I have to say that I'll take conservatives over so-called progressives. At least they are clearer, less ambiguous, and less hypocritical than those on the Left.

---

70 The Brazilian Workers' Party (Partido dos Trabalhadores, or PT) was founded by left-wing intellectuals, progressive Catholics, feminists, and union militants in 1980, just as Brazil was accelerating its protracted transition to democracy. The PT was the first party of its kind in Brazil, in that it strongly represented working people and its leadership did not emerge from the traditional political elite. Its ideology gravitated toward the political center during the administrations of Luiz Inácio Lula da Silva and his successor, Dilma Rousseff, yet it is still the primary organ of the Left in Brazilian electoral politics. Despite its otherwise progressive social agenda, the party maintained a somewhat conservative stance on matters relating to sexuality and reproductive rights, owing to its close proximity to the Church.

I met with Lourdes for the second time when the Health Ministry invited us to a meeting in Jundiaí, São Paulo, which ended up being entirely pointless, except that it served to bring us together again. She lived in Pará, and there was no email back then, letters took an eternity to arrive, and telephone calls were expensive as hell. There was no way for us to be in the close contact we needed so that we could begin articulating our movement.

In Jundiaí we talked a lot, and I convinced her to collaborate on organizing a meeting just for our community. But how could we do that without money? The ministry was the one with the money, but we couldn't do this with them. It had to be a meeting organized and attended exclusively by prostitutes.

Nostalgia for Simpler Times

I think deep down I knew it, but it took me a long time to acknowledge that Pantomime Carlinhos didn't love me. He was a tremendous womanizer, and he had never hidden this from me. But he also never tired of telling me that I was the only one of his women with whom he could speak openly about anything and everything.

Yet all of a sudden, he fell in love with some girl he was seeing and left the *zona* for a good while. That alone would have been enough to make me incensed. But the worst thing was, when he showed up again, he acted as if nothing had happened. That put me through the roof. I sent him packing, telling him that I didn't want anything to do with him anymore. But he just laughed and said: "But I like you a lot, and I won't stop seeking you out until we have a beer and sort it out." It was clear that he did like me a lot, but not in the same way that I liked him. I was longing for the type of companion with whom I could laugh and go all around town. I decided to retaliate, in the way that women often do when their lovers insist they are just friends in order to dodge commitment. I decided to give him some of his own medicine and make him feel really jealous.

There was a Black guy, a composer from Estácio, who in those days always flirted with me a fair amount. I thought to myself, *He's the one*. I invited him to have some soup with me in Vila Verde, knowing that, even if Carlinhos didn't see us together firsthand, he would find out that we had been there. I even kissed the guy, and that was when Carlinhos showed up.

He went nuts, yelling and gesticulating like a madman; it was clear he wanted to beat the guy up. At that moment, I regretted my decision. What was the point of doing such a thing to Carlinhos? But I had done it, and there we were. I had orchestrated a proper scandal. The guy perceived what was happening and left. I tried to talk to Carlinhos, but he refused to forgive me. It took us a very long time to be able to sit together as friends and have a beer. And after a while, he took off again.

A few years later, I had a little surprise. A psychologist friend of mine who worked in the Água Santa prison said to me, in the middle of a normal conversation: "Gabriela, you know there is a prisoner in Água Santa who swears that he is your friend? He won't stop asking me to bring you in to visit him." Normally, I wouldn't take this seriously, but, in that moment, something clicked. "What is his name?" I asked.

Carlinhos was in prison for robbing a bank. There were three guys involved; the other two were able to flee the scene but he was caught. He didn't rat on anyone, however. He served his time alone and was considered an exemplary prisoner. Carlinhos entertained everyone, helped out in the kitchen, and told stories left and right. I went to visit him and we both became overcome with emotion. He looked at my friend and told her: "We were very happy together back when times were simpler."

I adore Pantomime Carlinhos. He is a true friend, one of the most generous and kind-hearted people that I know.

Violence, the Crux of the Problem

In the mid-1980s, I was invited to participate in a debate about sexuality where I met Rubem Cesar Fernandes, the then-coordinator of ISER, the Institute for the Studies of Religion.[71] At the end of the debate, Rubem asked me if I was interested in formalizing my outreach work. He made a point of incorporating all types of work into the mission of ISER. If it was part of Carioca society, he made space for it. But it is one thing to make space, another to have everyone get on board once you're inside.

My great friend at ISER was Edda Mastrangelo. She was Uruguayan by birth but based in Rio, married at the time to a Presbyterian minister, Zwinglio Mota Dias, who had lived in exile in Germany during the dictatorship. Zwinglio was a modern guy with a phenomenal mind—a rare species among

---

71 Rubem Cesar Fernandes (b. 1943) is an anthropologist who served as the director of ISER from 1979 to 1991 and from 1995 to 2003. ISER, founded in 1970, was an ecumenical civil society organization that was actively involved in pro-democracy mobilizations in the 1980s during Brazil's political opening, focusing on human rights and religious diversity.

Protestant theologians. He went on to become the head of the Department of Social Studies at the Federal University of Juiz de Fora.

I started speaking with Edda about Lourdes's and my dream to have a national meeting of prostitutes, and she soon brought Zwinglio in on the plan. He had access to funding through the World Council of Churches based in Geneva, and he secured seven thousand dollars for our meeting, which was more than enough to put our plans into action.

Zwinglio, who was also an adviser to ISER, arrived from Geneva with the money needed to bring to fruition the project I had been long developing, but ISER said that I couldn't be the one to manage it. As long as it had had no funding, it was fine that I was in charge, but now that there was money involved, I was being edged out! They came up with some bureaucratic excuse—that in order to be the director of the project, I had to have a university degree. Have you ever heard of a university degree in prostitution? As an aside: that in itself is a pity.

The fight went all the way to the top administration. I had a meeting with Zwinglio, Rubem Cesar, and other important people who worked at ISER at the time. No one seemed willing to cede ground. So I decided to take a drastic measure. "Zwinglio, take that money back to Geneva, I don't want it and I won't organize the meeting," I said. That was enough for them to give in.

We started planning for the First National Meeting of Prostitutes, which would take place in July 1987. Edda lent a hand and acted as a wonderful producer. Flavio Lenz, at that time a mere friend of mine, married to my friend Regina, was the editor of ISER's publication and did an expert job as our press officer. He ensured that the meeting made a big splash in the media. Flavio offered to dedicate himself exclusively to that endeavor in the leadup to the meeting.

We encountered a lot of problems along the way, however. First of all, no hotel wanted to house our participants. When it came to a guest bringing a whore into his room, there was no problem, of course. But when the issue at hand was a national meeting of whores, they couldn't condone it. That isn't so much of a problem these days. But at that time, we were turned away by all the hotels. So we decided not to tell the whole truth about the meeting and just disclose part of the story. We went to the Hotel Flórida in Catete and told them that we were organizing a women's gathering. It was a deal.

Next, we needed a place to host the event itself, but, of course, no one was interested in helping us out. Until we met the director of the Calouste Gulbenkian, a cultural center in downtown Rio, that is. He was a great guy, open and curious.

He allowed us to use the center's theater. The only setback was that when he told the building staff that there was going to be a meeting of prostitutes there, they closed ranks. "On that day, we won't work," they declared. He told them: "Whoever doesn't come to work that day will be penalized a day's wages." We didn't know about any of this until the last day of the meeting.

Edda was able to arrange an evening of performances to open the conference at the venue Circo Voador, run by Perfeito Fortuna.[72] The evening, intended to introduce the event to the city, would have music and feature famous artists who supported our movement.

We made a list of all the topics we wanted to discuss: the profession, discrimination and stigma, schooling, and violence, among many others. But, in the end, even with efforts to broaden the discussions, we always came back to the same topic: violence. And it wasn't just any violence that we needed to discuss—it was police violence. Violations of prostitutes' human rights are almost always reduced to police brutality. But the prostitute experiences other types of violence as well. Our movement has made a concerted effort to widen the concept of violence in the prostitute's life. She needs to understand that a madam who doesn't provide good working conditions, for example, is also violating her human rights.

Tenth Commandment: You shall be proud of your profession . . . and you shall always use condoms.

From the Shadows to the Spotlight
The First National Meeting of Prostitutes was a resounding success. More than two thousand people showed up, including notable feminists Rose Marie Muraro and Lúcia Arruda, and the actress Lucélia Santos.[73] When we took the microphone to publicly thank our partners, the director of the Calouste told the story about the building staff, saying that in the end they had thanked

72 Perfeito Fortuna (b. 1950) is a Brazilian actor, producer, and event promoter who founded the famous Lapa venue Circo Voador in 1982.
73 Rose Marie Muraro (1930–2014) was a Brazilian sociologist and feminist who wrote about female sexual liberation, among other topics. Lucélia Santos (b. 1957) is an actress, director, and producer famous for playing an iconic role on the 1976 soap opera *Escrava Isaura*.

him because they loved meeting us and wanted to pay tribute to us. They all got up on the stage and gave us flowers.

The manager of the hotel had eventually discovered the truth about his guests, and he also ended up becoming our friend. Even he got up and thanked us for having stayed in his hotel. Darlene Glória, an actress and a singer who had become an evangelical Christian, made a beautiful speech. Zwinglio's son brought a rock band to play. The legendary singer Elza Soares put on an incredible show, and the samba musician Martinho da Vila closed out the event in style.[74]

The press came out in droves, from Brazil and elsewhere. Flavio planned a press conference before the show at Circo Voador, to disseminate our resolutions, which made a big impact. For the first time, society witnessed us as organized under the banner of our profession, and we came to see ourselves in that light for the first time as well. I had never dreamed small, though; I had always wanted to go places and was never reluctant to try. If we received a lot of Noes, at least we would have tried before failing. But, as it turned out, many people were drawn to help rather than impede our struggle.

It was a mature and well-executed event, and it came just at the right time. Our ideas were already percolating in the collective unconscious—the conviction that society needed to take a large leap forward in its treatment of the whore. We set about paving the way, stepping out of the shadows into what seemed almost like the spotlight.

Many people started seeking us out: universities, sociologists, and intellectuals. Scholars who studied prostitutes had always considered the prostitute to be a victim, and their research only served to confirm this thesis. There were a couple of good authors, like Magali Engel and Margareth Rago, but they were few and far between.[75] As time went on, the research on prostitution became more sophisticated, an evolution that I attribute to us, because we took the initiative to speak for ourselves. Today it is rare to come across

74 Elza Soares (1930–2022) was a widely popular Brazilian singer who produced music for over seventy years, much of which dealt with provocative and political themes. Martinho da Vila (b. 1938) is a singer and composer, considered a primary figure in the genres of samba and MPB (Brazilian popular music).

75 Magali Engel is a historian at the Universidade Federal Fluminense in Niterói, Brazil, and the author of *Meretrizes e doutores: Saber médico e prostituição no Rio de Janeiro, 1840–1890* (Prostitutes and doctors: medical knowledge and prostitution in Rio de Janeiro, 1840–1890). Margareth Rago is a historian at the Universidade Estadual de Campinas and the author of *Os prazeres da noite: Prostituição e códigos de sexualidade feminina em São Paulo, 1890–1930* (Pleasures of the night: prostitution and female sexual codes in São Paulo, 1890–1930).

research on prostitution in Brazil that doesn't cite us, and it all started with our meeting in 1987.

After the meeting, the girls went back to their cities, where they organized associations and with relative ease secured the support of students, intellectuals, and other segments of society. In the case of Belém, where most of the women were illiterate, the support of students was crucial in formalizing a collective project with some political clout. Ideas and statements were abundant, but turning these into political action wasn't so easy.

All of this happened in a time when society wasn't yet interested in the discourse of minorities. It was well before Lula's golden years, when social justice and the rights of minorities became fashionable.

Decadence without Elegance

Soon after the national meeting, my colleagues Clara, Eurídice, and I founded Brazil's first Prostitutes' Association, based in Vila Mimosa. Through ISER we secured the help of the lawyer Antônio Modesto da Silveira, who was famous at the time for defending political prisoners during the dictatorship. He helped us create our statutes, and we opened a space in an abandoned loft in one of the big houses on Rua Miguel de Frias.

We threw a big party to commemorate the founding of the association, and this caught the attention of the press. The local *malandros* put together a stage and set up a large grill for a barbecue. The staff at ISER invited the actress and dancer Adele Fátima, and my former boyfriend Carlinhos invited a *pagode*-singer friend who put on a fantastic show. It was none other than the famed *sambista* Zeca Pagodinho.[76]

Unfortunately, my presence in the association didn't last long—only eight months. The press always focused on me, regardless of whether or not I wanted their attention. As you might expect, this caused some jealousy among the ranks that made my life quite difficult.

The madams had a lot of power in the *zona*, and they didn't get along with the association. They came to regard me with a good deal of suspicion, and there is no way you can flourish in the *zona* if the madams aren't on your side. I loved Vila Mimosa, which made it hard to be treated as persona non grata there. Nothing major happened, really, but I came to be confronted constantly

76 Zeca Pagodinho (b. 1959) is a widely popular samba and *pagode* singer.

with the sort of gossip that thrives in close-knit environments. That was no way to live.

Simultaneously, other things complicated our work in the Vila. All of a sudden, a large number of young criminals appeared at the two entrances to the Vila and began robbing all the clients as they left. We started escorting our clients to the subway station because the kids wouldn't rob men accompanied by one of us. It was around that time that one of the brothels in the Vila became a drug sales point, using prostitution as a front.

One day, a Black teenager showed up who was handsome and always polite to the women. The son of a madam, his nickname was "Dentinho," and he had recently been released from jail. He drove the thieves out of the *zona*, and he killed those who didn't heed him. Every day someone would end up dead on the sidewalk in front of the bakery, and life in the *zona* became almost intolerable. The police would show up, they would exchange fire with the local guys, and the madams would be forced to close down the brothels. Clients didn't want to come by anymore, especially at night, and gradually the gang acquired more and more space, to the point that eventually there were armed men at every entrance.

That marked the beginning of the decline of the old Vila Mimosa. Some madams rented their houses out to unknown people who had no history with the place. Parallel to all of this, drug traffickers in the favelas were becoming more and more powerful, and, of course, their networks reached the red-light district as well.

Dentinho killed a lot of people, and then one day he was killed himself. Some say that it was the police, because he hadn't bribed them sufficiently, while others say it was a rival gang. We'll never know. But it was clear that Vila Mimosa as a place of work, collaboration, and companionship was slipping away.

It was around that time that the local samba school, Estácio de Sá, won Rio's Carnival contest with a parade that took its theme from *Paulicéia desvairada* (*Hallucinated City*), a book of poems by Mário de Andrade.[77] Until then, the fans of Estácio were people from the favela of São Carlos, the prostitutes and the *travestis*, who all loved to participate in the parade. When the school won the contest, people from the affluent part of town, the South Zone,

---

77 Mário de Andrade (1893–1945) was a writer from São Paulo whose *Paulicéia desvairada* (literally, "Frantic São Paulo," but often translated as "Hallucinated city") is considered one of the most important collections of Brazilian modernist poetry.

started coming to watch them rehearse, and the leadership decided to clean up the neighborhood. The prostitutes were soon barred entry to the neighborhood and the security guards started shooting into the air, for no reason, just to put on a show.

The *zona* was slowly becoming a zoo.

Back to Square One

In those days, my activism and work at ISER occupied a lot of my time, and Vila Mimosa soon became no more than my home and a place to rest.

I had lived in the *zona* for nearly twenty years, first in São Paulo, then in Belo Horizonte, and finally in Rio. I had given up a normal life to dive headfirst into that environment, whose bohemian culture had become ingrained in me. It was a place where people could experience things freely that only take place in secret in the outside world. Perhaps this was why my return to middle-class spaces with all their taboos after so many years wasn't so easy.

I didn't feel at home in the *zona* anymore, but neither was I at home anywhere else. I was lacking a natural habitat. I was also lacking patience, a sense of humor, and tolerance. In those days, I was difficult and ill tempered. I couldn't even tolerate myself. As a result, I gained a lot of weight and became a mess.

I couldn't bring myself to find a place to live. I moved all over town with a bag of clothes, not knowing where I would sleep each night. I spent a lot of time at Edda and Zwinglio's house, in Santa Teresa, and also in Laranjeiras with Celma, who was the secretary of ISER. A handful of times, I slept at Flávio and Regina's place on Rua Benjamin Constant, in Glória. Either that or I would stay in a hotel on Avenida Mem de Sá, in Praça da Cruz Vermelha. I wasn't turning tricks much at all, except occasionally, when an old client came around. My itinerant life lasted quite a long time; I spent more than a year that way, lost and wandering.

This continued until I hit rock bottom. But, at the bottom of the well, as the Brazilian saying goes, there was a spring that bounced me right back up. Upon emerging from the well, I made two big decisions. One was to go on a diet. The other was to rent my own apartment.

With my salary from ISER, I rented a studio apartment on Rua Hermenegildo de Barros, in Glória. I threw myself into my diet and lost ten kilos quickly, which, for a woman who was under five feet tall, resulted in a major change in my silhouette. From the ashes, I was reborn.

SOS *Vila Mimosa*

Not long after I had moved out of Vila Mimosa, to my great surprise I was sought out by a group of madams, who, ironically, needed my help.

Very close to the *zona* there was a large, abandoned house that the city government had given to Nelson Fanini, an evangelical pastor and entrepreneur, to be the headquarters of his new Christian TV channel. When he arrived and saw what he was up against in the neighborhood, the guy hired a bunch of henchmen to get people into line. These thugs entered the *zona* with weapons and beat people up to intimidate us and drive us out. They posted up at the entrance to the Vila, asking the clients to show identification. On the sly, the pastor offered a sum of money to any madam who wished to leave without making a fuss. Two madams had already accepted his offer, and the others were becoming desperate because, naturally, their client base had begun to dry up. That's why they came looking for me at ISER.

We held a meeting on a Saturday and invited a variety of religious leaders to discuss the matter. Zwinglio had an idea: since the guy was a pastor, we could hold an ecumenical celebration and invite him. We'd put him on the spot. Perfect.

We constructed a stage with a sort of altar on it and invited all manner of religious figures to attend. Zwinglio asked that they all come in their religious garb because, at the time, the evangelical churches weren't very widespread, and the public wouldn't perceive a pastor dressed in a suit as a man of the cloth. They all showed up in their robes, looking like Catholic priests. Sure enough, the owner of the TV station showed up in a suit. And right there on that stage, with the press as his witness, he committed to not bothering the prostitutes anymore.

In addition to this event, we held a public protest against the pastor and his TV station at Circo Voador, and soon after we were invited to a meeting with Saturnino Braga, Rio's mayor at the time. It was decided that the pastor could keep the house, but the mayor forbade him from expelling anyone from the *zona*. Problem solved! From that day forward, the pastor and his henchmen didn't lay a finger on the people of Vila Mimosa, and his TV station never got off the ground. It went bankrupt soon after it began broadcasting.

After all of this was resolved, the ladies didn't need me anymore. For the second time, I was prohibited from entering the *zona*, even just to sit and drink a beer. And that was all I wanted to do, really—to meet up with people, to drink and chat. I wasn't interested in doing politics there; the *zona* was my home, my backyard.

Unspeakable Pain

One day I received a call from the Palace Hotel saying that my father was very sick, and that he had been admitted to the local hospital. I left everything and went immediately to Caxambu.

He had suffered a stroke that left his entire right side paralyzed. I stayed with him until he was released from the hospital. When he returned to his hotel room, the staff took care of him, not letting him drink or smoke. Being the guy he was, he would hide in the bathroom and sneak a cigarette every so often, though. The staff made sure that he was eating at least a little bit, as food had never really been his thing. What he liked most was wine, chatting with people, the casino, of course, and his cigarettes. After being released from the hospital, he took to carrying around a ball, which he would squeeze to recover his motor skills. He was absolutely convinced that he would get better and go back to his life and his daily routine.

One day, once I was back in Rio, I received the news that he had died. The four-hour trip to Caxambu was blanketed in a suffering that I don't know how to measure. I just know that the feeling of losing my best friend, my adviser, my father, was something that I hadn't even been able to fathom before. It wasn't even a feeling, really; it was a numbness, a void.

The owner of the Palace Hotel had already taken care of the funeral arrangements and planned a wake in a house that belonged to the hotel. Gina, my brother-in-law, and my nieces and nephews had already arrived—the first time they had been to my father's corner of the world.

Gina wept a lot and asked me why he had chosen to live alone, without his family. That is my sister for you: so sweet and so different from me. She always believed that single people couldn't possibly be lonely if they lived with their families. In fact, she wouldn't give it a rest when the subject at hand was family. Thais, my other sister, used to visit my father, and they had their happy moments. But she didn't want to go to the burial. I understood her suffering, and her need to maintain an image of him alive and well, with a glass of wine in his hand, his Coke-bottle glasses perched on his nose, his immense love for us clear as day.

Late that night, I reckon that a large part of the city showed up to the wake. As if that wasn't enough, around three A.M. the croupiers from the city's clandestine casinos started to arrive. The wake turned into a celebration! They drank whiskey and wine served by waiters from the hotel and told stories about my father, who had been considered by all to be the best croupier in all of Brazil. I didn't know most of these stories because he had been quite discreet about his work.

A crowd accompanied the funeral procession the following day. As we walked through the streets, the shops closed their doors halfway in his honor. When we arrived at the Igreja Matriz, the bells began to ring, and there we had an open-casket funeral, the first and only Mass at which I paid attention in my entire life. Gina was next to me, and I took the opportunity to answer her question about our father's solitude. "He chose to stay here because he respected the locals and was respected by them," I said. "Look at how full this church is, and all of them, including the priest, lived alongside him and understood his great love of life." After the burial, we received so many condolences from so many people that I got overwhelmed and began responding automatically.

Back at the hotel, we were taken to my father's room to sort through his things. There, in that bright and spacious room, he had lived a significant part of his life. He didn't have money or property, just his clothes, which he cared for very well—his black shoes so shiny that you could almost see your reflection in them—his books, and some papers. I found his work identification booklet that had been issued in 1940, which contained records from casinos all across Brazil. It was a portrait of a time in which Brazil was more romantic and less moralistic when it came to life's pleasures. On the first page, there was a three-by-four-centimeter photo of a young, handsome man wearing glasses and dressed in the manner I remember him best: suit, white shirt, and tie.

I kept his work identification booklet and his glasses. That is the only material trace I have of my father, but he left me with an incalculable inheritance in terms of his way of life, his affection, and his friendship. I resemble him in my decision-making and my tastes, which include good wine, good restaurants, close friends, lively conversation, and a great love of life and bohemia, along with many other things that I have discovered as I move through my own life.

The Controversy Surrounding the Word Returns

There have always been people who say that I don't fit the profile of the Brazilian prostitute. People from the Workers' Party always compared me to Eurídice Coelho, an activist who is poor and Black and has little formal education.[78] That was difficult for me. They insisted on denying who I was.

---

78 Eurídice Coelho (b. 1946) grew up in the poor suburbs of Rio de Janeiro and became a prostitute in her late twenties. She cofounded the Associação de Prostitutas do Estado do Rio de Janeiro in Vila Mimosa in 1987 and represented Brazilian sex workers in national politics and abroad.

At the end of 1988, we decided to launch a newspaper, called *Beijo da rua,* or *Kiss from the Street*, in Recife, where we were hosting the First Meeting of Prostitutes of the North and Northeast. We even had support from the city's mayor, Jarbas Vasconcelos, who allowed us to put on the event in a theater.

The first issue of *Beijo da rua*, which was a big hit, included a poem by Carlos Drummond de Andrade called "A puta" ("The Whore"). At the launch party, I was standing around drinking beer when all of a sudden a prostitute appeared, furious, wielding a knife. She shouted, "I want to know who at this bullshit of a newspaper is calling me a *puta*!"[79] With difficulty, the owners of the bar were finally able to remove the knife from her hands. I explained that Carlos Drummond de Andrade was a poet from Minas Gerais, that the word *puta* wasn't a curse but, rather, a compliment. She still wanted to kill me. I told her, "This newspaper belongs to us!" She only responded by insisting that she wasn't a whore! Unknowingly, I had run the risk of having my throat slit right there at the newspaper's launch party. The woman must have suffered a lot from being called a whore, like all of us had, no doubt. But for her it seemed to be a particularly acute trauma. Eventually, she came around and understood our intentions, and everything turned out fine.

At the Third National Meeting in 1994, a number of issues came to the fore, like sexual fantasies.[80] The debate over terminology reappeared as well. The Third National Meeting of Prostitutes, we had originally wanted to call it. But, by that time, no one wanted to use the word *prostitute* anymore. Apparently, now that we were organized, we needed a more "serious" term. Fernando Gabeira, a politician from the Workers' Party, proposed the term *profission-ais do sexo*, or sex professionals. The Brazilian Network of Prostitutes came to be known as the Brazilian Network of Sex Professionals, and thus everyone started calling prostitutes *sex professionals*. For what it's worth, I'm against this. I believe that it is important to take ownership of the terms *prostitute* and *puta*, rather than shy away from them.

79 Similar to the word *whore* in English, in Brazil, *puta* is a fluid and transgressive term that can be used to describe any woman who doesn't conform to normative paradigms of gender and sexuality. As with *whore*, *puta* can be used derogatorily or as an empowering term of self-identification. Unlike *whore*, the word *puta* also has positive connotations as an adjective in Brazilian Portuguese—for example, a party could be called a *puta festa* (bitchin' party)—in addition to negative connotations related to being angry, such as "Estou puta," or "I'm pissed off."

80 While the text of Leite's *Eu, mulher da vida* says that this was the Second National Meeting, it was actually the third, as the second was in 1989.

At a meeting in Florianópolis, in southern Brazil, Roberto Chateaubriand, one of our allies, organized a panel to discuss the history of the word *prostitute*. I was also summoned to speak about it at the Faculty of Linguistics at the University of Campinas. They were thrilled with my presentation. It is certainly a juicy topic. Our colleagues elsewhere in Latin America consider us behind the times in relation to them, because they use the term *sex worker*, and we still haven't overcome the stigma by continuing to call ourselves *prostitutes*.[81] But I think they've got it all wrong; it seems to me that changing the term is more like an apology than an affirmation.

At a Latin American conference on AIDS in Buenos Aires in the mid-2000s, the organizers distributed a pamphlet with instructions for volunteers. A section titled "Words That under No Circumstances Can Be Used at This Conference" listed "prostitute." My panel was one of the best attended, as we had just launched our clothing line, Daspu, and everyone wanted to know who we were. There we were, surrounded by all the do-gooders of the UN and other organizations and institutions. The chair of the panel, the leader of an Ecuadorian prostitutes' organization, asked me: "How should I introduce you, Gabriela?" And I responded, "Say that I am from the national organizing committee of the Brazilian Network of Prostitutes," knowing full well what would happen. I was the third person to speak. The chair introduced me in Spanish: "I have the great honor of introducing to you all Gabriela Leite, one of our most senior leaders, who is a member of the organizing committee of the Brazilian Network of Sex Workers." When I took the microphone, I said: "I am very happy to be here, but I must correct my colleague from Ecuador. I would like to say that the name of our organization is the Brazilian Network of Prostitutes, and we would like it to be called that, so each time you refer to us, please call us the Brazilian Network of Prostitutes. We like to be called *prostitutes*." I repeated this, over and over again. I got pissed off as only a *puta* can.[82]

Everything is bold to those who dare nothing.
— FERNANDO PESSOA

---

81 *Trabajadora sexual* in Spanish.
82 The original expression is *fiquei puta*, a double entendre invoking the alternative meaning of *puta*, referring to anger.

Flavio Lenz, Love of My Life

I wouldn't have thought it was possible, but I must have spent about five years considering the love of my life just a friend.

I saw him as a great conversationalist, a comrade in activism, a formidable intellectual, and a highly competent journalist. In other words, he was everything, except the object of my desire. And if in those years you had told me that we would start dating and fall in love, I would have laughed in your face.

By the early 1990s, our work on *Beijo da rua* was in full swing. Flavio was the editor in chief, and our conversations in bars would last until the wee hours of the morning. We would discuss topics and come up with ideas, and we would invite our friends as well. We had great people writing for us, and we also managed to interview interesting characters. *Beijo* was a hit.

I met Regina, Flavio's wife, when she was pregnant with their son Rafael. After he was born, we all went out to a samba school together. Eventually we became great friends, and I would frequently have dinner at their house. Ever since he was a little boy, their son loved me. He was a sweet little kid, a real doll. ISER at the time had its offices at its third location, in a big house near Glória Hill, where we would have pool parties on the weekends. At that time, we were all quite close. One day Flavio and Regina showed up to a party with Rafael, and when he saw me, he ran over to give me a hug. I'll never forget that moment. I wondered to myself: "Why does this kid like me so much?" He would be glued to my side whenever we were together. I loved him, too; he awakened in me a very special feeling.

In those days, Flavio and Regina's marriage was on the rocks. As I was a friend to them both, I was privy to both of their complaints. It's true that Flavio was not an easy man to have as a husband. There was his ex-wife, who was painfully jealous and would make a scene in front of everyone. Not only that, there were various women who hung around him, smitten with his intellectual charm and elegance and constantly making trouble. Regina was getting fed up with all of that, and with good reason.

Regina is an extremely intelligent woman: a sociologist and a polyglot, and supremely competent. Just when things weren't going well with Flavio, she was awarded a scholarship to complete a course in the United States. It was a once-in-a-lifetime opportunity, and she and Flavio thought that it could be beneficial for their marriage for her to take advantage of it. She decided to go but gave herself some time to work out the details.

It was decided that Rafael, who was five at the time, would stay with his father. Flavio could provide him with a certain structure, as he had a maid and could count on his mother, who was crazy about her grandson and would certainly pitch in with his care. But Flavio had a busy schedule working as an editor at the *Jornal do Brasil*, and his maid didn't work full time. Because I was his close friend and loved Rafa, I agreed to pick the boy up at school and look after him once in a while. The days I spent with Rafa were wonderful, a genuine party! Somehow spending time with him fulfilled the maternal instincts I hadn't been able to express with my own daughters.

As soon as Regina left, Flavio became very depressed. He realized all the mistakes he had made in his marriage and started trying to repair the damage. He went to great lengths to be able to travel to the United States to make amends with Regina. He begged for a visa at the US consulate, managed to get vacation time from the newspaper, and left Rafael with me and with his mother.

We spent a lot of time together, Rafael and I, in my studio apartment. I would take him to school, pick him up, make dinner, and sleep with him in my bed. It was wonderful. But Flavio came back from the United States in worse shape than when he had left. Once he arrived there, he realized that Regina didn't have much faith left in the relationship. I tried to cheer him up, but I had seen the writing on the wall.

At the time, I was dating around. Since I had broken up with Pantomime Carlinhos, I hadn't met anyone I really liked. I would go out with guys, but I was much more focused on my work. That was my priority. So, even though I wasn't pining after anyone in particular, I didn't really mind.

One night I had arranged to go out with one of the guys I was seeing. It was Friday and a samba party in Mangueira was a tempting option.[83] Suddenly, Flavio called, saying that he was slammed at the paper. He asked if I could stay with Rafa until he got home, around two in the morning. I told him that I couldn't. I loved the kid, but it was too late to cancel my date. Flavio said he would reach out to another friend from ISER, Caetana, to see if Rafa could sleep at her house. In any case, I was still concerned, and I told him that I would be at the Taberna da Glória drinking until around eleven P.M., because the samba only started around midnight. If need be, he could find me there.

I had already perceived that Rafael was very sensitive. His life was complicated. His mother was abroad, and his father was in a bad place. Kids always perceive these things, and this case was no different. I was sitting drinking beer when I saw Caetana's car pull up and park in front of the Taberna, and out jumped Rafael, sobbing and yelling: "I want Gabi! I want Gabi!" There would be no samba for me that night. When he saw me, he hugged me, stopped crying, and said: "Let's go home!" I went to the bar, asked to use the phone,

83 Mangueira is a favela in Rio's North Zone, home to a famous samba school.

and called Flavio at the paper. What a mess. Flavio humbly asked me to take Rafa to his house, assuming that he would be all right there with Caetana. So off we went.

When we got to Flavio's house, Rafa said: "I don't want anyone here except Gabi." At that point my date was pretty fed up. The boy started crying again and the others left the apartment to wait for me at a café.

While we waited for Flavio to arrive, I made some food for Rafa and put him to bed. When Flavio arrived, I left, but at that point none of us wanted to go out. Needless to say, my date never sought me out after that. He was nice enough, but I never saw him again.

I went home that night and got to thinking that I didn't want to keep spending so much time with Rafa. I already had two children I couldn't raise, and now there was this kid who loved me and was attached to me, but only until his mother came back. I realized that I was very fond of him and that his suffering affected me as well.

I called Flavio and told him: "Listen, my friend, I hope you understand me when I tell you that I can't keep spending so much time with Rafa. Maybe eventually we can go out together once in a while, but things can't continue as they are." Flavio knew me well and understood exactly what I meant.

When Regina came back, she and Flavio decided to officially separate. I didn't really follow what happened between them, since I had decided to focus on other things. Once some time had passed, Flavio came to see me. He said that he was finally managing to move beyond his fixation on Regina, that he had accepted that their relationship had come to an end. In fact, he did seem much better—more calm, more carefree. And then, after I don't even know how many beers, came the big surprise.

Flavio told me that he was interested in having a closer relationship with me. I found that very odd—the thought of going out with my friend of so many years. He was charming, very polite and refined, and I saw how women would throw themselves at him, but I couldn't imagine that for myself. Moreover, I had never had any type of romance or flirtation with anyone from ISER. I had witnessed all manner of things happen within the organization, but no one ever approached me in that way. Among everyone else, I was the prostitute, and a troublemaker with few friends. I didn't quite know what to think of Flavio's proposal; I found it curious, but I decided not to dismiss it out of hand. Because, after all, this soft-spoken, skinny guy with blue eyes was certainly not the type of man you come across every day.

We started going out every so often, but we were still somewhat shy and nervous. Soon enough I had to go on a trip. I was to attend a conference in

Florence, and I decided that I wanted to see Venice as well.[84] Terrible idea. Once I set foot in Venice I discovered that it wasn't all it was cracked up to be. It was at that moment that I realized that I was completely in love with my friend Flavio Lenz. I sent him a postcard nearly every day because everything reminded me of him; I wanted to tell him about every single thing I saw! I came down with a terrible case of missing him and couldn't wait to get back to Rio.

When I arrived two weeks later—which felt like an eternity—Flavio was waiting for me at the airport. He told me about his definitive separation from Regina, that he had left home and was staying in a hotel for single men in Santa Teresa. My first day back, Flavio didn't go to work at ISER, and we spent the day together, chatting and drinking beer. We were completely smitten with one another. It almost seemed as if we hadn't met before, but, of course, we already had the intimacy of five years of friendship. It was a surprising combination and somehow perfect.

At four in the afternoon, Flavio went in to work at the newspaper and I stayed in the hotel room. I collapsed into bed after twenty-four hours out and a lot of beer. When Flavio arrived late at night, he knocked on the locked door but I was fast asleep and didn't hear. So as not to wake me up, he borrowed a ladder from the hotel manager and entered the room via the window. When he told me the story the following day, I thought it was incredibly romantic.

Regina and I were never rivals. Many people wanted us to be and went to great lengths to make it seem as if we were. But we never competed for Flavio's affections. We are great friends to this day; I like her a lot and she likes me. But, even more than friendship, I admire her, and I love her son, which I think brings us even closer together.

It is true, however, that I was confronting yet another taboo. I was dating the ex-husband of a friend of mine, but without fighting with her or even going behind her back. This made a lot of people uncomfortable, especially the women around us. I knew it wouldn't be long before there was some sort of backlash. But in those early days I was on cloud nine; I couldn't even imagine the possibility of the situation catching up with us.

Eventually, Flavio decided to leave the hotel and rent an apartment so that Rafael could spend the weekends with him. At that moment, my landlord decided to terminate my lease, because he needed a place to live. In such a situation, at least in those days, the tenant was obligated to hand over the apartment immediately. I put my belongings in a storage unit and once again

84 This was the Seventh International Conference on AIDS, held in June 1991.

began to live an itinerant life. Because Flavio's hotel room was so large, at first I decided to stay with him. Then he moved to an apartment on Rua Cândido Mendes. At the time, Rafael was six years old and very sad because his parents had just officially divorced. That was when Flavio and I were first dating, and Rafa decided to reject me. Even for us, the transition was fast, so imagine what it was like for a child.

Soon after Flavio moved, and while he was still setting up his apartment, I received an invitation to go to Strasbourg, France, to attend a conference on prostitution and migration, a topic that is still widely discussed today. As the conference proceedings would be conducted in English without simultaneous interpretation provided, I decided to pass along the invitation to Flavio, since he was well qualified to speak on the subject and understood English. He spent about two or three weeks in France, and during that entire time I didn't see Rafa in Rio. He stayed with Flavio's mother, Dona Maria Luiza. When Flavio was due to arrive home, I arranged to have a beer with her before I went to pick him up at the airport. It was time to fess up to what was happening between us.

Maria Luiza was a serious and elegant woman, a fierce Protestant who had always been less than satisfied with her son's choice of wives. It had taken her a long time to accept Regina, and by the time she finally had, the couple was on the outs. As if this wasn't enough, her son soon fell in love with someone even less appropriate in her eyes, a prostitute. It was a tough situation. She treated me with indifference, which upset Flavio, and the whole situation was unpleasant. But by that point I really liked Flavio, and things couldn't continue on those terms with his mother. Before meeting her, I went to a boutique and bought a beautiful blue linen outfit and then headed to the Taberna da Glória.

One of the most trademark characteristics of the woman who would become my mother-in-law was her directness. "I don't like you. I think that you're getting in the way of my son's life," she said to me as soon as we sat down. Her words didn't intimidate me; to the contrary, I like people who express themselves bluntly.

"Look, this is a surprise for me as well," I told her. "It all happened very fast. And it could be something minor that comes and goes, but I really like Flavio. He is a great companion and a very special person." I explained that I didn't want to complicate his life and told her how much Rafael and Regina meant to me and how long we had been in each other's lives. What I wanted was to continue on good terms with everyone as long as things were going well between me and Flavio. But the most important thing was to make clear that I had had nothing to do with Flavio and Regina's separation.

After about an hour, Waldo, Flavio's father, stopped by the Taberna in his car with Rafael to pick up his wife so that they could all go to the airport to meet Flavio.[85] I paid my bill and said goodbye to Maria Luiza with the intention of hailing a taxi. But she surprised me by saying, "No, no. You can come with us." From that day on, she treated me very well. We were very direct with one another, and our relationship found its own path forward. Flavio was shocked when he arrived at the airport and saw all of us together. He had never expected to be greeted with such a sight.

That night, we went to his house, and his parents left soon after, leaving the three of us to have dinner alone. I made my usual spaghetti dish and Flavio went out to buy some wine at the corner store. That very day he invited me to move in with him.

On Cloud Nine (And a Bit of Jealousy Here and There)
Whoever witnessed things happening so quickly between me and Flavio probably wouldn't have imagined that our relationship would last.

Flavio's apartment was small, and, as he had only asked me to move in with him once it was all set up with his things, my belongings remained at the storage unit.

Even before I started dating Flavio I had nearly stopped seeing clients, but once things solidified with him I abandoned the profession altogether. Activism and continuing to work as a prostitute seemed irreconcilable. I was also in better shape financially, because, after the First Meeting of Prostitutes in 1987, I had started receiving grant funding.

An American NGO called Ashoka had its offices in the same building as ISER. The organization, which is based in Washington, DC, supports social entrepreneurs and is funded entirely from donations from American citizens. They took their fundraising very seriously, and the organization had grown a lot in Brazil, but always maintained its focus on individuals, not institutions. The director, Lene Silverstein, an American who had lived in Brazil for many years, suggested that I submit a proposal for funding after she saw the work I had done for the 1987 gathering.

85 Waldo Aranha Lenz César (1923–2007) was a Protestant theologian, sociologist, and journalist and an important civil society leader during Brazil's long democratic transition. He also served as the first president of Davida, the NGO Gabriela Leite and Flavio Lenz founded in 1992.

The situation was the following: the grantee received a monthly sum to support their work for a period of three years, with the possibility of extending the grant for one additional year. I received the grant for the full four years. After that, you stop receiving money but you maintain your affiliation with the organization. During those four years, every three months I received a check for $1,200.

A while after I had moved in with Flavio, Regina decided to give up her apartment on Rua Benjamin Constant and go live with her parents in Niterói, a neighboring city. As Rafa was studying at São Vicente School, in Cosme Velho, he started living with us in Glória during the week. Flavio would take him to school in the morning and I would pick him up in the afternoon, feed him lunch, and stay with him until his father came home. Then he would spend the weekends with his mother. That was a happy time. Flavio proved himself to be a wonderful companion, always attentive and available. He is the prince who never turned into a frog. Today, all these years later, he is the same guy that he has always been.

When we were first together, however, we fought a lot. After all, I knew that he was a ladies' man. So I made sure to stake out my territory, and things got tense from time to time, but eventually they ironed themselves out.

The funniest and most absurd story of that phase happened when we had just moved to the house where we still live. It is a big, old house with three floors: the bottom floor, which has a separate apartment; the middle floor, where we live; and the attic, where our guests stay and where I set up my jigsaw puzzles and other things like that. Flavio still worked at *Jornal do Brasil* at that time and would always get a beer to unwind after work in Praça Mauá with his friends from the editorial team. I started getting annoyed with his habit of arriving home at dawn. One night, I arrived home around eleven P.M., as I had also gotten some beers with my friends, and Flavio wasn't home. I was already rather drunk and I got angry. I decided to go look for him in Praça Mauá.

I left home and hailed a taxi, but I soon realized that I didn't have any cash on me, only a single blank check. I asked the driver to stop at the local airport so that I could take some cash out of the ATM. But when we got there the ATM wasn't working because it was after hours. I asked if the driver would accept a check and he agreed. He left me in Praça Mauá and drove off with my only check. When I arrived at the bar, Flavio wasn't there, meaning that he could only be at Capela, an old traditional restaurant in Lapa where journalists tended to hang out because you could still smoke inside. I was lucky in that it was almost Carnival season, so there were lots of men working on the street decorations, meaning I didn't have to worry about my safety. I walked from Praça Mauá to Lapa in the middle of the night, drunk and cursing Flavio.

When I arrived at Capela, I encountered Flavio's friends, but not him. "Where is Flavio?" I asked in a scolding tone. A friend of his, a layout designer, a really nice guy, could sense I was upset and tried to calm me down. "Gabriela, sit with us for a bit, have a beer. Flavio already went home, you'll find him there," he said. "No way," I told him. "I was home and he wasn't there! He must be with another woman!" And so on. The guy very discreetly gave me some money and hailed a cab for me. When I arrived at home and approached the gate, I could see that the lights were on in the top-floor apartment. I felt ashamed. As I ascended the stairs, I decided to let go of my anger. When I arrived, I saw Flavio asleep with a book on his chest. Turns out he had been there reading all along, even at eleven, when I had first come home. It was embarrassing, to say the least.

We had a couple of other mishaps here and there, but, for the most part, Flavio and I were over the moon. Yet we began to suspect, but had not yet confirmed, the extent to which our relationship would provoke envy and resentment in the people around us.

A Fit of Poolside Rage

It was around Christmastime in the early 1990s, and ISER decided to put on a party for us.[86] More than a hundred people showed up to a poolside barbecue. Flavio had to work, so I went ahead with Rafa. When I arrived, some employees were distributing a letter signed by ISER's female employees. As I walked in, I perceived that the mood was tense, but I couldn't put my finger on why. I sat down and started reading the letter, which in fact was more like a death sentence. My death sentence.

In the document, the women of ISER claimed that I was dangerous, because, if you can believe it, I had stolen Regina's husband from her. They even had the gall to justify their demand to fire me with technical reasons. The first reason was that prostitution didn't fit with the mission of the organization. Second, they said that an NGO couldn't receive money from the government, and I was negotiating a grant with the Ministry of Health to orchestrate an AIDS prevention project and trying to get ISER to accept the money. Need-

---

86 This section's heading is a reference to a 1978 novella by Brazilian author Raduan Nassar, *Um copo de cólera*, literally translating to "A cup of rage," or (as for the title of a 1999 film adaptation) *A Fit of Rage*.

less to say, within a few years not only ISER, but almost all Brazilian NGOs started accepting public funding. Edda Mastrangelo was the only woman who didn't sign the letter. And Regina immediately came out against it. It was completely absurd, a total violation of her privacy.

I sat there next to the pool, taking it all in in disbelief. The mood was dark, and Rafa, even without knowing what was going on, sensed something was wrong and didn't leave my side. When Flavio arrived and read the letter, he simply said: "Let's get out of here."

We spent Christmas that year with his parents. Maria Luiza and Waldo were indignant at what was happening to me. After all, Waldo was one of the founders of ISER. Flavio spent the following week in bed. He became terribly depressed, nearly catatonic and unable to work. On New Year's Eve, he got up and said that he was going out. I became worried, but an hour later he returned home with a bottle of nice champagne and said: "Let's celebrate. Let's head to the beach to ring in the new year." In those days, Copacabana was still the best place to spend New Year's Eve.

There are those who say that the secret reason for my expulsion from ISER, which had been authored exclusively by employees of the female persuasion, was that Flavio Lenz was now off the market. This theory is amusing, and, of course, he is worth all that. But I believe that there was something else going on. The letter was a response to my defiance in the face of the social norms carefully maintained by the women who worked at the institution, most of whom were sociologists and scholars of religion. A prostitute should not have the right to shack up with a middle-class intellectual, unless she is a character in a film played by Julia Roberts. A prostitute should never end up with a guy who successful and intelligent women are competing for, unless, again, she is Julia Roberts. Moreover, a prostitute shouldn't shack up with the ex-husband of a friend without at least having committed some terrible and sordid act of betrayal that her colleagues could accuse her of. It was the fact that Regina had no beef with me that made them squirm.

One aspect of Jesus's teachings that Christianity has embraced and that I can't condone is the idea of turning the other cheek. I won't do it. I strike back. If I didn't, I wouldn't be able to live with myself.

We're Bad, but We Could Be Worse
That whole episode of the letter was spearheaded by an anthropologist now based in the United States who, at that time, was responsible for the AIDS work that ISER did. She had been a student of Rubem Cesar in the anthro-

pology department of the Federal University housed at the National Museum and she was really thriving in ISER, in part thanks to my help, because I had worked on AIDS projects for some time and had shown her the ropes. Several years later, I ran into this woman. Our encounter was like a scene from a movie.

I'll set the scene: I was in Chile at a conference on AIDS, and when the last session was over, the panelists decided to go out for a pisco sour, Chile's national drink. Before leaving, I went to the bathroom. As I was crossing the empty convention center, I heard high heels clicking behind me. I turned around and there she was. Just looking at her filled me with the same rage I had felt that day sitting around the pool in Rio. I knew just what to do. I spat on the ground in front of her. Yes, I spat right at her feet. She stood there, motionless and silent. She watched me walk away without saying a word. She knew she deserved it.

By the way, that woman was one of the first people in Brazil to receive government money—and a lot of it—as the project coordinator for ISER's AIDS work. That has become commonplace today, for NGOs to receive and be sustained by public money.

A Step Backward but in the Right Direction

After New Year's, Flavio, Rafael, and I went to Olinda for a vacation.[87] It was there that Rafael baptized me with the name that he calls me to this day. We were at the airport, and because he was chattering away happily, the airline agent checking us in took an interest in him: "Are you happy? Because you're going on a trip with Mommy and Daddy?" Rafa responded in his characteristic way, looking sweetly and intently into the eyes of the agent: "I'm happy, yes. This is my dad but she isn't my mom. My mom is at home. This is my almost-mom." I loved the title, and, of course, I'm crazy about my almost-son.

Rafa went back to Rio a couple of days before we did, with Rubem Cesar, who was also in Olinda. Flavio and I stayed on, enjoying a little improvised honeymoon, to put the negative energy behind us. Those days in Olinda were wonderful, and they proved to me that it made no sense whatsoever to return to the hell that ISER had become.

As soon as we arrived in Rio, I received a terrible piece of news that only confirmed my feelings. Every Tuesday my prostitute colleagues and I had

87 Olinda is a picturesque colonial town outside of Recife, the state capital of Pernambuco, in Brazil's northeast.

the habit of meeting up to discuss how our movement was progressing on the patio outside ISER's offices. On a Tuesday while I was still on vacation, the girls showed up only to be told by the ISER staff that they couldn't enter the building, not even to go to the bathroom. They had to stay outside the building. I considered this a terrible act of disrespect—cowardly, really. I flew into a rage. Much smaller offenses had caused me to reconsider my life trajectory, so I knew that under no circumstances would I put up with something this egregious.

I scheduled a conversation with the administrative director. We met up at the Taberna da Glória, and I told him that I would be leaving the institution. He resisted my resignation and tried to convince me to reconsider. He proposed that we rent a room just for me so that I could work in peace and not be affected by the negative environment that had descended upon ISER. I wasn't interested. Finally, he accepted my decision, telling me that, like any dissatisfied employee, I was free to settle up my accounts and quit.

But I wasn't just any employee—I was the founder of the project that I managed. If I left, I knew I needed to take everything with me, every last document from the projects that I had planned and developed. The director said that if it came to that, I would have to hire a lawyer. For me, that wouldn't be a problem.

I went to the ISER offices and told Flavio and everyone else who I had worked with that I was leaving the organization and that I was going to the Taberna to celebrate my newfound freedom. What a relief it was when Flavio showed up at the bar one hour later with his arms full of file folders, shouting, "I'm free! Free!" It was a beautiful thing to witness. He said, "Gabriela, I quit, too! Let's start our own organization." That day, we stayed up until dawn drinking.

Davida

Our next challenge was founding our own institution with the mission of defending the rights of prostitutes and prostitution as a profession, one that also worked to diminish the risks to which prostitutes were exposed and to promote other issues that were crucial for the realization of their citizenship.

The name "Davida," which was brilliant, was Flavio's idea.[88] Waldo drafted the statutes step-by-step in conversation with us, and he agreed to serve as

88 The phrase *da vida*, which literally translates to "of the life," is a euphemism used to refer to prostitutes, as in "women of the life."

the president, a position he maintained until his death. We had everything except money.

We planned a show to celebrate our founding with the aim of raising money to reimburse us for the startup expenses. Ângela Leal let us host the event onstage at the Rival Theater.[89] Sandra de Sá agreed to sing and Zeca Pagodinho not only showed up, but he brought his entire band.[90]

We took over the ticket booth. When Zeca arrived, he said to me: "So, Gabriela, I brought my whole crew, and we need to have some beers." Of course we provided them with beer and had a few ourselves. In the end, we ended up spending as much on beer as we made in ticket sales, but the event was worth it in terms of getting the word out, especially because we were supported by such wonderful artists.

Next up was securing a place to have our office. Lima, president of a samba school in São Carlos, had a massive lot in Estácio where his group rehearsed. He offered us a space where we could construct a building that would temporarily function as our office. And that's how we started out. To take care of the legal matters with ISER, we hired a good lawyer who agreed to take on our case pro bono. The arbitration dragged on for a year. But I refused to give up; I wanted to keep everything I had worked so hard on. Even the furniture I had bought for my office I wanted to take with me. Ultimately, we won the case, and we filled up two trucks with paperwork and took it all to Estácio. After all that time, I was back in Estácio, right near Vila Mimosa, where I had started out all those years before.

The Cesar Family

Occasionally, good things happen in life. Along with Flavio came the wonderful gift of his family, who took me in and taught me a lot.

Once I had broken the ice with Maria Luiza, she and I became close friends. We started having lunch together every Sunday. At first it was quite strange for me, because they were Protestants, and I couldn't smoke at their house. But, within no time, I started enjoying spending time there, even though at first I didn't like to cook. Maria Luiza would always make some special dish, so I decided to start reciprocating, and I eventually did so with pleasure. Until the day he died, Waldo gave me the nicest compliments about my cooking.

89 Ângela Leal (b. 1947) is an actress famous for her appearances in a number of soap operas.
90 Sandra de Sá (b. 1955) is a singer and instrumentalist whose music spans many genres, including MPB (Brazilian popular music), samba, and soul.

Waldo was the friendlier one, while Maria Luiza was more reserved. She was a Portuguese teacher, and an excellent one, serious, rigid, and absolutely passionate about her work. Her students loved her; they were inspired by her pedagogy and learned a lot. She spoke French and English very well. At a ripe old age she even decided to learn German. One day I went to pick her up from her class at the Goethe Institute and found her surrounded by young people. Seemingly a bit cold at first, she was actually quite affectionate.

Waldo Aranha Lenz Cesar was a great sociologist of religion. The son of a Presbyterian minister, he was highly respected in his field. It was he who taught me how to find passages related to prostitution in the great works of literature and history. It was he who showed me the effects of religion on the archetype of the prostitute. Essentially, it was Waldo who revealed to me my own life's work.

Maria Luiza died first, of sadness. There was no other way to explain it. After the death of their daughter, Ana Cristina Cesar, one of Brazil's greatest poets, whom I unfortunately never met, she was never the same.[91] Around the time of Ana's birthday each June, Maria Luiza would get very depressed. One day, right around that time, she stopped eating, and her heart could no longer bear the sadness.

Ana was a very special woman, beloved in fact. She translated Shere Hite's *The Hite Report* into Portuguese, and her poems are moving and beautiful. Flavio used to say that if we had had the chance to meet, we would have been great friends. I take this as a true compliment.

Felipe is the third sibling of the family. He is a good friend of mine, even though we don't see each other much. From time to time I was able to help him and Flavio move past their differences. Like the rest of the family, Felipe is very dear to me.

When Waldo was already quite sick with cancer, he decided to go live in the family's country home in the mountains. He still loved the food I prepared for him, so even when I was on vacation I would give up time by the pool or at the waterfall to make lunch for my father-in-law, which he liked to eat at the same time each afternoon. Cooking for him gave me a lot of pleasure. It was as if I had taken up the mantle of Maria Luiza after her death.

The effects of chemotherapy became very difficult for Waldo to tolerate, and at a certain point it was no longer possible to leave him in the country-

91 Ana Cristina Cesar (1952–1983), known artistically as Ana C., was a poet, translator, and literary critic who committed suicide at age thirty-one.

side by himself. He spent his final month with us in our house, sitting in his favorite armchair. Once, when he hadn't been able to eat in days, I made polenta with a simple bean sauce. He ate it all with his trembling hands, weary from so many years of life, but he gave me a thumbs up to communicate that it was delicious.

Two hours later he complained that his tongue was swollen. The ambulance came and took him away. The following day, he was gone.

One of the great privileges of my life, without a doubt, was knowing Waldo. He was a friend first and foremost, and then a father-in-law. He was loving and a lover of life, just like my own father.

Self-Sustainable

In the early days of Davida, one of our funders pulled out, alleging that our organization was too green and didn't have the credibility needed to receive significant investments. Another philanthropic institution from the Netherlands went so far as to show genuine discrimination toward us. An unfortunate staff member said to Flavio in a meeting that he wouldn't give money to prostitutes or their pimp. How humiliating for that guy. On the other hand, Oscar Bolioli, who ran an American institution that gave us funding—not much but some—stuck by our side.[92] We had a good reputation because of what we had done so far, especially when it came to press coverage and public opinion, but the bulk of our funding hadn't come through yet.

We were rapidly running out of money and saw that we would soon have to give up on our projects. That was when I decided to open a restaurant on the lot where the samba school rehearsed. I invested the small bit of money we still had and, thankfully, it paid off. Since there were a lot of print shops in the neighborhood and the employees needed to have lunch somewhere, our venture quickly became a success. As soon as we started up we were firing on all cylinders. We soon realized that it was possible to be a bit more ambitious with the space, so we began organizing *pagode* shows on Friday nights, an easy task since I knew all the musicians in the vicinity. The shows were a huge hit, and there was always a line out the door to come in. Just like that, we had become entrepreneurs. Although the money was pouring in, we were left with little time to dedicate to Davida. We had to choose, and that was how our brief but prosperous business venture came to an end.

---

92 Oscar Bolioli (1934–2017) was a Uruguayan Methodist minister and an important ecclesiastical leader in Latin America.

In the mid-1990s, we received our first major grant from the National AIDS/STD Program under the auspices of the Ministry of Health to develop a project focused on disease prevention among prostitutes.[93] This was the beginning of a partnership that lasted for many years.

When anthropologist and first lady Ruth Cardoso launched the Community Solidarity Program, we applied for funding for a new project that we designed. Together with the samba folks and the local youths, we created a project called Carnival Industry. It was selected to receive the grant, and we spent four years running a school that offered workshops on sculpture-making, metalwork, and costume and prop construction. It was cutting-edge work, the first of its kind and much praised by Ruth herself. But, after four years of running it, I was exhausted. Working with young people isn't easy, in part because you have to make sure that they stay in school. Furthermore, our organization was still focused on advocating for prostitutes, which generated some friction with the students' mothers. Once, a boy took home a flier with AIDS prevention information designed for prostitutes and showed it to his mother, who was an evangelical Christian. The evangelicals showed up promptly and pulled all their kids out of the school. After that episode, our patience started to wear thin.

In that time, Zwinglio, my friend Edda's husband and an ISER adviser, worked for an ecumenical institution called Koinonia, which had some free space in its building on Rua Santo Amaro in Glória. We ended up renting that part of the building and moved Davida to Glória. In Estácio it had been difficult to maintain a functioning institution, as there were always people coming and going, telling us about their problems and looking for advice. Moreover, the place was surrounded by bars, which lured us away from our work.

On Rua Santo Amaro, we were able to better concentrate on our mission of advocating for prostitutes. Since leaving ISER we had had to get creative in order to sustain ourselves financially. There had been no other way — either we expanded our activities or we perished. But it was high time that we returned to our official mission.

93 This partnership, called PREVINA II, was based on a pilot project initiated in 1989 (PREVINA I).

Lourdes in Amapá

As I mentioned, in the mid-1990s, I began working directly with the Ministry of Health, which had begun to take its work with prostitutes very seriously. Without a doubt, the position taken by the federal government vis-à-vis our community was the beginning of a new era for us. By collecting official data on the profession, the state was able to initiate a series of beneficial public-health measures that it maintained for a number of years.

To gather this data, I embarked on a number of work trips with my great friend Lourdes, who quickly became an important activist and one of the primary figures in our movement. I could write an entire book just filled with the stories that Lourdes told me on these trips. Here is one that happened to us way up north.

The Ministry of Health sent us to the Amazonian state of Amapá, to map out the workflow of prostitutes in the area. On our team was Lourdes, me, an assistant to the governor, and our driver, who took us around in a Jeep that would have looked more at home in a war zone. One of our stops was a mine, a fascinating place, magical and strange, with a culture all its own.

The only women who frequent the mining camps are prostitutes. The whole place is a veritable shrine to gold. The prostitutes, just like the miners, have gold teeth and wear gold necklaces, rings, and bracelets by the kilo. Entering the camps, you feel as if you are walking into the gilded halls of King Solomon, except that the people are very poor; they don't have decent clothing, nothing luxurious other than the gold, not even proper sanitation. The contrast is brutal to witness. And, of course, Lourdes, who had worked in a mining camp, was convinced that for us to really understand the mine we would have to spend the night there. There was only one hotel in the camp, and Lourdes dragged us there, insisting that it was perfectly decent.

We entered the rainforest aboard our Jeep, its four-wheel drive engaged to move us across the difficult terrain. When we finally arrived at the hotel, it turned out to be a far cry from perfectly decent. Among other horrors, the governor's assistant ran out of her room screaming because she had seen a feline-size rat. We tried reasoning with Lourdes, saying that it could be dangerous for our health to stay there because of the contagious diseases, such as malaria, circulating in the area. It was no use. Lourdes looked me in the eyes and laid down the gauntlet: "You aren't a real *puta* if you don't sleep here, Gabriela."

We managed to drag Lourdes back to the Jeep, her curses raining down on us. She called us bourgeois, stuck-up, prejudiced, and so on and so forth.

When we arrived in the next city, the only hotel in town didn't have towels.

The bathroom, instead of a shower, just had a pipe where cold water poured out. Was it worth it? We had to spend the entire evening listening to Lourdes tell us that she had told us so, that the second hotel was worthless and that she preferred the rats in the first a thousand times over.

When we were on our way back the following day, we needed to stop somewhere to eat. Up in the remote north of Brazil they don't have the type of gas stations with an adjacent restaurant and gift shop that are so common in the south. The driver carried gallons of gas in the Jeep, and when we wanted to eat, we would have to stop at the home of a family. It's customary in the north for families to sell plates of food to travelers.

That day, we stopped at an Indigenous family's small home on a reservation, and the woman of the house received us warmly. Lourdes very politely examined the entire house, meticulously scouring each room top to bottom, giving particular attention to the kitchen. When it was time to order food, she only asked for a small piece of cornbread. No one understood why, since we were all starving. The food was abundant, and we sat with the family while digging in to a gigantic and scrumptious Amazonian fish complemented with rice and beans. Lourdes simply said: "No, thanks, I'm not really hungry."

Three hours later, all of us, except Lourdes, were terribly sick. I was taken to the hospital and had to call off the rest of the trip. Lourdes, victorious, declared: "It's one thing to speak about the Amazon rainforest, another thing entirely to live in it."

Lourdes in Oiapoque
When we arrived in Oiapoque, the northernmost municipality in Brazil, also located in the state of Amapá, the governor's assistant proudly showed us a plaque that read, "Here ends Brazil," as if the people around those parts didn't know that the earth was round. I soon discovered that Oiapoque is a very strange place, difficult for an outsider to understand.

The city is tiny, and even though the state government had given me a mobile phone, it didn't work up there because it didn't have an antenna. The mayor at the time was the owner of the only telephone switchboard in the city, which maintained the strange practice of employing someone to listen in on people's conversations.

Despite its beautiful-sounding Indigenous name, Oiapoque is a very dangerous place, since it is located along a drug trafficking route and is close to the mines. That means there are a lot of prostitutes as well. They were all under the thumb of a single pimp, a very young guy from São Paulo who owned a nightclub full of beautiful women whom he brought up from the southeast. The guy wore so much gold around his neck that he slumped under the weight.

One day, we went to visit the girls, to chat with them and gather data, but we forgot to bring the condoms that we always carried around in large quantities. We told them we would come back the following day. That night, we decided to go out and ended up going to the nightclub owned by the rich kid from São Paulo. There were only women inside, and the beer was very expensive—in other words, not really worth our time. But, as it happened, Lourdes became fixated on some girl she met there.

This girl was beautiful but clearly a troublemaker. Lourdes, who was already drunk, cozied up to her and offered her a beer. We barely had any money, but Lourdes wasn't fazed. "What would you like to drink?" she asked. The girl responded: "I don't like beer. I like martinis with a cherry." Lourdes responded: "Go ahead and order." The girl ordered one, and then another, and then another . . . When Lourdes ran out of money, the girl lost interest.

At that point I was already outside the bar, drinking beer at a kiosk. I went back to look for Lourdes and found her on the sidewalk sobbing like a baby. Insisting that the girl would come back, she made a real scene sitting there. Then she said she wanted to go back to the hotel in a cab. "Lourdes, look where we are! There are no taxis in Oiapoque!" I had to drag my friend, who is almost three times my size, the three blocks back to our hotel.

The following day, she woke up smiling and said: "That girl, Gabi! She tricked me!"

Soon after breakfast, we returned to the nightclub to distribute condoms to the prostitutes. There we found them locked inside the building. When we confronted the pimp about it, he said simply: "If I leave the building open, they flee." We didn't hesitate: we denounced him to the state government, his nightclub was shut down, he was thrown in jail, and we never again set foot in Oiapoque.

Lourdes in Brasília

We have a very beautiful friend, Tina, who is also an activist in our movement.[94] She is from the south of Brazil and has a dark complexion, a real knockout. I've never met a man who didn't do a double take at Tina.

94 Tina Taborda of Porto Alegre was one of the chief figures in the prostitutes' rights movement in southern Brazil. She is a long-time member and the leader of the NGO Center of Prostitution Studies (Núcleo de Estudos de Prostituição, or NEP).

On one of our trips, Tina, Lourdes, and I were having dinner together at a hotel in Brasília, and we were contemplating going elsewhere for drinks because the hotel bar was so expensive. But as we were about to leave, Lourdes, being the bird of prey that she is, identified a very well-dressed guy at the back of the restaurant who was drinking Johnnie Walker Black Label. She said: "See that guy over there? He is a congressman from up north, I know his type. Ladies, tonight we're going to drink from the top shelf."

Lourdes approached the guy and told him that Tina was very interested in him. Without missing a beat, the guy invited us to join him. We drank about three full bottles of whiskey, the guy champing at the bit to take Tina to his room. But Tina, in addition to having a flight to Porto Alegre at five A.M., was not the slightest bit interested in the guy. Lourdes made a plan: "Tell him that you're going to his room to shower, and that as soon as you're ready you will call down and wait for him upstairs. Got it? The rest you can leave to me." Tina did exactly what Lourdes had advised.

After waiting for some time the guy remarked: "Wow, she is really taking a while!" And Lourdes replied: "You really are crazy about her, aren't you? No wonder, she is quite something. You'd never know that she has AIDS." The guy nearly fell off his chair. He tried to disguise his reaction, but he quickly paid the bill and left.

While all this was happening, Tina was already flying over Brasília on her way home to Porto Alegre.

She did the same exact thing with a certain mayor of a state capital in the north of Brazil . . .

Anything for Money? Not Quite

There is an American government agency called USAID. They invest money in social impact programs in countries in the so-called Third World. At the end of the 1990s, they decided to award a large sum of money, $48 million, to AIDS prevention efforts in the Brazilian states of Rio de Janeiro, São Paulo, and Rio Grande do Sul.

In 2004, George W. Bush was reelected, and his AIDS policies became more hardline. One of the new rules stipulated that any government receiving money from USAID had to sign a pledge stating that they wouldn't work with organizations that supported prostitutes. Of course we considered this to be a reactionary and conservative stance. When I found out, I immediately requested a meeting with the Ministry of Health in Brasília. I talked with my friends who also had projects with USAID and we laid out our position clearly: either they retract the new rule, or we would refuse to accept the money.

The Ministry of Health asked us to participate in a meeting put on by the AIDS Council about this very issue. Because of the pledge, the Health Ministry was considering following in our footsteps and canceling its partnerships with USAID. On the day before the meeting, as soon as I arrived in Brasília, a USAID employee I knew asked me to have dinner with him. At dinner, the first thing he said to me was: "The ministry isn't going to refuse the money from USAID, is it?" I responded: "If you refuse to remove that stipulation, it's likely they will. We have dedicated our lives to this profession. We prefer to pass up on the money rather than violate our principles." Visibly upset, the employee, who I knew would lose his job if our partnerships fell through, left me at my hotel. Before getting out of the car, he said to me, with tears in his eyes: "I've never met anyone like you." I knew what he meant, but I decided to brush it off as a joke. "Well, of course not!" I said. "Every person is unique!"

That night I couldn't sleep. After all, we and the other NGOs would be giving up the chance to be awarded a lot of money. The following morning, I headed to a meeting with the AIDS Council. Pedro Chequer, who at the time was the coordinator of the National AIDS and STD Program of the Ministry of Health, said: "Since prostitutes are the ones directly targeted by this new rule of USAID, I want Gabriela to share with us the movement's position." Without hesitation I said: "We don't accept this new rule." We spent the entire day in discussions. Finally Pedro stated: "It's been decided that Brazil will not accept this money."

The reverberations of this decision at the international level were immediate. A correspondent for the *New York Times*, Larry Rohter, came to Davida's offices and interviewed me. The *Washington Post* called me on the phone. People are still interested in this episode to this day. Since then I have been invited to participate in many conferences on AIDS around the world.

Because of the positioning of the Brazilian prostitutes, Brazil became the only country in the developing world that didn't receive money from USAID. It wasn't easy to send all those dollars back to the United States. But there was no other way. The hypocrisy would have been intolerable for us.

Friends Forever
Years passed, the movement became stronger, and I started traveling a lot, all around Brazil and abroad as well. I came to see very little of my great friend Vera, of Vila Mimosa. One day I went out dancing at the Elite dance hall and

saw Danilo, her husband. He told me that Vera had cancer and that she was undergoing chemotherapy.

I went to visit her and, despite the circumstances, she was in good spirits. We talked a lot, reminisced about our times together, and had dinner. She told me that she was starting to believe in my dream of organizing the prostitutes. She also said that the worst thing about being sick was that she couldn't go to the *zona*, because there was nothing quite like the intoxicating ambiance of the red-light district.

I invited her to have lunch with me and Flavio at our house. I made spaghetti, we drank wine, and Vera took home some of my books to read. It was the last time I saw her. Still beautiful, but thin, with her head wrapped in a scarf because she had lost her hair, she bade me farewell.

Vera Tarragô Rodrigues, my great friend and protector, left this world. She made me believe in friendship, camaraderie, and the dignity of our profession.

Daspu: A Coup

One of our activists, Imperalina, who sews very well, had the idea to set up a business making clothes. At one of our endless meetings in which we deliberated how to make money for our NGO, Imperalina suggested: "Gabriela, let's set up a clothing workshop." That was a great idea, but I wanted to take it even further. "Not just a workshop," I said. "Let's launch a label."

In 2005, on the anniversary of Davida's founding, we put on a party and got to scheming about our label over beers and snacks. It was exactly at that time that Daslu, the luxury women's clothing store based in São Paulo, was making news because of a money-laundering scandal it was wrapped up in. Sylvio de Oliveira, our designer, came up with an inspired name. "I've got it! Daspu!" he said. Everyone laughed, and there was no doubt about it. Daspu, or "of the *putas*," which spoofed the name of the high-end brand, would be the name of our label.

Daslu unintentionally helped us gain visibility when they sued us for copyright infringement. I must confess, it was the best thing to happen to us. It created a fascinating contrast between us and them that actually made us look great.

Daspu is the apogee of all my years of work. I always believed that social outreach shouldn't be dry, joyless, or solemn. I hate that style of activism in which a militant goes to a seminar and complains about everything, using expressions like "pertaining to." For me this type of work has to be carefree, beautiful, feminine, inspired by art.

On the runway, the girls who model our clothes show their faces, speak out, and rid themselves of stigma. The international press has followed our fashion shows, interviewed us, and amplified our voices. Elaine Bortolanza, a friend of mine from Brasília, wrote a piece for the *Revista Global* whose title sums up perfectly what Daspu is: "Runways of Resistance."[95]

In the past, I had tried to get the women in Praça Tiradentes to stop showing up to work so badly dressed. I was quite happy when my friend Thaddeus, an anthropologist who researches prostitution, told me: "Gabriela, did you know that the girls in Tiradentes are looking more put together?"[96] Perhaps Daspu helped with this.

I love beauty. My aunt, my grandmother, my father, all of them appreciated the beautiful things in life. I think it was Lenin who said that the masses should emulate the good taste and refinement of the bourgeoisie. That was what I decided to take with me from my aristocratic ancestors. Watching the girls walk down the runway wearing beautiful clothes and working the crowds breaks down prejudice. That is what I believe in. Beauty triumphs over hypocrisy.

Different Yet the Same

My personality is such that I don't really harbor a sense of guilt. I'm not sure why I'm like that. My sisters, even though all three of us had the same upbringing, experience guilt from time to time. But my father never did. In that sense, I take after him. I love the fact that at this point in my life, looking back on my trajectory, I know exactly what gives me pleasure. I am a woman who only sleeps with men; I have never felt desire for another woman. If I had, I would have certainly acted on it. I like men, and, even more importantly, I insist that men surrender to their desires when they are with me. If a man doesn't know how to give in to his desires, I teach him.

My pleasures are simple. For me, the best orgasms come when I'm spending all day in bed, having sex and talking. Drinking wine, laying around doing nothing, just the two of us naked all day. I love spending the day wrapped up in a sheet. Making breakfast like that, like a fairy, or a Grecian lady.

For most of my life I have felt sexually free. Even if you are working, it is horrible to go to bed with a guy if you don't feel like coming. And I never spent

95 The original title was "Passarelas passeatas."
96 Thaddeus Blanchette, an anthropologist and a professor at the Universidade Federal do Rio de Janeiro, Macaé.

the night with a client. I consider this to be too much of a sacrifice. But I had the back of each and every one of my clients.

I came a lot, throughout my entire life. Abundantly, in fact. I attribute my professional success to this. Men loved to see me come. They knew that it was for real. Things aren't like that for me anymore. Lower hormone levels as one ages is a real thing; it compromises your libido. I tried replacement therapy, but it made me sick. I decided to just accept the changes going on in my body. I can't come as easily anymore, but my desire and the feeling of letting go of inhibitions—no lack of hormones can take those away from me.

Today I feel trapped by my role as the director of an NGO. I need to find a way out somehow, which I know I will discover in due time. When I was a girl, all I wanted to be was a crooner with a band behind me. I didn't need to be a star, just a singer in some nightclub somewhere. These days I'd like to open a restaurant in Penedo, in the countryside of the state of Rio, where I could cook all the dishes I love.

If it works out, I hope to keep living with Flavio until our final days. I want to live in Rio forever, and I'm sure this will happen, as where I live is up to me. I'd like to make a bit more money in order to live exactly how I do now, but still have ample funds left over to buy my favorite Chanel 19 perfume, as it's too hard to live without.

When it comes to my family, there are some things I regret and other things I don't.

I should not have had children. Motherhood didn't come naturally to me, but I ended up giving in to the social pressure that dictates that all women should have children. That doesn't mean that I am speaking poorly of my daughters. They are wonderful people, and, to be perfectly honest, they never burdened me. I know that I have burdened them, however—of that I am sure. I know that I am not a good mother. I am not a mother that anyone would wish for themselves, although I am a very good "almost-mom" to Rafael, Flavio's son. This issue has occupied my thoughts throughout my life. As a mother—and now I am a grandmother—I was never able to provide the love and care to my daughters that I was able to give to others. I am sad that it was me who had to be my daughters' mother. It is strange to say that, but it is true.

On a similar note, I regret not being able to understand my own mother better. My feelings toward her were always complicated and paradoxical. My sister Thais and I have spent endless hours in the backyard drinking beer and talking about our mother and her strange ways. She was never one to give us hugs and kisses. She put up a wall around herself, and we were all afraid of getting too close. Thais was able to breach that wall from time to time; she knew how to overcome our mother's anger with kisses and affection. I was never able to do this, and I don't think Gina was, either. But there was one day—on Christmas, in fact—when, after we had spent hours talking outside about our mother, Gina and I went into the house to find her sleeping. I woke up that woman who had always been an enigma to me, with hugs and kisses. She laughed, but maintained her composure and said: "Otília, what is all this nonsense?" My mother refused to call me Gabriela, my chosen name. At that moment, for the first time in my adult life, she hugged and kissed me, and I let all our pain and disagreements fall away. She and I reconciled and have remained on good terms ever since.

It took me a long time to understand what an incredible woman she is, a fact that today I am well aware of. She is supremely intelligent, strong, and courageous, and I never fully appreciated her or showed her my love. My father was charismatic and wielded the power of seduction and I imitated him in everything. But without my mother I would be no one. My character comes from her, my strength, my strong voice, and my convictions as well. All this and to think that for so many years all I did was butt heads with her. Despite our differences, my sisters say that no one else in the family resembles her as much as I do. And it's true.

Time to Move Forward

It is a fact that all prostitutes, like me, have had orgasms with their clients. Even though they are usually strangers, once in a while one comes along who appeals to our particular fantasies, and we don't even have to say a word. He might even be the kind of guy who makes your heart beat faster. In my case, my greatest fantasy was always to encounter a total stranger who would make me come with a regular old fuck, nothing fancy. Everyone knows what this is like; we've all felt strong attractions out of the blue.

Prostitution is not an easy profession. Passion is fundamental in order to tolerate the contradictions and the downsides of the job. But to this day I have never met a *puta* who left the profession because she didn't like it. The Church has gotten sex and love all mixed up. Love originates in the ego; it pertains to the individual, but sex—sex gives us life.

The world is not composed of victims. Everyone negotiates his or her own place in it. Some do this well while others do it poorly. But everyone knows, at the very least, what they want and how much it is worth. And they know how far they will go to get it. This is no different for the prostitute.

In the realm of fantasies, the desire to be a *puta* hovers over all women, whether it is in the bedroom or just in their imagination. But this is a different story than working as a *puta* as your profession. What do *putas* have that other women don't? Nothing. What do other women have that *putas* don't? Nothing.

What I know is that all great *putas* discover that men are immensely fragile. My years in prostitution taught me this. In those small rooms, men offer themselves up to us. They are not cruel, not by nature. I believe that women are more innately cruel. Men are used to coming first in society, whereas women have had to covertly get by, resorting to all kinds of tactics to advocate for themselves.

When I hear a woman speaking badly of a man and blaming him for all the wrongs in her life, I recognize that she is hiding behind a story that society has established as true. Even modern, independent women are often incapable of making their sons wash their own underwear, do the dishes, or cook. Mothers tend to raise their sons in such a way that they grow into the type of men they resent.

Most men don't know how to fuck. They depend on their sexual partners to teach them about the mysteries of their own bodies. They opt for quantity over quality in sex. They are scared to death of not getting an erection, and they only start truly using their imagination when they take their money to the red-light district to expand their sexual horizons.

They think that being virile means always having a hard dick. It doesn't. A truly virile man is one who is generous. A guy who always has a hard dick only thinks about his own pleasure. A big dick can turn into an impediment if a man doesn't know how to be generous in sex.

Because she knows all this, a *puta* is more like a friend to a man than a lover. Lovers aspire to be wives. A *puta* will never advise a man to leave his wife and family. She will talk with him about all the things that he doesn't share with anyone else. In fact, I've witnessed a lot of *putas* who have kept families together.

Oftentimes, in the *zona*, sex is just an excuse for a man to have a conversation with his favorite prostitute. Even though he may speak badly of prostitutes out in the world, he knows that he can speak to her in complete confidence.

We humans have an innate desire to sexually satisfy one another. In ancient Greece, women were assigned low status because men preferred to have sex with one another. But there were women who were afforded the highest respect, and these women were prostitutes. They could discuss philosophy, art, and science, meaning they were intellectually capable of circulating among men. These women had a window into the society of men that others of their gender didn't have. The Romans had similar traditions. The discovery of Pompeii, which was destroyed when Vesuvius erupted, gave us the chance to observe what brothels were like in the Roman Empire. They were beautiful, elegant spaces with art adorning the walls.

When it comes to prostitution, it seems as though we are moving backward. I believe that only a great society is capable of fixing this predicament. Now, I'm not certain if ours is a great society, but what is society if not the sum of the individuals who make up its ranks? Perhaps the changes we need to make are closer at hand than we might imagine. It is time, therefore, to move forward.

Selected Further Reading

There is a vast body of literature, films, digital resources, and visual art on sex work and sex-worker activism, of which a large part is produced by and for sex workers. Here, we suggest a selection of anthologies, articles, monographs, and memoirs that have influenced our work. As this list cannot possibly be comprehensive, we encourage readers to consult the social media networks of local sex-worker rights organizations and the extensive writing produced by sex workers available online and in print.[1]

SEX WORK IN BRAZIL

Barreto, Lourdes. *Lourdes Barreto: Puta Biografia*. Edited by Leila Barreto and Elaine Bortolanza. São Paulo: Editora Paka-Tatu, 2023.

Blanchette, Thaddeus, and Cristiana Schettini. "Sex Work in Rio de Janeiro: Police Management without Regulation." In *Selling Sex in the City: A Global History of Prostitution, 1600s–2000s*, edited by Magaly Rodríguez García, 490–516. Leiden, Netherlands: Brill, 2017.

Calabria, Amanda de Mello. "Life Story, Prostitution and Activism: Challenges and Possibilities of Research in Co-creation." *Global Public Health* 17, no. 10 (2022): 2512–20.

Carrier-Moisan, Marie-Eve. *Gringo Love: Stories of Sex Tourism in Brazil*. Toronto: University of Toronto Press, 2020.

Corrêa, Sonia, and José Miguel Nieto Olivar. "The Politics of Prostitution in Brazil between 'State Neutrality' and 'Feminist Troubles.'" In *The Business of Sex*, edited by Laxmi Murthy and Meena Saraswathi Seshu, 175–211. New Delhi: Zubaan, 2013.

De Lisio, A., P. Hubbard, and M. Silk. "Economies of (Alleged) Deviance: Sex Work and the Sport Mega-event." *Sexuality Research and Social Policy* 16 (2019): 179–89.

---

1 For a survey of Anglophone writing, websites, and films produced by sex workers, we recommend that readers consult the Sex Worker Syllabus and Toolkit curated by Angela Jones and PJ Patella-Rey, available at this link: https://docs.google.com /document/d/1ziubffIk5wqueSDB6p0OfsajfyyscYsNyWSzT0bXuDc/edit?usp=sharing.

Donini, Angela, Laura Murray, Natania Lopes, Naara Maritza, and Patricia Rosa, eds. *Puta Livro*. Rio de Janeiro: Coletivo Puta Davida, 2022. https://repositorio.iscte-iul.pt /bitstream/10071/27713/1/bookPart_94552.pdf.

Engel, Magali. *Meretrizes e doutores: saber médico e prostituição no Rio de Janeiro, 1840– 1890*. São Paulo: Editora Brasiliense, 1989.

Guider, Margaret Eletta. *Daughters of Rahab: Prostitution and the Church of Liberation in Brazil*. Minneapolis, MN: Fortress, 1995.

Kulick, Don. *Travesti: Sex, Gender, and Culture among Brazilian Transgendered Prostitutes*. Chicago: University of Chicago Press, 1998.

Leite, Gabriela Silva. *Eu, mulher da vida*. Rio de Janeiro: Editora Rosa dos Tempos, 1992.

Leite, Gabriela Silva, Laura Murray, and Flavio Lenz. "The Peer and Non-Peer: The Potential of Risk Management for HIV Prevention in Contexts of Prostitution." *Revista brasileira de epidemiologia* 18 (2015): 7–25.

Lenz, Flavio. *Daspu: a moda sem vergonha*. São Paulo: Aeroplano Editora, 2008.

Mitchell, Gregory. *Tourist Attractions: Performing Race and Masculinity in Brazil's Sexual Economy*. Chicago: University of Chicago Press, 2016.

Moira, Amara. *E se eu fosse puta*. Sorocaba, Brazil: Hoo Editora, 2016.

Murray, Laura Rebecca. "Puta Politics / Putapolítica: The Innovative Political Theories and Protest Praxis of Putas." In *Rio as Method*, edited by Paul Amar. Durham, NC: Duke University Press, 2024.

Olivar, Jose Miguel. *Devir Puta: Políticas de prostituição de rua na experiência de quatro mulheres militantes*. Rio de Janeiro: Editora UERJ, 2013.

Olivar, Jose Miguel, and Flávia Melo. "The Jaula and Racialization of the Amazon: Reflections on Racism and Geopolitics in the Struggle Against Human Trafficking in Brazil." In *White Supremacy, Racism and the Coloniality of Anti-Trafficking*, edited by Kamala Kempadoo and Elena Shih, 103–16. London: Routledge, 2022.

Perlongher, Néstor Osvaldo. *O negócio do michê: a prostituição viril em São Paulo*. São Paulo: Brasiliense, 1987.

Piscitelli, Adriana. "Shifting Boundaries: Sex and Money in the North-East of Brazil." *Sexualities* 10, no. 4 (2007): 489–500.

Piscitelli, Adriana Gracia. "Love and Anger: *Putafeminismos* / Whore Feminisms in Brazil." *Global Public Health* 17, no. 10 (2022): 2401–14.

Prada, Monique. *Putafeminista*. São Paulo: Veneta, 2021.

Rago, Margareth. *Os prazeres da noite: prostituição e códigos de sexualidade feminina em São Paulo, 1890–1930*. São Paulo: Paz e Terra, 2008.

Ribeiro, Fernanda Maria Vieira. "Pleasure and Protagonism: An Interview with Maria de Jesus Almeida Costa, a Black Sex Worker Activist from Brazil's Northeast Region." *Global Public Health* 17, no. 10 (2022): 2468–77.

Santos, Betania, Indianarae Siqueira, Cristiane Oliveira, Laura Murray, Thaddeus Blanchette, Carolina Bonomi, Ana Paula da Silva, and Soraya Simões. "Sex Work, Essential Work: A Historical and (Necro)Political Analysis of Sex Work in Times of COVID-19 in Brazil." *Social Sciences* 10, no. 1 (2021): 2. https://doi.org/10.3390 /socsci10010002.

Silva, Ana Paula da, Thaddeus Gregory Blanchette, and Andressa Raylane Bento. "Cinderella Deceived: Analyzing a Brazilian Myth regarding Trafficking in Persons." *Vibrant: Virtual Brazilian Anthropology* 10 (2013): 377–419.

Simões, Soraya. *Vila Mimosa: Etnografia da cidade Cenográfica da Prostituição Carioca.* Niterói, Brazil: Editora da UFF, 2010.

Siqueira, Indianarae. "Travestirevolutionary Occupy Movements/Ocupações Possessórias Travestirevolucionarias: Solidarity Economies, Anticapitalist Housing Politics, and Nonbinary Worldmaking." In *Rio as Method*, edited by Paul Amar. Durham, NC: Duke University Press, forthcoming.

Surfistinha, Bruna. *The Scorpion's Sweet Venom: The Diary of a Brazilian Call Girl.* New York: Bloomsbury USA, 2007.

Teixeira, Esther. "A narrativa de prostitutas por um viés literário: contraste entre as obras de Bruna Surfistinha e Gabriela Leite." In *Perspectivas críticas da literatura brasileira no século XXI: prosas e outras escrituras*, edited by Rafael Climent-Espino and Michel Mingote Ferreira de Ázara, 81–98. São Paulo: EDUC, 2021.

Teixeira, Esther. "Prostitución, colonización crítica y revolución teórica: La reflexión de Gabriela Leite y demás trabajadoras sexuales organizadas y el canon." *A Contracorriente* (forthcoming).

Vieira, M. A., ed. *Guaicurus, a voz das putas.* Belo Horizonte, Brazil: Fundo Estadual de Cultura de Minas Gerais, 2018.

Williams, Erica Lorraine. *Sex Tourism in Bahia: Ambiguous Entanglements.* Champaign: University of Illinois Press, 2013.

SEX WORK BEYOND BRAZIL

Bell, Shannon. *Reading, Writing, and Rewriting the Prostitute Body.* Bloomington: Indiana University Press, 1994.

Berg, Heather. *Porn Work: Sex, Labor, and Late Capitalism.* Chapel Hill: University of North Carolina Press, 2021.

Bickers, Matilda, Peech Breshears, and Janis Luna, eds. *Working It: Sex Workers on the Work of Sex.* Oakland, CA: PM Press, 2023.

Cabezas, Amalia L. *Economies of Desire: Sex and Tourism in Cuba and the Dominican Republic.* Philadelphia: Temple University Press, 2009.

Chapkis, Wendy. *Live Sex Acts: Women Performing Erotic Labor.* New York: Routledge, 1997.

Chateauvert, Melinda. *Sex Workers Unite: A History of the Movement from Stonewall to Slutwalk.* Boston: Beacon, 2014.

Delacoste, Frédérique, and Priscilla Alexander, eds. *Sex Work: Writings by Women in the Sex Industry.* Jersey City, NJ: Cleis, 1998.

Despentes, Virginie, and Frank Wynne. *King Kong Theory.* New York: Farrar, Straus and Giroux, 2021.

Grant, Melissa Gira. *Playing the Whore: The Work of Sex Work.* New York: Verso, 2014.

Hennig, Jean-Luc, and Ariana Reines. *The Little Black Book of Grisélidis Réal: Days and Nights of an Anarchist Whore.* Cambridge, MA: Semiotext(e) / MIT Press, 2009.

Jameela, Nalini. *The Autobiography of a Sex Worker*. Translated and with an introduction by J. Devika. Chennai, India: Westland, 2007.

Kempadoo, Kamala, and Jo Doezema, eds. *Global Sex Workers: Rights, Resistance, and Redefinition*. Abingdon-on-Thames, UK: Routledge, 2018.

Leigh, Carol. *Unrepentant Whore: Collected Works by Scarlot Harlot*. San Francisco: Last Gasp, 2004.

Mgbako, Chi Adanna. *To Live Freely in This World: Sex Worker Activism in Africa*. New York: New York University Press, 2016.

Nagle, Jill. *Whores and Other Feminists*. New York: Routledge, 1997.

Pheterson, Gail. *A Vindication of the Rights of Whores*. Seattle: Seal, 1989.

Orellano, Georgina. *Puta feminista: Historias de una trabajadora sexual*. Buenos Aires: Sudamericana, 2022.

Rodriguez, Juana María. *Puta Life*. Durham, NC: Duke University Press, 2023.

Smith, Molly, and Juno Mac. *Revolting Prostitutes: The Fight for Sex Workers' Rights*. Brooklyn, NY: Verso, 2018.

Weeks, Meg. "A Prostitutes' Jamboree: The World Whores' Congresses of the 1980s and the Rise of a New Feminism." *Journal of the History of Sexuality* 31, no. 3 (2022): 273–301.

DAVIDA: WEBSITES, SOCIAL MEDIA, AND FILM

Beijo da rua. "About the World Cup." 2014. https://issuu.com/prudha/docs/beijo _preview_final3/1.

Beijo da rua. "Celebrating 30 Years of the Brazilian Prostitute Movement." 2017. https:// issuu.com/flaviolenzcesar/docs/prova06.

Beijo da rua. "30th Anniversary Edition." 2018. https://issuu.com/flaviolenzcesar/docs /beijo_30_2018_rgb_final.

Coletivo Puta Davida Instagram: @coletivoputadavida.

Coletivo Puta Davida YouTube Channel, https://www.youtube.com/@coletivoput adavida2855.

Daspu Instagram: @daspubrasil.

Monti, Valentina, dir. *DASPU: Putas pret-a-porter*. 2009. Brazil. 52 mins. https://www .youtube.com/watch?v=IHrIMu2kA74.

Murray, Laura Rebecca, dir. *A Kiss for Gabriela* (*Um Beijo para Gabriela*). 2013. United States. 30 mins. https://www.youtube.com/watch?v=LqgwDysJjY0.

What You Don't See: Prostitution as We See It. Participatory audiovisual project. 2016. http://oquevcnaove.com.

Contributors

CAROL LEIGH was born in 1951 in Queens, New York, and often described her parents as "disenchanted ex-socialists." Her father, Alfred, repaired televisions from their home, and her mother, Augusta, did the billing for the family business. At Boston University, Leigh attended the Creative Writing Program and cofounded a feminist writing group. In 1978, she moved to San Francisco, where she worked at the Hong Kong Massage Parlor on O'Farrell Street and joined the fledgling prostitutes' rights group COYOTE. In the early 1980s, Leigh developed a one-woman show, *The Adventures of Scarlot Harlot*, in which she told stories from her working life and suggested that sex for money was perhaps not so different from other professions. A beloved and world-renowned sex-worker activist, Leigh famously coined the phrase *sex work*, served on a commission on prostitution created by the San Francisco Board of Supervisors, and advocated for Proposition K, a ballot measure that sought to decriminalize prostitution in the city. Leigh founded the San Francisco Sex Work Film and Art Festival, made a number of documentaries, and in 2003 published *Unrepentant Whore: The Collected Work of Scarlot Harlot*. She died on November 16, 2022.

LAURA REBECCA MURRAY is associate professor at the Center for Public Policy Studies in Human Rights at the Federal University of Rio de Janeiro (NEPP-DH/UFRJ). She has a PhD in sociomedical sciences from Columbia University and completed a postdoctoral fellowship at the Institute of Social Medicine at the State University of Rio de Janeiro. She is a member of the Coletivo Puta Davida, the Brazilian Network of Prostitutes, and a founding member/researcher of the Prostitution Policy Watch / UFRJ, where she coordinates a project that organizes and disseminates the archive of Davida, the nonprofit founded by Gabriela Leite in 1992. She has written a number of academic and nonacademic publications about sex work, politics, state violence, HIV/AIDS, and sex-worker activism in Brazil. A documentary filmmaker, Murray directed the film *A Kiss for Gabriela* (2013) and co-coordinated the participatory audiovisual project *What You Don't See: Prostitution as We See It*.

ESTHER TEIXEIRA is associate professor in the department of Spanish and Hispanic Studies at Texas Christian University. Her research focuses on the representation of prostitution in Latin American narratives and testimonies from the late nineteenth to the twenty-first century. The impact of her work can be measured by its publication in important journals in her field, including *Bulletin of Hispanic Studies*, *A Contracorriente*, *Journal of the Midwest Modern Language Association*, and *Journal of Gender and Sexuality Studies*. Teixeira has worked closely with the Sex Workers' Association of the state of Minas Gerais, Brazil, and the Women's Ministry, a Catholic institution dedicated to assisting sex workers in Belo Horizonte. She has conducted interviews with organized sex workers and carried out archival research at the Public Archive of the State of Rio de Janeiro and the National Library, focusing on documents related to the newspaper *Beijo da rua*, created by and for sex workers in 1988.

MEG WEEKS is a writer, translator, and historian. She holds a PhD in history and the studies of women, gender, and sexuality from Harvard University. She has published widely on art, literature, feminism, and politics in Latin America and beyond for a variety of academic and nonacademic publications, including the *Journal of the History of Sexuality*, the *New York Review of Books*, *n+1*, *frieze*, *Baffler*, and *Artforum*. Her translations of Brazilian fiction and nonfiction have appeared in *Two Lines*, *piauí*, *Asymptote*, *Revista Rosa*, and *Adi*. She is assistant professor of Latin American studies at the University of Florida.

Index

Note: page numbers followed by *f* refer to figures.

La Licorne, 63, 69

Left (traditional), 1, 52

Leigh, Carol, 6–7, 25

Lenz, Flavio, 10, 11*f*–14*f*, 19, 21, 24, 135,
137, 140, 146–59, 166, 168; *Fala, mulher
da vida*, 8*f*–9*f*, 17*f*. See also *Beijo da rua*

lesbians, 85, 94

liberation theology, 5, 7, 129

literature, 1, 24, 40, 45, 48n17, 87, 158;
Brazilian, 60

Lobo, Beth, 123–24

Lula. *See* Silva, Luiz Inácio Lula da

Machado de Assis, Joaquim Maria, 1, 45–46,
60, 62

madams, 30, 68–69, 71, 81–82, 91–93,
105–6, 109, 138–39, 141; pimps and, 70;
police and, 67, 73, 119; poor treatment by,
116, 136

malandros, 74, 81, 103, 106–7, 111, 118–19,
138

Marcos, Plínio, 50, 62

Mastrangelo, Edda, 134–36, 154

men, 29, 32, 38, 51–54, 60, 68–70, 78,
90–94, 99–100, 102, 108, 110, 114, 127,
167–68, 170–71; Black, 53; fantasies of,
65; fragility of, 31, 170; gay, 3; married,
74, 77; poor, 94; rich, 63, 66n29; single,
149; from the south, 107

Michel, 63–64

Minas Gerais, 3, 36, 75, 88–89, 91–92, 131,
144. *See also* Belo Horizonte; Caxambu

Ministry for Marginalized Women (Pastoral da Mulher Marginalizada, PMM), 5, 7,
129–32

Moon, Scarlet, 125–26

moralism, 1, 23

Murray, Laura, 19; *A Kiss for Gabriela*
(film), 18*f*

música popular brasileira (MPB), 126n63,
157n90

National Meeting of Prostitutes, 8*f*, 82,
135–36, 144, 151

Network of Brazilian Prostitutes (RBP), 7,
130

Neves, Tancredo, 92, 95n46

NGOs, 15–16, 78, 153–55, 163, 165, 168. *See
also* Davida—Prostitution, Civil Rights
and Health

nightclubs, 1, 63, 66, 100, 163. *See also* La
Licorne; Michel

Oiapoque, 162–63

Oliveira, Silvio de, 21*f*, 166

Olympic Games (2016), 19, 21

orgasms, 9*f*, 31, 167, 169

pagode, 53, 138, 159

Pagodinho, Zeca, 138, 157

Pará, 130, 133

Pastoral da Mulher Marginalizada (Ministry for Marginalized Women, PMM), 5, 7,
129n65

pills, 30–31, 55, 79, 91

pimps, 67, 70–76, 118, 159, 162–63

pleasure, 7, 19, 116, 158, 167, 170

police, 2–3, 47, 58, 71, 73–74, 79–82, 103,
119, 139; brutality, 2–3, 136; domestic violence and, 123n59; favelas and, 98; federal, 57, 75; military, 42n10; payment to,
67; prostitution and, 10, 11*f*; repression,
3, 70, 81, 89n42. *See also* violence: police

pot, 43–44

pregnancy, 55–56, 58, 83–84, 86–87

prejudices, 57, 67, 70, 77–78, 107, 161, 167;
Blackness and, 55; classist, 39; prostitution and, 16, 19, 23; racial, 54; samba and,
53; traditional Left and, 52

prostitutes, 7, 11*f*, 23, 30–31, 63–65, 68–70,
74, 99–100, 108–9, 114, 119, 122–24,
126–31, 144–45, 169–70; autonomous
movement of, 132; clients with physical handicaps and, 78; disease prevention among, 160, 163; Estácio da Sá and,
139–40; goal of, 78; lesbian, 94; Ministry
of Health and, 161; national meeting of,
135–36; national movement of, 4–5, 16;
organized actions of, 3, 6, 133; police and,
80–82; political organization of, 116,
166; rights of, 156; scholars of, 137;
USAID and, 164–65. *See also* Davida—
Prostitution, Civil Rights and Health;
Lenz, Flavio: *Fala, mulher da vida*; madams; pimps

prostitution, 1–4, 10, 11*f*, 16–17, 19, 30, 64, 66–68, 90, 98, 105–6, 112, 129, 135, 158, 169–71; AIDS relief and, 15; in Belo Horizonte, 90; Brazilian Penal Code and, 71; in Campo de Santana, 117; conference on, 150; decriminalization of, 2, 4, 6, 70, 71n31, 177; drug sales and, 139; economic necessity and, 124; ISER and, 153; low-end, 71, 77; luxury, 93; in Marcos's work, 50n19; moral panic surrounding, 21; neoabolitionist view of, 5; police repression and, 70; as profession, 156; research on, 137–38, 167; Sunday and, 74. *See also* madams; pimps; Rio de Janeiro: Mangue; *travestis*

puta, 19, 144–45, 161, 169–70

red light districts (*zonas*), 4, 10, 24, 65n28, 75n33, 100, 103, 108, 118. *See also* Rio de Janeiro: Mangue; São Paulo: Boca do Lixo; São Paulo: Boca do Luxo; Vila Mimosa

Redondo Bar, 49–52, 62–64, 69, 79

Regina, Elis, 101–2, 125

revolution, 49; sexual, 49, 52; socialist, 48

Rio de Janeiro, 3–4, 23, 53, 65, 88, 90–92, 95–105, 108, 111, 113–16, 122–23, 132, 140, 142, 143n78, 149–50, 155; Archdiocese of, 128; Avenida Brasil, 95, 98; Avenida Mem de Sá, 113–14, 140; Baixa do Sapateiro, 98–99; Botafogo Beach, 102, 128; Calouste Gulbenkian, 135; Cinelândia, 117; Copacabana, 95–97, 99–101, 104, 108, 154; Estácio, 14*f*, 101, 111n55, 124, 127, 133, 157, 160; Glória, 140, 152, 160; Ilha do Governador, 112–13; Jacarepagúa, 78; Leme Beach, 97, 99; liberation theology and, 129; Madureira, 96–97; Mangue, 3, 11*f*, 75–76, 100–102, 105–6, 118, 147; Mangueira, 157; National Meeting of Prostitutes in, 8*f*, 82; National Meeting of Sex Workers in, 15*f*; *Noites Cariocas*, 125–26; Praça da Cruz Vermelha, 112, 140; Praça Mauá, 152–53; Praça Tiradentes, 24*f*, 167; real estate prices in, 19; Rua Miguel de Frias, 123, 138; Rua Prado Júnior, 95, 99–100; Salgueiro, 54; São Carlos, 105, 111, 139, 157; sex worker organizations in, 10;

South Zone, 96, 139; Vila Verde, 114, 133. *See also* Daspu; Davida—Prostitution, Civil Rights and Health; *pagode*; samba; Vila Mimosa

Rio de Janeiro (state), 43, 78, 122n58, 164, 168

St. James, Margo, 6–7

Salvador, 129–31

samba, 53–55, 60, 74n32, 83, 87, 98n49, 111, 119, 147, 160; *gafieira* and, 99; musicians, 3, 106, 137, 138n76, 157n90. See also *pagode*; Rio de Janeiro: Estácio

samba schools, 23, 45, 54n23, 83n38, 146, 147n83, 157, 159. *See also* Estácio de Sá

Santo Aleixo, 115, 122

São Paulo, 1, 3–4, 11*f*, 23, 30, 36, 38, 44, 47, 56, 65, 79–80, 86–92, 95, 98, 101–2, 105, 112, 126, 140, 162–63; Avenida São João, 53, 61, 73, 75; Boca do Lixo, 1–2, 66, 69–71, 73–74, 79–82, 107, 115; Boca do Luxo, 64, 66, 81; bohemian, 34, 67; Brasilândia, 85; bus station, 61; Casa Verde Alta, 82; counterculture in, 2; *Folha de São Paulo*, 81; Guarulhos, 115; industrial regions surrounding, 124n61; Jabaquara, 39, 43; Largo do Arouche, 60, 79; periphery of, 123; pimps in, 75; prostitution in, 68; Rua Consolação, 45, 48; Rua Major Sertório, 63, 74; Rua Maria Antônia, 47–48, 50; Rua Vitória, 54, 68, 72; samba in, 53, 83n38; São Paulo Biennial, 18*f*; Vila Mariana, 32, 37, 39, 59. *See also* Daslu; University of São Paulo

São Paulo (state), 32, 33n2, 95n45, 97, 164

sex, 2, 16, 25, 42, 44, 49–52, 54–55, 63–66, 70, 76–78, 104, 113–14, 116–17, 119, 167, 169–70; appetite for, 92; capitalism and, 7; commercial, 2, 5; with men, 94; oral, 111; philosophy of, 23; with strangers, 72

sex professionals, 14, 144

sexuality, 10, 19, 49, 63, 132n70, 134, 144n79; female, 23, 31, 55, 70

sexual rights, 17, 19

sex work, 6, 23

sex-worker movement, 1–2, 4–7, 10, 16, 20, 23, 71n31

sex-worker organizations, 10, 14, 17–19, 145